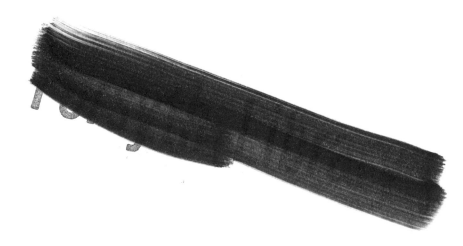

D1560195

Ellen and Irene Kossoy with Woody Guthrie, Greenwich Village, 1959
(Photo by Photo-Sound Assoc., courtesy of Aaron Rennert)

"WASN'T THAT A TIME!"

Firsthand Accounts of the Folk Music Revival

edited by
RONALD D. COHEN

American Folk Music and Musicians, No. 1

The Scarecrow Press, Inc.
Metuchen, N.J., & London
1995

British Library Cataloguing-in-Publication data available

Library of Congress Cataloging-in-Publication Data

"Wasn't that a time!" : firsthand accounts of the folk music revival /
    edited by Ronald D. Cohen.
        p.   cm. — (American folk music and musicians ; no. 1)
    Includes bibliographical references and index.
    ISBN 0-8108-2955-X (acid-free paper)
        1. Folk music—United States—History and criticism. I.
    Cohen, Ronald D., 1940- . II. Series.
    ML3551.W38   1995
    781.62'13—dc20   94-24902

Dedication

To: Pete Seeger

Table of Contents

Editor's Foreword

The purpose of the American Folk Music and Musicans series is to present important and interesting materials relating to the field that are encompassed by the term *folk music* used in its broadest sense.

In common usage as opposed to scholarly definitions, the meaning of the term *folk music* has been broadening throughout the twentieth century, especially since the advent of nonfolk urban folk singers in the 1920s and 1930s and the urban folk revival of the 1950s and 1960s. This broadening definition comprises material ranging from folk music and performers who fully satisfy old academic definitions to composed materials of urban folksingers, and along substantial borderlines with pop music, country music, blues, jazz, and rock. It seems in the interest of readers and the music to avoid semantic tangles and take a liberal view.

In spite of definitional uncertainties, the center of gravity of folk music lies in an area that often receives less general attention than other major musical forms. Books in this series will be chosen for their value in overcoming this problem and contributing to increased understanding and enjoyment of this area of music.

It is a pleasure to present this book as the first in the series. The Richard Reuss Memorial Folk Music Conference was itself the first event of its kind. Presenters at this conference were actual participants in the urban folk revival of the 1950s and 1960s. The conference was sponsored by the Indiana University Folklore Institute and was funded by the Indiana Humanities Council.

The conference was conceived by Ronald D. Cohen, Professor of American History at Indiana University Northwest, who edited the conference proceedings for this book. It is significant that Dr. Cohen's specialty is American history rather than folklore or musicology. His interest in the urban folk revival signals increasing recognition that the meaning and importance of the Revival extend beyond the domains of folklore and music specialization and constitute an important feature of recent American social and cultural history.

Ralph Lee Smith
Series Editor

WBAI CLUB & BROADSIDE

magazine

present

"CITY SINGERS in CONCERT"

with

PHIL OCHS
JOHN HAMMOND
MARK SPOELSTRA

FRIDAY, MARCH 8

AT THE C.C.N.Y.   8:30 PM

FINLEY STUDENT CENTER

(GRAND BALLROOM - 133rd and Convent)

TICKETS:

ALL SEATS $1.25
at FOLKLORE CENTER
110 McDOUGAL
GR 7-5987

SUBWAY: B·way. 7th Ave.
IRT to 137th

Introduction
Ronald D. Cohen

On May 17 and 18, 1991, "Wasn't That a Time!": The Richard Reuss Memorial Folk Music Conference was held at Indiana University in Bloomington, Indiana. Twenty-five musicians, folklorists, editors, and folk music activists from the 1950s and 1960s gathered to share their memories and understandings of the Revival. In addition to nine panels and keynote presentations, the conference included a hootenanny on Friday night, emceed by Doctor Demento (Barry Hansen) and featuring many of the participants along with local performers, and a square dance on Saturday night energetically called (and danced) by Izzy Young. The large, enthusiastic crowds appreciated the wealth of information and memories as well as the many vigorous (and sometimes heated) exchanges among the panelists and between panelists and audience members. Most of the panelists remained throughout the conference, switching roles from presenters to listeners and continuing various personal and ideological dialogues that had certainly begun decades earlier.

The conference was held in honor of Richard A. Reuss (1940-86); his wife, JoAnne, and his brother, Burt, were in attendance. Reuss had received his B.A. in history from Ohio Wesleyan University in 1962 and his Ph.D. in folklore from Indiana University in 1971; his dissertation, "American Folklore and Left-Wing Politics, 1927-1957," is a dispassionate, scholarly study of the connection between folk music and communist politics during those three turbulent decades. While yet unpublished, it remains the foremost study of the subject, a landmark in folk music and folklore scholarship.

In addition to numerous articles, Reuss also published *Songs of American Labor, Industrialization and the Urban Work*

Experience: A Discography (1983) and *Woody Guthrie: Bibliography* (1968). Indeed, Reuss was one of the foremost Guthrie scholars. (Almost forgotten is his 1965 Indiana University M.A. thesis, "An Annotated Field Collection of Songs from the American College Student Oral Tradition," a sampling of bawdy tunes recently cited by Ed Cray in *The Erotic Muse*.) After teaching for several years at Wayne State University, he became a mental health therapist.

A noted historian and folklorist, Reuss was also a zealous cataloger and collector of folk music books, articles, recordings, tapes, and periodicals connected with his research interests, particularly the folk music revival in the United States (as well as in Canada, Australia, and England). Jo Reuss donated the bulk of his extensive collection of primary and secondary materials to the University Archives and the Archives of Traditional Music at Indiana University at Bloomington, a gold mine of primary materials for studying folk music in the United States from the 1930s into the 1980s. (Other materials wound up at the Archive of Folk Culture of the Library of Congress.) This conference was, therefore, fittingly held in Bloomington, his home for many years and the repository for most of his expansive collection.

In his essay on Reuss, presented at the conference and now published in Archie Green, ed., *Songs About Work: Essays in Occupational Culture for Richard A. Reuss*, David King Dunaway has written: "Dick Reuss participated in the folk-cultural revival movement starting in the late 1950s as a subscriber and, eventually, as a volunteer at both *Sing Out!* and *Broadside* magazines in the early and mid-'60s. In the 1970s, as I interviewed one figure after another from the revival, many said that this was the *second* time they'd been interviewed on these matters—mentioning a tall, shy kid with ruffled hair and inside information, the Kilroy of the revival, Dick Reuss." Reuss, indeed, seemed to appear everywhere: in various archives, at the *Sing Out!* office, and interviewing performers and activists, as well as at numerous concerts.

Recently, JoAnne Reuss sent me a bound volume of Dick's folk concert notes from 1958 to 1963, his undergraduate years and his first year of graduate school at IU (although if he could not be present at a concert, he had others take the notes). In his papers are scattered concert critiques from later years. (The concerts were initially mostly somewhere in Ohio or in New York City, then in Bloomington.) "The purpose of taking and preserving such notes is essentially to more accurately perpetuate the real spirit and details of each performance more readily in mind," he wrote in the preface to the bound volume, "and to serve as a storehouse of information for cross checking purposes." He described each performer and selection, often followed by an insightful or pointed discussion of the event. For example, regarding a Pete Seeger concert at Carnegie Hall on December 17, 1960: "The audience seemed to enjoy posing as a liberal leftist audience—anytime Seeger mentioned anything that could possibly coincide with a position taken by varying degrees of liberals, the audience cheered or clapped (some of them). I think it unlikely that very many actually made a big cause for these positions outside the theater in regular life, but rather just enjoyed cheering on any cause because of Pete's reputation as a liberal, and just for the plain heck of it. Pete actually was much less partisan than the audience." Following a poorly attended Joan Baez concert in Cleveland on October 29, 1961: "Considering that Joan is only 20 or 21, her achievements and future are fantastic. Some people have all the breaks! Her outlook on life is the product of some rare environment which it would be interesting to discover, in view of this neurotic generation." Reuss remained an avid, yet always scholarly, fan.

Considering his interest in folk music and in left politics, he was known neither as a musician nor as particularly left-leaning. Jonathan Kwitny, a well-respected writer and friend of Dick's who attended the conference, has written me: "Dick signed up for a summer tour with the National Student Association the same summer I did, and we wound up on the same ship to Europe. He brought his banjo. Every night several dozen of us would stay on deck till sometime between midnight and dawn singing to Dick's leadership. Every day, he would explain the interaction of folk music and politics to me, and I would explain the interaction of the Dodgers and Yankees to him. He would argue the baseball. I never did the music." Kwitny also remembered that Dick, perhaps curiously, in 1964 believed that Nelson Rockefeller "would make the best President; his mother was shocked that he had picked a Republican." Despite his "liberal" political leanings, Reuss apparently failed to get tenure at Wayne State University because his research interests tainted him as a "Red." On the other hand, his distance from the (Old and New) Left allowed him a critical detachment from his subject matter, which is clear in his disserta-

tion and various published writings and certainly rare considering
the controversial nature of his subject matter.

Reuss continually puzzled over the relationship between
academic folklore scholarship and the folk song revival throughout
the 1960s, as he attempted to legitimate and bridge both worlds.
"One reason there is so much confusion is that except for people
like Archie Green and D.K. Wilgus—maybe a half dozen people in
all—most folklore scholars are totally devoted to their own (often
pedantic) projects, and have not concerned themselves with help-
ing those folk buffs outside the academic discipline who are
genuinely interested in their relationship to folksong these days (I
exclude the Madison Avenue hucksters) to comprehend the present
scene," he wrote to Sis Cunningham from Bloomington on November 9, 1964.

> And I can testify that this has hurt the folklorists'
> image outside of their own profession. By ignoring the
> world around them they have left themselves open for
> every kind of charge that all folklore and folksong study is
> nothing more than beatniks and left-wingers playing gui-
> tars in Greenwich Village—you know, the old stereotypes.
> . . . Here at Indiana University about ten or fifteen students
> at least, have come into the Folklore program in the last
> three or four years directly from the folksong revival (or at
> least as a result of its influence). This runs maybe a third
> of the students (and more if the foreign students are
> omitted) in the total program. It seems to me that when this
> large a percentage of your students come to you from one
> source, the least you could do is to pay some attention and
> find out something about what that source is all about.

Fortunately for Dick, he usually combined his love and appreciation
of the music with his scholarly penchant and even earned the
support of Richard Dorson, his dissertation advisor, notorious for
his hostility to the folk revival.

Unfortunately, Dick Reuss was not in Bloomington during
those sparkling May days in 1991, but his spirit infused the
conference, which attempted to comprehend the Revival from a
broad range of personal experiences and academic perspectives.
The time seemed ripe for such an overview. The key participants in

the conference had all played important roles in the Revival, and while some had been extensively interviewed (by Reuss, Dunaway, and myself, at least), most were keen to share their memories and insights and exchange views. Some old wounds had healed over the years, but others still festered, giving the numerous verbal exchanges a refreshing bite that didn't immediately end. In his published postmortem on the conference in *Folk News* (Summer 1991), the always pungent Lou Gottlieb wrote: "Looking back at the event, . . . I would say any rational reader of this publication would have found it sadistically boring in the time-honored tradition of all academic symposia. . . . The ego mania, world class nit-picking and gold medal kvetching characteristics of tenured, time-serving mediocrities on every university faculty were all given equal time." After rehashing his three-decade-old dispute with John Cohen (see essays by Cohen and Gottlieb) and his public apology—"Professor Cohen graciously accepted the apology thereby tactfully circumventing a major confrontation"—Gottlieb thanked me for "the opportunity to hang out with many dear hearts . . . [and] the opportunity to experience the LAST folk conference I will ever voluntarily attend during this lifetime."

The Gottlieb-John Cohen imbroglio, during the morning of the first day, set a certain tone for the remainder of the conference, leading to various apologies, mostly (all?) sardonic. The presentations and exchanges were generally more elevated, however, presenting a broad range of valuable insights and information. And despite Gottlieb's delightful animadversion, academics did not constitute the bulk of the participants. Indeed, most of the essays are reminiscences—firsthand memories little tinged by theoretical or analytical insights. They furnish pinpoints of light on the Revival, illuminating particular experiences and stories and thereby furnishing raw materials for future studies and interpretations. A few, however, do broaden our understanding of the Revival, a complicated phenomenon that has yet to be fully explicated. Hopefully, this volume will stimulate further thinking on the larger subject as well as entertain.

The conference was divided into seven separate panels—on Richard Reuss, Popular Folk Music, Record Reviewing, Folk Music Journalism, Singer-Songwriters, Greenwich Village, and Bloomington and Other Local Scenes—along with two individual presentations by John Cohen and Oscar Brand. For various reasons, all of the talks were not suitable for publication in this volume, but a large number are included. They do not appear, however, as originally delivered. A few had been previously composed, but most were improvised from brief notes and detailed memories, often shaped by the immediate setting and the dynamic give-and-take of the affair. All of the sessions were taped and the tapes subsequently transcribed; then the essays edited and re-edited by both myself and the authors, often going through numerous versions and substantial rewritings until acceptable to all concerned. After further copyediting and additional corrections, they reached their final, publishable form. I have attempted to retain as much as possible of the flavor and immediacy of the original presentations, where possible: the speakers' delightful styles and inflections as well as their spontaneous outbursts. I believe their unique personalities are often evident, although the written word cannot substitute for the actual event. Moreover, it must be stressed that these essays are all based on the individual authors' views, memories, arguments, and interpretations; they should not be taken as historical truth or verified fact. They have been edited for style, continuity, readability, and interest but not checked for their "factual" accuracy. I have added a detailed current bibliography, which should be consulted by those seeking further information and confirmation.

In order to facilitate the reader's access and comprehension, the sixteen essays have now been grouped, somewhat arbitrarily, under four general headings: Overviews, Folk Magazines, Performance Stories, and the New York Scene. In the first category, John Cohen, Joe Hickerson, Ed Kahn, Neil Rosenberg, and Dave Samuelson add considerably to our understanding of the development of various folk music styles and their connection to the Revival, generally focusing on white southern string music. Their discussions perhaps supply more questions than answers, hopefully stimulating an ongoing dialogue. Kahn and Samuelson, for example, explore the confusion over attempting to draw a hard and fast line between traditional and popular, authentic and commercial, folk music.

Specialized folk magazines were instrumental in shaping and promoting the Revival. Both Jon Pankake and Barry Hansen analyze their singular, feisty publication, *The Little Sandy Review*, while Irwin Silber presents important insights into the characteristics and politics of the *People's Songs* bulletin and *Sing Out!*, which he edited through the peak years of the Revival. Others might prefer the memories and anecdotes of the commercially oriented performers Dick Weissman and Lou Gottlieb, members of two of the more successful folk groups of the 1960s, the Journeymen and the Limeliters. Len Chandler and Frank Hamilton, both accomplished, influential musicians, discuss their careers, the former increasingly caught up in the civil rights movement as an activist and singer-songwriter, the latter temporarily committed to establishing the Old Town School of Folk Music in Chicago. Roy Berkeley, Izzy Young, John Cohen, and Ellen and Irene Kossoy furnish idiosyncratic stories of the piquant Greenwich Village folk scene, generally considered the hub of the Revival.

In putting together the conference and this book, I have attempted to approach an understanding of the Revival from various perspectives. I believe that the performers—popular acts, singer-songwriters, string band revivalists, etc.—were most important, so they have been included, but there are so many other perspectives and aspects that need attention. Folk music journalism, both mainstream and specialized, was crucial in creating and molding the audience—not just *Sing Out!* and *The Little Sandy Review* but also the *New York Times*, *Caravan*, *Broadside*, and the plethora of national and local publications that sprang up throughout the 1960s. These publications not only reviewed records but also promoted concerts, discussed performers, analyzed the changing folk scene, and in general pushed and probed the changing musical panorama. The folk scene, moreover, existed not just in Greenwich Village, which garnered the bulk of the attention, but throughout the country—in Chicago, Cambridge, Philadelphia, Berkeley, Los Angeles, and Denver as well as in Bloomington, Indiana, and Oberlin, Ohio. Indeed, practically every city and college town spawned folk clubs, concerts, and magazines, at least during the mid-1960s.

These are only a few of the important topics covered in this volume and during the conference. But there are many more that need considerable attention and are only occasionally touched upon here, if at all. Activist politics became part and parcel of the various folk music revivals, particularly during the 1930s, when Old Left politics and folk music became intertwined. By the 1960s, many of the key performers and promoters were politically active and saw folk music as one vehicle for furthering their left agendas as well as being entertaining. (The political Right seldom evinced an interest in folk music—except modern country music—and indeed usually attacked it as a left-wing plot, but in 1964 there was at least one album, *The Goldwaters Sing Folk Songs to Bug the Liberals* [Greenleaf Records].) While much (most?) of the Revival was strictly commercial, as the music became increasingly commodified, there remained various political aspects, particularly the early singer-songwriters and the civil rights movement, which need additional study. More broadly, issues of race and gender should be explored, through the study of individual performers as well as through an understanding of changing musical styles and audiences. Moreover, unfortunately, none of the conference participants were traditional musicians, black or white, whose appearances on concert stages and in record albums by the mid-1960s signaled the revivalists' recognition of their own musical roots. The importance and role of traditional performers, or those who bridged the gap between old and new, such as Doc Watson, warrant considerably more reflection.

I am particularly interested in those individuals, normally behind the musical scenes, who had immeasurable influence: the record company producers and executives, folk club and store owners, concert promoters, festival organizers, agents and managers, editors and writers. Virtually all white men, with the exception of concert promoter Mary Ann Pollar in Berkeley, and often veterans of the political and labor battles of the 1940s and 1950s, they had a dual commitment to changing society as well as encouraging folk music; they were also commercially savvy. Individuals such as Moe Asch (New York), Kenny Goldstein (New York and Philadelphia), Manny Greenhill (Boston), Frank Fried (Chicago), and Herb Cohen (Los Angeles) represented a shrewd combination of the entrepreneurial spirit and a Left/labor commitment, somehow shaped by their Jewish identity. They also dominated the record business: Moe Asch (Folkways), Maynard Solomon (Vanguard), Jac Holzman (Elektra), and Orrin Keepnews (Riverside). There were, of course, many other local personalities who were key to the success of the Revival—for example, Ed Pearl (Los Angeles), Ray Nordstrand (Chicago), Izzy Young (New York), Barry Olivier (Berkeley), Gene Shay (Philadelphia)—but they had slightly more particular concerns.

Introduction 9

The changing nature of what was fashionable and considered folk music also needs more study and reflection. Anglo-Saxon ballads, popular into the 1950s, faded away during the next decade, except for the interest of Joan Baez and a few others. Bawdy songs, international folk music (French, Israeli, etc.), and calypso also had a commercial market during the later 1950s, only to quickly disappear. Throughout the 1960s folk styles proliferated—the singer-songwriters, blues, gospel, old-time music, bluegrass, Cajun, and so much more— in addition to the popularity of folk-rock in mid-decade. The music changed because the times and the audience changed, growing larger and younger from the 1950s through the 1960s. Just as we need to know much more about the music's production, we also must study its consumption. Why was folk music commercially popular for a few short years, roughly from 1958 to 1964? Why were young people, in particular, attracted to it at that time?

These are just a few of the topics that spring to mind when considering the phenomenon of the multifaceted Revival, an important and fascinating musical, cultural, political, and social period in our history. Popular musical tastes and styles are shaped by a multitude of factors, and through their understanding we can better understand the modulating demographic, political, social, cultural, and economic topography. The Revival did not start in the late 1950s nor end in the mid-1960s, but stretched backward many decades and has continued to the present. As a collection of variegated musical styles—lumped together as "folk music"—it has existed for many decades. But only for a few short years did folk music attract considerable popular interest and commercial success.

I would like to acknowledge the many people who made the conference, and this book, a success. First, I want to thank those who formally participated in the conference but who do not appear in this book for a multitude of reasons: Bernie Asbell, David Dunaway, Bob Gibson, Paul Tyler, Burt Feintuch, Richard Bauman, Pat Sky, Mimi Fariña, and Oscar Brand. They all made invaluable contributions. In preparing the conference I had the warm cooperation and support of Richard Bauman, Henry Glassie, Joe Hickerson, John McDowell, Judy McCulloh, Neil Rosenberg, Ellen Stekert, and Ruth Stone, who composed the rather informal advisory committee. Inta Gale Carpenter of the Folklore Institute at Indiana University was particularly helpful, indeed invaluable, and the Institute was the sponsor of the conference. Inta went way beyond the call of duty, which I greatly appreciate. Ilana Harlow devoted untold hours to making the conference a success, and Nora Dial of the Archives of Traditional Music audiotaped the entire conference. Mike Jasiak of Indiana University videotaped the conference, and I hope to produce a film at some point. The Friday night hootenanny was professionally audiotaped by Bob Burkhardt and Tim Stockman. Robert Cohen copyedited the entire manuscript, with his usual care and folk music expertise. Rich Remsberg photographed the conference, and I thank him for the photos that appear in the book. Liz Faier and Steve Miller transcribed the conference tapes. I owe special thanks to Terry Lukas of Indiana University Northwest, who designed and prepared the manuscript for final publication. I also want to thank Ralph Lee Smith, editor of the folk music series of Scarecrow Press, for his faith in this book.

Funding was provided by the Indiana Humanities Council for both the conference and the book, and I want to thank them, particularly Nancy Comer, for making this all possible. Additional support came from Indiana University at Bloomington and Indiana University Northwest. I particularly want to thank and acknowledge the contributions of Velma Carmichael of the Folklore Institute. She not only devoted innumerable hours before and during the conference to making it the success that it was, but she has also done most of the computer work on this book. Her cooperation and patience have been considerable, and this whole project—conference and book—could not have been completed without her wonderful, always cheerful, assistance. Thank you, Velma!

Overviews

The Friends of Old Time Music
present

ROSCOE HOLCOMB
Traditional singer of Kentucky

&

JEAN RITCHIE
the
GREENBRIAR BOYS
the
NEW LOST CITY RAMBLERS

FEB. 11, 1961

P.S. 41
8:30 P.M. at 11th. st. & 6th. Ave.
Tickets $1.50 at Folklore Center
110 Mac Dougal St. GR 7-5987

a non-profit organization

1 Joe Hickerson

Richard Reuss was from Long Island. His undergraduate work was at Ohio Wesleyan University in Delaware, Ohio, where he obtained his B.A. in history in 1962. I do not remember exactly when I met Dick; perhaps it was when he visited Indiana University in search of a graduate school or when I performed at his institution. He was a folk singer too, albeit a laid-back one, who was forced into performing during two years of entertaining kids at a summer camp. He was so intrigued with the process of singing and leading camp songs that he contributed a very interesting article on the subject to the June/July 1961 issue of *Sing Out!* He wrote about being influenced by a group called the Folksmiths, which I was part of at Oberlin College. The Folksmiths had made an LP for Folkways in August 1957 (*We've Got Some Singing to Do: The Folksmiths Travelling Folk Workshop*); it was issued in February 1958, perhaps illustrating the oft-stated surmise that Moe Asch would record anyone.

Dick came to Indiana University in September 1962. He received his M.A. in folklore in 1965 with a thesis on college songs. He finished his Ph.D. in folklore in 1971, with a dissertation on American folklore and left-wing politics, and was editorial assistant for the *Journal of the Folklore Institute* as well as a folklore research assistant. Subsequently, he taught at two campuses of Indiana University and at UCLA, Wayne State University, and the University of Michigan. He was chair of the American Folklore Society Historiography Committee, where he was instrumental in compiling a series of recorded oral histories, which are now at the Archive of Folk Culture at the Library of Congress. He was also involved in launching the journal *Folklore Historian*, and he served as vice president of the Michigan Folklore Society.

Dick had a wide range of research interests, including the left-wing uses of folk song, the historiography of folkloristics, the folk song revival, labor lore, and urban folklore. He was one of the premier scholars of Woody Guthrie; one of his three books was a bibliography of Guthrie. His others were a discography of labor songs on LPs and a Festschrift, which he edited, for Richard M. Dorson. As a bibliophile, Dick amassed a large collection of books and periodicals on folklore and the folk revival. Many of his periodicals are now at the Library of Congress, while others are at Indiana University, along with his papers. Outside of folklore he was very active with the committee to combat Huntington's disease and an avid collector of baseball cards. He and his wife, Jo, were married at The Ark, a coffeehouse in Ann Arbor, Michigan; the Reusses were devoted supporters of The Ark (one of the country's quintessential venues for folk music over the last twenty-five years) during their residence in Ann Arbor.

* *

At the beginning of this century, a folk song "revival" began in England with an effort to collect local folk songs and dances, arrange and publish them, and then get kids in schools and others to perform them. This was called a "revival" because folk songs that were dying out in England were being "revived" and sung by English people. But already we find this notion to be a bit askew. What was actually occurring was that songs were being collected from rural folk in England and then were being sung by children and adults in the cities of Newcastle, Liverpool, and London. This was certainly not a revival from one's own immediate tradition.

Nor was that the case with respect to what we call the folk revival in this country, which I maintain began in earnest during the second half of the 1930s and has been developing apace ever since. This early interest in folk song was achieved through certain important conduits. The idea of conduit is significant because what was happening was not a revival at all, but rather a kind of transfer or transplant. Songs, instruments, and certain aspects of style were adopted and adapted from such regions of America as the upper and lower South, the Southwest, Appalachia, and the Mississippi Delta. These songs were then enjoyed, learned, and sung by people outside of those areas, mostly in the Northeast. They were transplants from one part of the country to another.

Chief among these early conduits was the Library of Congress Archive of American Folk Song and the efforts of John and Alan Lomax from 1933 through 1942. The Lomaxes published songs and books, presented performers in concert, broadcast on the radio, and fed songs to the young folk singers of New York and Washington. Alan Lomax was by far the most prolific of the two in these regards and was, as well, an active performer himself. He was also influential in effecting another early conduit—namely, the contact between true folk singers such as Woody Guthrie, Leadbelly, Aunt Molly Jackson, Josh White, Sonny Terry, and Brownie McGhee and the new folk singers of New York City, Washington, D.C., and other urban centers.

What I refer to as the folk revival is not limited to what many people, including some scholars, consider to have occurred in the late 1950s and early to mid-1960s. The Revival began in earnest in the late 1930s. From the beginning, it was not a mainstream cultural activity; rather, it was, and still is, primarily an underground, non-mainstream cultural phenomenon that has seen continuous growth in terms of participants and activities from the late 1930s up through the present time. I call this steady growth an "undergroundswell." There have been local wanings and revitaliza-tions, but the overall seed has flourished and increased over the past fifty-five years.

Over the past thirty or so years, one of the reasons for this growth has been increasing diversification and specialization. Whereas folks used to be content to just sing songs and play the guitar and banjo, now hordes of people concentrate on one or more very specific styles or instruments, such as clogging, old-time music, Irish music, the fiddle, the hammered dulcimer, storytelling, and shape-note or Balkan singing. The cultural phenomenon of the late 1950s through the 1960s, which some have called the "folk boom" (others have called it the "folk scare"), involved what I would describe as solar flares of songs, people, styles, etc., springing from the underground folk revival into the mainstream of popular culture. This has occurred more than once in the past fifty years. For example, it happened in 1950-51 with the popularity of the Weavers on Decca Records and in concert. The Weavers sold millions of recordings of "Goodnight Irene" and other songs before they were blacklisted in 1951-52.

Two other such "flares" occurred in the mid-1950s. Remember skiffle, with Lonnie Donegan's million-selling recording of "Rock Island Line" in 1956? (The catchphrases at the time were "Don't knock the rock," "Don't joke the folk," and "Don't piffle the skiffle.") Calypso and Harry Belafonte became popular around the same time. But the biggest and most influential eruption of all came in 1958 with the Kingston Trio's recording of "Tom Dooley," which sold upwards of three million copies. It made "folk," "folk music," and "folk song" household words like, as Bob and Ray would say, "slopbucket." As a result, everybody did their "folk" thing. Record companies added "folk" to their categories of products, hiring artists and groups from the folk revival and elsewhere. Participants in the Revival aspired to recording contracts, and some were successful with their auditions; a few, indeed, were *very* successful. Record stores began to have "folk" sections for these new products of the recording industry. Many recording artists, pop and otherwise, made one or more "folk" LPs. This popularity of "folk" lasted several years.

Meanwhile, underground folk revival activity continued apace. In fact, it often flourished as a direct result of an antagonism to and retrenchment from the "boom." Folk song societies developed which offered venues, performers, and activities that were abjured by the commercial arena. In other words, the noncommercial revival of the late 1930s through the mid-1950s continued growing in size, aided in part by the sudden popularity of the commodity called "folk music."

The following is an outline of a number of topics that I consider important for discussion and research about the Revival. These themes are meant to be suggestive, not inclusive; the first two topics are covered above.

1. **Antecedents** (in the U.S., U.K., etc.).

2. **The Revival as "Underground" Activity, with "Solar Flares" into Mainstream Popular Culture**.

3. **Repertory**. Where did individual songs sung by Revival singers come from? This question has always fascinated me. For example, Burl Ives did not grow up with "The Blue Tail Fly." Alan Lomax brought it to his attention for one of his many radio programs in the early 1940s. It soon became Burl's theme song.

4. **Performance Styles**. How did the Almanac Singers come up with their style of playing and singing? How and when did solo and ensemble revival styles develop during the next few

decades? The questions of authenticity, imitation, and interpretation of traditional styles became especially important in the 1960s
and are still a lively source of debate.

5. **Left-wing Use and Influence.** This was one of Dick
Reuss's favorite topics. Also important are the reactions to the
activist aspect engendered by the left-wing elements of the Revival.
For example, we had *The People's Song Book*, but then we also had
The Bosses' Songbook: Songs to Stifle the Flames of Discontent, in
reaction to and as a parody of the original.

6. **Topical and "Contemporary" Songs; Songwriting.**
A. Specific Social and Political Issues and Causes. This
category, which overlaps with the previous one, introduces the
concept of composition as part of the Revival: that is, the "topical"
or "contemporary" folk song and, more recently, the "singer-
songwriter." The reworking of old songs and the making up of new
ones was part and parcel of the folk revival from the beginning, as
the fledgling folk singers from the North became acquainted with
the authentic folk singers from the South, whose repertoires
included songs that they had made up and were continuing to make
up. Leadbelly, Woody Guthrie, Aunt Molly Jackson, Sarah Ogan
Gunning, and Jim Garland were the role models for songwriting in
the early revival. It was only natural that when aspects of the Revival
went pop in the late 1950s, songwriting, particularly of the topical
sort, went along with it.

B. The "Make Up Verses As You Go Along" Phenomenon.
A subset of song composition in the Revival was the idea of making
up verses as you go along. Pete Seeger exhorted us to do this in
concerts at least since the early 1950s, when I and many other
aspiring folk singers fell under his sway. He would encourage us
with "Lots of verses to this song, Hey li le li le lo, Make them up as
you go along, Hey li le li le lo." Where did this idea come from? Well,
for this Bahamian song, which Alan Lomax had collected in 1935,
Woody Guthrie made up additional verses following the "Married
man will..." and "Single man will..." pattern of the original verses;
his and Cisco Houston's rendition of this appears on a twelve-inch
Stinson LP. Did Pete extend this to introduce the spontaneous
addition of two-line verses?

7. **The "Singing Along" Phenomenon.** Pete Seeger exhorted us to join in, and so we all did. Where does this practice come
from? The Library of Congress folk archive has recordings made in

November 1937 in the Chevy Chase, Maryland, home of Charles and Ruth Crawford Seeger in which staff members from the Resettlement Administration join in on choruses of (and take turns singing the verses of) "Cindy" and "Skip to My Lou." On a recording of a "Columbia School of the Air" broadcast from 1940, Woody Guthrie and the Golden Gate Quartet are reading a script about the boll weevil. "That's not a bug, that's the boll weevil. Well, ah, isn't there a song about that? Why yes there is. Why don't you sing it?" And just before Woody starts singing the song, Alan Lomax says, "and all of you out there sing along, too."

     8. **The "Scenes."** This topic would explore the kinds of communities where the folk revival took place, such as those listed below, and the linkages between them.

     A. Specific Cities or Parts Thereof. E.g., "the Village."

     B. Colleges and Universities. Pete Seeger has said that his first concert at Oberlin College in February 1954 was a benchmark in his career, opening up a new audience of college students to his performances and to folk music.

     C. Summer Camps. How many of us were involved with folk music at summer camps such as Camp Woodland, Buck's Rock, Killooleet, Idyllwild, and Circle Pines?

     D. Outing Clubs. E.g., the MIT Outing Club ("MITOC") and its mimeographed songbooks, which led to Dick and Beth Best's *Songfest.*

     9. **Venues**. What kinds of contexts has this music been performed in?

     A. Living Rooms/Lounges/Campouts/Sessions/Parking-lot Jamming/"After Hours"/Washington Square. These are the most informal gathering places.

     B. Hoots/Folksings/Sings/"Singer Circles." These are generally a bit more formal.

     C. Coffeehouses/Folk Clubs/Open Mikes. I remember "The Quiet Answer," the first coffeehouse in Bloomington (1958), with the best name of them all.

     D. Stores/Centers. Some of these were important hubs of activity, such as Izzy Young's Folklore Center in Greenwich Village.

     E. Concerts. We sought to present ourselves and others in these formal situations.

     F. Festivals. Here's an example of the influence of festivals. In April 1957, two carloads of us drove from Oberlin, Ohio,

to Swarthmore, Pennsylvania, to attend the Swarthmore Folk
Festival. Oh, the youth and energy we had in those days! Within
three weeks we had conceived of, organized, and put on the first
annual Oberlin Folk Festival. We had out-of-town singers like Tony
Saletan from Boston, Ellen Stekert from Cornell, and a carload of
performers from Ann Arbor.
      G. Retreats/Getaways. The weekend "Getaway" of the
Folklore Society of Greater Washington has been an annual event
(and model) for almost thirty years.
      H. Workshops/Teaching Camps. These have proliferated
in the past fifteen years.
      I. The Media: Radio and Recordings. Folk music on the
radio began in earnest with the CBS' "Columbia School of the Air"
and "Back Where I Come From" series, conducted by Alan Lomax
from 1939 through 1942, and network broadcasts featuring Lomax
and Burl Ives in the later 1940s. WNYC in New York City also had
a folk music show, beginning with Henrietta Yurchenco's in 1940
and another for the past forty-eight years (the longest continuous
radio program hosted by one person), Oscar Brand's. The influence
of published recordings flourished under the aegis of Alan Lomax,
Moe Asch, Kenneth Goldstein, and others beginning in 1940.
      10. **Attitudes and Values of Revival Participants**. Here I
will touch on certain kinds of attitudes that I have encountered.
      A. We/They (Esoteric/Exoteric). There has often been the
idea that folk music is something special and exciting that "we" are
doing, while "they," the masses, are not. It's esoteric, rather than
exoteric.
      B. Elite or "Better" Than Pop Music. Coupled with the
previous attitude is the value that is placed on folk music—namely,
that it is better than pop or elite music. I have observed chagrin and
consternation when a folk song escapes our grasp and becomes
incorporated into mainstream popular music. This was exemplified
by an incident in 1956, when a student at Oberlin College, weaned
on folk music in New York City, was seen running into the lounge
of Grey Gables Coop (the chief venue for folk singing at Oberlin at
that time), tears streaming down her cheeks. She had just heard the
million-selling recording by Lonnie Donegan of "Rock Island Line,"
and she was screaming, "They've taken 'Rock Island Line' away
from us! What will they take next, 'Midnight Special'?" (As it turned
out, it was "Tom Dooley.")

C. The Desire and Need to Proselytize. For many people folk music was so special and so good we didn't just want to keep it to ourselves; we wanted to proselytize. We didn't want to have our folksings just in the basement of GRC here at Indiana University; we wanted to have them in the lounges of Reed and Oak Halls and other dormitories. So, as Pete admonished us to do, we spread the word wherever we could (just so long as it remained "folk" and did not cross over into "pop"). Note the contrast between this attitude and the two previous ones.

D. Life Style. E.g., clothing, foodways, and habitat.

E. What Constitutes the "Folk?"/What Constitutes the Revival? Ask people in the Revival: Who are the folk? What is folklore? Twenty to thirty years ago, many revivalists' conceptions of folklore matched what folklorists thought folklore was and the folk were fifty or more years previously. Revivalists have generally been conservative in regard to these perceptions as compared with folklorists of the past two or three decades. This attitude has altered somewhat in recent years as people in the Revival have had access to actual folk musicians and singers through festivals, concerts, recordings, and videos.

F. Revivalist Attitudes Toward Academic Folklore and Folklorists (and Vice Versa). Among many folk revival people, I have observed an incipient anti-intellectual feeling accompanied by a suspicion of academic folklore and folklorists. Of course, this has worked both ways.

11. **The People Who Created and Influenced the Revival.** Who were the stars, the idols, the role models of the folk revival? Who were the entrepreneurs? Who were the conduits?

12. **Organizations and Publications of the Revival.** The first organization I know of was the American Square Dance Group, organized in New York City around 1936 by Margot Mayo, along with its newsletter, *Promenade*. What other groups and ephemeral publications arose in New York City and elsewhere before and during the tenure of People's Songs in the late 1940s?

13. **Differentiation and Conflict as to What Is "Folk."** These have been the subjects of many a discussion and diatribe.

A. Interpreters vs. Roots Musicians. If you look at the letters and columns in recent issues of *Bluegrass Unlimited, The Old-Time Herald*, and *Sing Out!*, you will see that this is not a dead issue.

B. "Trad" Interpreters vs. Innovators. Did the message of

the New Lost City Ramblers devaluate the message of Pete Seeger?
C. Hardcore (Underground) Revival vs. the "Folk Boom."
(Some still seem to consider that only the latter constitutes the
Revival.) Back when the "folk boom" was occurring in the late
1950s and early 1960s, there was tension between those who
stayed in the underground revival without going boom and those
who went into the boom.

14. **Resources for the Study of the Revival.** What and
where are these resources? There's a lot out there and the published output is increasing.

A. Bibliographies, Discographies, and Other Reference
Works. In 1969 I compiled and published a comprehensive bibliog-
raphy on the Revival. It ran to nine pages and contained 112 items.
How large would today's version be?

B. Articles, Books, Recordings, and Manuscripts. There
were a number of articles written during the boom by people in the
folk revival, partly as a reaction to what was happening at the time.
Over the past ten years the subject has once again been flourishing.

C. Libraries, Archives, and Research Centers. Certain
archives and libraries have been accruing books, periodicals,
recordings, manuscripts, photographs, and ephemeral publications on the Revival. We have a vast collection at the Library of
Congress Archive of Folk Culture and would like to acquire more.

15. **Specialization and Diversification Within the Revival.**
As I mentioned before, there is the aspect in recent years of
increased specialization and diversification within the Revival.

16. **Relation to Craft, Dance, and Other Revivals.**

17. **Nomenclature (The Lexicon of the Revival).** A special
vocabulary has been used in the Revival, such as "folkie" and
"folkni(c)k." Was it Izzy Young or John Cohen who coined the latter
term, or was it a combination of the two? "Folksing," "hoot,"
"hootenanny"—such terms have come and gone and have been
used in different ways. In the late 1950s, "folkni(c)k" was a pejorative term, but when it reached San Francisco a short time later it
became the title of the newsletter of the San Francisco Folk Music
Club. In recent years many people in the the music industry and the
folk revival-derived subculture have been reluctant to use the word
"folk" for singer-songwriters and their product and performance.
The phrase "acoustic music" has been used, and more recently
"new acoustic music." In a way I like that, for this reason. For many

years, when people have asked me, "Joe, what kind of folk songs do you sing?," all I could think of saying was, "I sing folk songs and allied forms in the English language that I like and can remember," which is quite accurate, but a bit wordy. Now I can say I play "old acoustic." Heck, some might even say I play "paleo-acoustic."

18. **Personal Narratives**. We need to explore the autobiographies and personal reminiscences of Revival participants.

A. How Did People Discover and Get Into the Revival? How did people get into folk music? What was the occurrence or the accident that triggered it?

B. How Did People In the Revival Become Students and Scholars of Folklore and Ethnomusicology (and, Specifically, of the Revival)? I found that this was a very fruitful topic for a discussion a few years ago at a meeting of the Northeast Chapter of the Society for Ethnomusicology. I asked those assembled how they had made the transition from participation in the Revival to the study of folk music or ethnomusicology. Of the eighteen people participating in the roundtable of the whole, all but one had a story to relate about their own experience in moving from participation to academia. Dick Reuss's Festschrift for Dorson also includes several reports of similar transitions.

19. **Fiscal Considerations**.

A. How Did Participants Choose to (or Not to) Make Money Within and Outside the Revival?

B. How Did Non-Participants Make Money from Folk Music, Including the Revival?

C. Funding of Revival Musicians and Events, and Its Relationship to Funding of Non-Revival Folk Musicians and Events.

* *

In the beginning there were the folk, and they sang songs. They did not sing folk songs; they did not know that term. They sang songs. Along comes the collector, who collects the song and calls it a folk song. The collector sometimes is a singer. In the case of "Tom Dooley," Frank and Ann Warner collected the song from Frank Proffitt in Beech Mountain, North Carolina, and brought it to New York City, where they lived. Warner began to sing it around and eventually recorded it as a folk singer singing a folk song. It soon got picked up by other participants in the folk music revival of New York City. Young pickers and singers sang it with great gusto and rudimentary Scruggs licks on the banjo.

The folk revival spread, partly through Pete Seeger concerts on college campuses, beginning with his February 1954 concert at Oberlin College, and the Weavers' 1955 Christmas reunion concert at Carnegie Hall. It got so that every northern college campus had a folk song trio, quartet, or whatever. In 1957, one such trio got a big break with a night club stint in San Francisco and a Capitol Records contract. The Kingston Trio released "Tom Dooley" in 1958. This recording sold millions and made "folk music" a household word, and suddenly everybody was doing folk music, including choral groups and rock singers.

I conclude by taking a sip of water from the left-handed mug which was presented to me when I left Indiana University in 1963 and which is inscribed: "Founding father, IUFC" (Indiana University Folksong Club).

BRANDEIS UNIVERSITY 2ND ANNUAL FOLK FESTIVAL

SATURDAY, APRIL 25, 1964 at BRANDEIS UNIV., WALTHAM

EVENING CONCERT · 8 P.M. TICKETS: $2.25

REV. GARY DAVIS
GEORGIA SEA ISLAND SINGERS & DANCERS
with BESSIE JONES
ROSCOE HOLCOMB
JIM KWESKIN & THE JUG BAND
NEW LOST CITY RAMBLERS

AFTERNOON EVENTS

CHILDREN'S CONCERT
1 P.M. • $1.00
REV. GARY DAVIS
IRENE KOSSOY
TONY SALETAN

FILMS
1 P.M. • 50¢
HAZARD,
KENTUCKY COAL MINERS
and
"TO HEAR MY BANJO PLAY"
with PETE SEEGER

GUITAR WORKSHOP 3 P.M. • 50¢

ALL KINDS-A BLUEGRASS
3 P.M. • $1.00
CHARLES RIVER VALLEY BOYS
LILLY BROS. & DON STOVER
NEW LOST CITY RAMBLERS

MAIL ORDERS FROM:
BRANDEIS FOLK FESTIVAL
BRANDEIS UNIVERSITY
WALTHAM, MASS.
OR.
FOLKLORE PRODUCTIONS
P.O. BOX 227
BOSTON, MASS. • HU 2-1827

ORDER COUPON
☐ $2.25 ☐ $1.00
ENCLOSED, FIND CHECK / MONEY ORDER FOR $____
(I AM ENCLOSING A SELF-ADDRESSED STAMPED ENVELOPE.)
NAME____
ADDRESS____
CITY____ ZONE____ STATE____

2 John Cohen*
I

Within the folk song revival the presence of old-time string bands has been a continual gadfly and source of musical enrichment. The role of traditional music within the Revival had a history and development, with precedents in the '30s, philosophical and political issues, an academic component, and a network of festivals, clubs, magazines, record collectors, and record companies. Although the cognitive roots of the folk song revival were within the disciplines of anthropology and folklore, during the '60s the discussion expanded and interfaced with popular culture. This took several forms: the popularization and commercialization of the folk boom, on the one hand, and the movement for traditional music, on the other.

For me the Revival was a dynamic process, an expansion of horizons, a crusade and an opportunity to learn from traditional artists and to play good fiddle music with friends on stage and at home. Only the last items continue to this day.

The acceptance and diffusion of traditional music has been the one aspect of the folk song revival which has outlasted the Revival itself. Traditional music, as defined by the Revival and by scholars, existed before there was any Revival. The contribution of the Revival was to make people outside of the traditions more aware of what they had been missing, and it served as a corrective. It was also necessary to break down boundaries and definitions that the Revival had constructed. It was those definitions that had created the need for a revival in the first place.

*Parts of this essay were previously published as "The Folk Song Revival—A Historical Perspective" in *The Old-Time Herald*, vol.3, no. 3 (Spring 1992), 27-32, and no. 4 (Summer 1992), 34-40. Reprinted by permission.

Implicit in the concept of "revival" is bringing to life something which is dying out. This ethnocentric concept—as applied to
traditional music—was more a reflection on the revivalists than on
what they were reviving, for in its inevitable manner of constant
change, traditional music never dies out.

The Revival gave a distinct representation of American
traditional music to the rest of the world. For example, in 1964,
when I was in Peru recording Andean music for Folkways, I met a
young man who worked in the Peruvian National Institute of
Culture. He defined American folk music for me: "It is two beards
and a blonde singing about a Negro with a chain on his legs, and
he is *very* far from home."

Before the 1960s, folklore scholars collected and studied
from traditional sources as well as in libraries. Some made field
recordings for the Library of Congress, or for the Brown Collection
of the University of North Carolina. These collectors (with the
exception of a few like Bascom Lunsford, who was singularly
involved with the people and the culture) were working within an
institutional framework—academic or archival, or a recording
company. They received a salary for their efforts. Within this group
I would include D. K. Wilgus, Kenneth Goldstein, and Alan Lomax.
By contrast, when Ralph Rinzler, Mike Seeger and myself started to
make "field" recordings in the late '50s, it was not within any such
framework. There was no Ph.D., no salary, no need to publish or
perish. There wasn't any commercial outlet for our activity. Our
arrangement with Folkways Records was seen as an opportunity to
do something, not as a contract. I think we had been raised on the
earlier field recordings and commercial hillbilly records and viewed
them with some kind of awe, just as a poet or artist might view their
sources of inspiration. The opportunity to visit traditional artists in
their homes was seen as a privilege, an activity of reaching out, a
dynamic process that might bring meaning and music to one's own
life.

On the field recordings done for the Library of Congress you
hear the voice of the "collector" at the end of each song: "This was
recorded in Hazard, Kentucky, on October 14, 1937, by Alan
Lomax, for the Library of Congress in Washington, D.C." Possibly
this was spoken to assure the performers that the recording wasn't
just for the collector. Yet one is impressed by the power, authority,
and permission given to Lomax as representative of the Govern-

ment. It also must have made a big impression on the farmer seated before the microphone.

Early cylinder recordings of American Indians begin with the "collector" shouting into the recording device: "This is an example of a Sioux ceremonial song sung by Mr. William Little Eagle," followed by, "All right, start singing." One wonders to whom the collector is shouting. From the syntax, you know his intro is not directed to the Indian informant but rather to some imagined academy or archive, to History, or perhaps with some sense of the importance of the act of documentation itself. By contrast, the tapes and field recordings made by young collectors with portable equipment in the 1960s sounded like a hushed and mumbled request: "Like, well, I mean, like the machine is running and well, uh, maybe you might want to play something?"

My first field recording of a traditional artist was on a front porch in eastern Kentucky in June 1959. At the end of every song, before the final note was completed, the musician announced, "This was composed and recorded by Banjo Bill Cornett of Hindman, Kentucky." He had been to the National Folk Festival and was warned about the acquisitive practices of folk song collectors, so he made his own copyright claim right there on the record.

Earlier folk song collectors followed diffusion theories which were built on regional distribution of song variants.[1] By contrast, our emphasis was on the music and the people it came from. The idea of crediting the artists was important and integral to our collections and performance. We set a model of activity which encouraged many other young people to do similar work in the field: collecting, recording, meeting and getting to know traditional musicians as people and as friends, as well as learning to play their music as a form of personal enrichment.[2]

Underlying all our activity was an interest in "style": how the music sounded vocally and instrumentally, as heard from its traditional sources. We were encouraged by Alan Lomax's concerns in his Cantrometrics project. We felt that playing music with traditional artists created a closer bond than just collecting texts and tunes. This distinguished us from earlier folk singers such as John Jacob Niles, Cynthia Gooding, Burl Ives, and Richard Dyer-Bennet, who made theatrical and commercial interpretations of the songs. In this, we were different from the Weavers and the Kingston Trio. Eventually, our message was taken up by people younger than

ourselves at the universities, who not only studied the music but
formed bluegrass bands on campus and went on to legitimize the
study of popular culture (including hillbilly and race records) as part
of the American Folklore Society.

In our concern with traditional musicians we had to deal
with the Revival's prior political reputation and its connections with
the Left.[3] Although we were part of the system of folk festivals and
recordings, we had to find ways to shelter our traditional informants
from any guilt by association on the part of blacklisters, the FBI, or
Congressional committees. We had to determine whether by
knowing us the traditional fiddlers and banjo players would be
tainted. We evolved an intricate scheme to test the possibility that
one of the musicians who worked in a highly sensitive electronics
position might have his job jeopardized by recording for Folkways.
Through a legal friend in the entertainment business, we submitted
a list of folk artists (all of whom had recorded for Folkways) as
possible entertainers on a network TV show. Our legal friend
submitted this list to a blacklist organization that was pressuring the
networks at that time. Our traditional musician's name was not
included, and neither was Pete Seeger's. Since the list of artists was
okayed by the "censors," we concluded that recording for Folkways
was not in and of itself viewed as an act of political subversion.

In spring 1961, Mike Seeger and I made a recording trip
through the South, starting with the Union Grove Fiddle Convention
and ending up with a visit to Earl Scruggs and *The Grand Ole Opry*
in Nashville. We saw in the newspapers that Pete Seeger had been
called to a hearing in federal court for defying the House Un-
American Activities Committee. We wrote Pete. I said that I
wondered whether we should be out collecting music at this time,
when it might be more important to be home with him supporting
his case. He wrote back saying that what we were doing was as
important, and part of the same pursuit of freedom of expression.

In 1963, the ABC-TV *Hootenanny* show submitted to the
demands of the blacklist. Pete Seeger was not allowed to appear,
and the folk song revival was put to the test once again. The
argument within the folk song community was that if you appeared
on the ABC show you were supporting a system that acquiesced in
the blacklist. Folk song artists were pitted against folk singers as to
where they drew their political lines. It was quite amazing to us (the
New Lost City Ramblers) that we were even considered for this

John Cohen I   29

show, and we went through a great deal of soul searching to arrive at our decision. Central to our argument was to balance our repugnance at the blacklist industry with the opportunity to bring traditional music, played in a traditional style, to the widest possible audience.

However, there was another type of blacklist at that time, a musical blacklist. It manifested itself in our conflict with the commercial folk singers, their driving desire for exposure, and their total disinterest in traditional music or traditional musicians. From our point of view, they were our enemies.

One of the most humiliating experiences we ever went through was at the rehearsal for the ABC-TV *Hootenanny* show, which we participated in at Ann Arbor, Michigan. The show was to be filmed in a ballroom where we had performed earlier for the college folk song society. The students already knew us personally, yet in the national TV media circumstance we were made to feel like outsiders. I can never forget our "audition" before Lou Gottlieb of the Limeliters, who was charged with deciding which of our songs we would be allowed to perform. We played him a slow one, then a very traditional one, and since there was no response, we tried the most up-tempo Uncle Dave Macon number imaginable. During the song, Bob Gibson entered the ballroom and Gottlieb went over to greet him, gave him a big hug, and left us singing our hearts out to nobody. It was pretty clear where the allegiances and power were at that time. Eventually we performed "New River Train" on the show, and Mike Seeger heard from some old people in Galax, Virginia, that they enjoyed our straightforward performance done in the manner of Ernest Stoneman and his Mountaineers, just as it was always played around Galax.

The agendas within the traditional music aspect of the Revival were also fascinating. At the first University of Chicago Folk Festival in 1961, Richard Chase's introduction of Horton Barker and Frank Proffitt suggested that the singers were still Anglo-Saxon yeomen from Merry Old England, transplanted to the Appalachians with their values intact. Horton Barker had sung ballads at the Whitetop Festival in Virginia in the late 1930s.[4] I had heard that singers there were screened so that the hillbilly tradition was excluded and only pure old English songs were permitted. I was sensitive to a connection between John Powell, who helped organize the festival, and his racial bias and anti-black stance in Virginia

politics. I became determined to re-examine that premise about the
Anglo-Saxon purity of the ballad singers, and made the film *The
End of an Old Song* to show as realistically as possible how a
traditional ballad singer living in the oral tradition could also live in
beer joints and pick up women in bars around Asheville.

We argued about the relationship between the commercial
traditional musicians, such as Flatt and Scruggs, and the "authentic"
back-porch variety, like Roscoe Holcomb. Behind the argument
was a definition of what is "pure folk." However, in contradiction
to these definitions, Roscoe Holcomb listened to Flatt and Scruggs
on the radio and was a big fan of Dolly Parton on *The Porter
Wagoner Show*.[5] We talked of the importance of homemade music
in a world of mass media. We treasured old "lassie-making songs,"
such as Clarence Ashley's "Coo Coo Bird," but our own research
showed that Ashley had lived essentially as a medicine showman
doing stage performances.[6]

For us, it was a struggle to convince the Revival of the
validity of both the back-porch *and* the commercial traditions.
Eventually our point of view prevailed, and within a few years
country music and home-grown musicians were accepted as part
of the folk music revival. The earlier movement was forced to
widen its horizons.

Perhaps our initial reason for seeking traditional sources
had to do with the urban/rural polarity. This could be viewed as a
"romantic" notion reflecting earlier dichotomies between industrial
vs. agricultural, evil vs. good, etc. Yet for me there was another
motive. In 1951, I would listen to *The Wheeling, West Virginia
Jamboree* on WWVA late at night and was intrigued by the music
and the advertisements for plastic tablecloths imprinted with a
picture of the Last Supper. Coming from a middle-class suburban
experience, this was an introduction to what I had been missing. It
became my awakening and, for me, the Discovery of America.[7]

The need to open up our cultural horizons was manifested
in our love for string band music, just as the Beatles needed the
blues. The opening of cultural horizons eventually exploded into
the notion of the '60s counterculture. Traditional music was part of
the total mix—so, for example, autoharps were heard at hippie
communes along with rock 'n' roll. Folk singing found a natural
affinity with the back-to-the-earth movement.

However, there were implicit collision courses and philosophical minefields along the way. The presence of city revivalists at southern fiddle contests made for a new interchange. Documenting the conventions on records made them better known to a wide audience. Northern bands won prizes in southern contests.[8] In response, the fiddle contests grew in size and proliferated. There was a resurgence of interest in fiddle contests from Idaho to Vermont, and especially in the South. *The New York Times* reviewed them. At the University of Chicago Folk Festival in the early 1960s, Archie Green hypothesized about the inevitable clash of values in his talk, "Traditional Music at the Crossroads." In his scenario, college students playing banjos and fiddles meet the Ku Klux Klan at a bluegrass festival.

The idea of knowing traditional musicians firsthand and playing music in an authentic way was not inherent in the earlier folk song movements. Collectors viewed the singers as "informants" and "source material" rather than as artists. The shift in awareness came later. Alan Lomax played an indispensable part in this.[9] There were also others who came from the country and devoted their efforts to introducing traditional music to the city.

In the late 1930s, Ralph Tefferteller arrived in New York at the Henry Street Settlement[10] and brought with him the tradition of Tennessee Running Sets. Margot Mayo also came to the city, taught at the Walden School, and formed an organization called the American Square Dance Group (ASDG),[11] which along with the dances presented a spectrum of folk singers (including Pete Seeger) in the '30s and '40s.[12] Margot was related to Rufus Crisp, an old-time banjo player from Allen, Kentucky, and she made recordings of him for the Library of Congress. She gave Rufus's address to Pete Seeger, and he visited Rufus while hitchhiking around the country. She also took various members of ASDG from New York to Kentucky to meet Rufus. Stu Jamieson was one, and Woody Wachtel was another. I met Woody in 1948, and that was my introduction to the five-string banjo. Woody showed me how to build fretless banjos, which he had learned from Rufus Crisp, using a tree branch for the neck and tacking a cat skin onto a hexagonal wooden box for the banjo head. Woody's singing conveyed great joy. He played banjo in the frailing style and used a lot of different modal tunings. This was a new realm of music for me, accessible in a personal way rather than as a stage performance, and totally different from Burl Ives (who was popular at that time).

Another important source for traditional music in the folk music revival was a summer camp in the Catskills called Camp Woodland, formed and directed by Norman Studer, who was from rural Ohio.[13] The program which he established there in the 1940s was a paradigm and precedent for much of my later outlook (I worked at the camp in 1953 and '54). The camp was located on the site of an old lumber mill, and some of the old structures became the sites of bunkhouses, kitchens, and recreation halls. Each summer they would present a Folk Festival of the Catskills, with singing by the campers, and including guest performances by local people from the region singing old songs. I recall two little local girls singing the traditional Irish folksong "If I Were a Blackbird" followed by "Mockingbird Hill," which was a top ten song on the radio. Every weekend there were square dances with local callers, such as George Van Cleet. The musicians also were local and included fiddlers and banjo players (four-string) as well as button and keyboard accordion players. Musically it was like reliving early New York State old-time string band music.[14]

Earlier the camp had "discovered" George Edwards, who had spent his entire life in the mountains and was a wealth of old Scotch and Irish ballads, as well as songs about the lumbering, tanning, slate, and barrel hoop industries, which had flourished in the Catskills during the past century. I got to know Mike Todd, an old-time lumberjack, who was invited to stay at the camp to tell stories and share his knowledge of the woods and of local crafts, such as how to split and shave wooden shingles. The campers, who were children from the New York City area,[15] were taken on bus trips through the mountains to visit families and villages that were being moved in order to build the New York City reservoir system. The children (and myself) were impressed and touched by the way local people's homes and valleys were being flooded so that we in the city could have drinking water. Local singer and fiddler Grant Rogers was welcomed at the camp, and one summer the musician in residence was a black woman folklorist named Louise Bennet from Jamaica who introduced many Jamaican songs, such as "The Banana Boat Song," which later became part of Harry Belafonte's basic repertoire.[16]

Between 1950 and 1957 the first festivals devoted to folk music were held at Cornell University, followed by the one at Swarthmore.[17] In 1952, we held the first hoot at Yale; Tom Paley and myself formed a core, and many other guitar players "appeared" at the first gathering. The first dozen guitars which arrived were all closely in tune with each other. This was never repeated. Tom, with his background in New York City playing guitar and banjo with Harry West, gave a decided old-time musical direction to the hoots.

Guests included Peggy Seeger from Radcliffe, fretless banjo player Woody Wachtel, and an early performance by Yale's Russian Chorus. Jackson Pollock's nephew played flamenco and classical guitar. Logan English from Kentucky learned to sing folk songs at Yale, and Charlie Faurot was singing with guitar (he later made field recordings of banjo players and Texas fiddlers for County Records). The grandson of James J. Hill, who had owned a railroad line, astounded us by singing "Hallelujah, I'm a Bum!" including the verses that mentioned his grandfather. Then there was Bob Mamis, from Wesleyan University, abandoning his violin training in order to learn to play fiddle. We gathered every few weeks for five years.[18]

We were learning our songs and instrumental styles from old phonograph records of southern music. There were a few anthologies of these on LPs. These reissues became the central influence in shaping the direction of the traditional music aspect of the Revival. They offered access to and continuity with an oral tradition—style, tune, and text intact. They bypassed earlier folk song collections, which used music notation and piano arrangements.[19]

One cannot underestimate the visionary importance of early reissues on Decca and Victor. Smoky Mountain Ballads, issued in 1941, was the first. Its contents were selected and edited from earlier hillbilly records by John Lomax. Later in the 1940s, Alan Lomax issued Mountain Frolic and Listen to Our Story. The most influential reissue was Harry Smith's three-volume, six-record set on Folkways (1952), the Anthology of American Folk Music.[20] Via commercial recordings it introduced us to old-time music (the Carter Family, Dock Boggs, Clarence Ashley, etc.), to early blues (Mississippi John Hurt, Gus Cannon, Sleepy John Estes), to Cajun music, and to authentic cowboy singing. The significance of these recordings extended beyond folk festivals and eventually provided an invigorating infusion of "folk" into mainstream commercial music. They provided us with insights into the development of bluegrass as well as the rationale for the blues revival. The

artists presented on this series became a pantheon of old-time
heroes. Various artists first heard on the *Anthology* became the
subjects of intense searches. The reappearance of Tom Ashley,
Mississippi John Hurt, Dock Boggs, and others became an event at
folk festivals in the 1960s and brought great satisfaction to these
musicians, who had originally recorded in the late '20s and early
30s.

The literary critic Stanley Edgar Hyman roughly put it this
way: "Why do you choose to learn off old hillbilly records, which
are from a tradition outside your upbringing, when you could be
playing blues, which are such better music?"[21] Eventually the blues
revival took its own course when it interfaced with and was
absorbed by the commercial rock 'n' roll scene of the '60s. Blues
elements are clearly heard in the music of the Rolling Stones, the
Beatles, and Cream (Eric Clapton) and eventually found ultimate
apocalyptic expression in heavy metal (an antisocial form of
adolescent fantasy and revolt which many Americans youths pass
through as a stage of development). Recently Studs Terkel observed that if it had not been for the McCarthy era, we would not
have the Rolling Stones. He postulated that during the 1950s Alan
Lomax left for Europe to get away from the political climate of the
witch-hunting and blacklisting and brought with him his Library of
Congress recordings of early blues along with early commercial
records, which he played on his radio shows in England. These
shows were heard by the youthful John Lennon and Mick Jagger.

In 1957, on my return from Peru, Izzy Young opened the
Folklore Center on MacDougal Street in Greenwich Village. By 1958
I had re-established an earlier acquaintance with Ralph Rinzler, who
took me along on his weekend jaunts to Sunset Park and New River
Ranch in Maryland to hear bluegrass shows. At that time Ralph was
already intrigued by the artistry of Bill Monroe and eventually
engineered his entrance into the folk revival.[22] As part of the Folklore
Center, Izzy put on a series of small concerts (Peggy Seeger was the
first) which helped galvanize the small community of New York City
folksingers and offered some kind of a stage.

The seeds for the New Lost City Ramblers (Mike Seeger,
Tom Paley, and myself) and the ensuing old-time string band
movement had its roots in the universities, its heart in the country,
and its historic convergence in Greenwich Village in 1958. The
musical scene at Washington Square on Sundays probably was our

first public performance (consisting of a few songs and a rumor that we were forming a band); we had once performed earlier on FM radio in Washington, D.C. In conjunction with Izzy Young, we put on our first concert at Carnegie Hall (originally in the small Chapter Hall, which quickly sold out, so we moved to the Recital Hall). That same weekend we made our first record for Folkways, with Moe Asch as the recording engineer.[23] Most of the audience at the concert were already players of guitars and banjos, and the concert introduced the Autoharp, mandolin, Dobro, and fiddle and exhibited different instrumental and vocal configurations as well as presenting a range of musical possibilities from an ensemble. In appearance we were scattered and disorganized. The audience could empathize with that.

Over the following months we edited the record, did some retakes, and wrote individual essays as to what the music meant. I created the name New Lost City Ramblers from echoes of former string bands and names of fiddle tunes. The image on the cover of the album was a photo by Russell Lee from the Library of Congress Farm Security Administration files, and the designer was Robert Benton (then art director of *Esquire*, who went on to make Hollywood movies).[24] Later, cover photographs of us were taken by my neighbor Robert Frank, who went on to become one of the most influential and renowned photographers of the century.

Our repertoire was largely drawn from old hillbilly records of the 1920s and '30s, and although many people thought that we sounded exactly like the old records, we didn't. We introduced the name "old-time music" on our second album, *Old Time Music for Children*. We stood in opposition to the commercialization of folk music which was being exploited by the Kingston Trio, the Limeliters, the Highwaymen, the Chad Mitchell Trio, and other groups with collegiate appeal.

Within a year of the first concerts by the New Lost City Ramblers, there was a mimeographed fanzine *Gardyloo* which spotlighted us in New York. Our record was released in early 1959, and before summer we had done two more New York City concerts,[25] recorded two more records, and were invited to the first Newport Folk Festival, where we performed from the same repertoire. As we traveled doing our initial concerts, something unexpected happened. People who were not from the universities nor from the folk music revival would show up. Record collectors who

had been fans of this kind of music long before us volunteered to
make their collections available because we were performing a kind
of music they liked. Archie Green became an early theorist and
advocate for us and introduced us to some of the collectors.
Possibly he was as affected by us as we were by him, and we
intersected with him many times throughout the next ten years. At
colleges and in the cities we met newly formed string bands who
drew from the same musical sources and who created their own
old-time names, such as the "Kings County Outpatients" and the
"Denver Public Library." Revival bluegrass bands were forming,
and groups would travel to southern fiddle conventions to com-
pete. I believe the Greenbriar Boys were the first to do this, and the
New York City Ramblers were the first to win a contest prize.

In the spring of 1960, against the counsel of Harold
Leventhal (Pete Seeger's manager, who was trying to advise us),
we accepted three jobs in the Midwest, without any guarantee that
we would be paid. Traveling as three men in a Volkswagen beetle
with suitcases and seven instruments (two guitars, two banjos,
fiddle, mandolin, and Autoharp), we played at Oberlin College, in
Ann Arbor, and at the University of Chicago. The Chicago concert
was put together on three days' notice. From our meeting with
enthusiastic students there (foremost was Mike Fleischer), the
seeds for the University of Chicago Folk Festival were planted, and
that festival, which is dedicated totally to traditional music and
traditional musicians, started the following year. Thirty years later
it is still running. During the '60s it became a mecca for folk song
societies throughout the Midwest, and it helped give birth to many
small festivals and concerts during the next decade.

The weekend of our initial appearance at the University of
Chicago, we also auditioned for a commercial club, the Gate of
Horn. The UC students packed the place and cheered us on, which
led to another serious venue for our music. As a condition of our
employment at the Gate of Horn we had to look respectable. So we
considered the attitude of old-time farmers who might have gone
to town to perform a show and decided to dress in our best, rather
than in bluejeans or work clothes. We studied old photographs of
early rural performers from the pre-cowboy suit country music era
and came up with white shirts, ties, and differing vests as our garb.
Years later, in August 1969, when we did a benefit square dance for
the Family Dog on the Great Highway, the last of the psychedelic

dance halls of San Francisco, where everyone else was dressed in the swirling rainbows and tie-dyes of the counterculture, I didn't know how to respond to a musician who approached me, looked at the vest and tie, and said, "Far out!"[26]

By the summer of 1960, copies of our first album (which had sold 400 copies) had reached people on the West Coast, and we were invited out for the Berkeley Folk Festival. We also played our first engagements at the Ash Grove in Los Angeles. Our relationship with Ed Pearl at that club was ongoing, and for more than a decade he served as a presenter of traditional music and also (along with other serious political positions) attempted to bridge the gap between the country music and folk song constituencies of Los Angeles. He also ceased hiring commercial performers, like the Limeliters and Bud and Travis. Instead he built a following for Lightnin' Hopkins, Doc Watson, and Maybelle Carter. He presented the first L.A. appearances of Flatt and Scruggs and Bill Monroe, gave the Country Boys (aka the Kentucky Colonels) their first urban stage (the Byrds met Clarence White there), and had a profound influence on young persons such as Ry Cooder, David Lindley, and others, who used the Ash Grove as their schooling in traditional music.

Throughout all our performing years we never stayed at hotels. Rather, the organizers of concerts would put us up in their homes or in college dorms, and much of our sleeping was done on couches and spare beds. We developed friendly connections everywhere, from which emerged an intricate nationwide network of musicians dedicated to traditional music. I recall the sense of having ongoing personal dialogues with people in Boston, New York, Washington, Chicago, Minneapolis, Los Angeles, and Berkeley, and for a decade we would retravel this circuit and keep the conversations going.

Our stage performances were characterized by long periods of tuning a large array of vintage guitars and banjos. We devised "folklore" to cover the tuning, most of it improvised, and instructed the audience about the cross-disciplinary aspects of folklore, including discography.[27] One trialogue went, "Hey, your guitar is sharp, Cecil." The response was, "Yours is flat, Lester," followed by, "Don't be such a child, Francis." Most of the audience did not know enough to understand whether this was funny or not, but they had to learn.[28]

Besides performing and preparing our records for Folk-

ways, the members of the NLCR kept busy in other ways. Even
before the formation of the NLCR, Mike had produced three records
for Folkways which shaped the direction of the Revival: 1)
American Banjo Scruggs Style, which offered an alternative to Pete
Seeger's banjo picking, and moved the listener or urban banjo
picker out of the folk song movement and through the five-string
banjo's folk roots into the more unfamiliar area of commercial
country music (Scruggs played regularly on *The Grand Ole Opry*);
2) *Mountain Music, Bluegrass Style*, which was a survey of raw and
excellent bluegrass bands.   This album introduced the name
"bluegrass" to the urban public, and also by its presence on the
Folkways label effectively challenged the earlier definition of the
sound of folk music and legitimized bluegrass as a folk form (this
was going on simultaneously with the Kingston Trio's hit record
"Tom Dooley"). The album also included bluegrass performances
by "citybillies" (a phrase coined by Mike's father, Charles Seeger);[29]
and 3) *American Banjo Tunes and Songs with the Stoneman
Family*. Pop Stoneman was a 1930s hillbilly Galax musician. Other
artists on the album included Louise Foreacre, Mr. Sutphin, and
Hilary Dickens (father of Hazel Dickens).[30] It was on this project that
Ralph Rinzler first got involved; he wrote the extensive notes for the
songs, including biography, bibliography, and discography.

       Once the NLCR started, we considered doing a few "theme"
albums. The idea of *Songs of the Depression* was one; there were
many references to the Depression in the old records. In order to
experience an economic depression firsthand, I visited eastern
Kentucky and made photos and field recordings for six weeks in
1959.[31] From this came my documentary album *Mountain Music
of Kentucky* and the "discovery" of Roscoe Holcomb. Roscoe
became the most profound influence on me, and his music and life
suggested emotional depths and meanings within the tradition
which hit me (and others) very hard. It was with some ironic sense
of symmetry that I offered copies of my tapes to the Library of
Congress, and it took them several days to decide whether to accept
them. I don't think I was considered sufficiently legitimate at that
time.

       The process of "producing" this record of field recordings
entailed the research on the songs, writing liner notes, designing the
booklet to include a portfolio of my photographs, and designing the
cover of the album. Moe Asch of Folkways never said no to any of

these steps. He just set limits on how much he could spend on the production. I was not paid for my efforts, but in the process Moe Asch gave me all the responsibility for the material, the documentation, and the interpretation along with the visual representation. This established a pattern of independence and setting values for myself that made it difficult for me ever to work in any other fashion.

I brought Roscoe Holcomb to various festivals and concerts, and though he was well received I was not totally satisfied with the form of communication. I felt something more profound in my visits to Kentucky than what I could convey on records, with photos, or through his concert appearances. So in 1962, in order to bring all the elements together, I returned to Kentucky to make a movie. The film focused on the life around Roscoe. It was called *The High Lonesome Sound* and set me in a direction which I have continued on for the next twenty-nine years, making films about traditional music performed in its own home context. That first film is still shown in university folklore courses across the country, from Harvard to UCLA.

Another ongoing effort of the NLCR was to do research with the record collectors who so generously made the music available to us. From their collections we made selections which were meaningful to ourselves, and hopefully to our "audience." (I think from the outset we never considered this audience as listeners, but rather as musicians looking for material and ways to play.) Most of the record collectors were not affiliated with the Revival or with academia. The list includes Eugene Earle, Bob Pinson, Dick Spottswood, Willie Foshag, Harry West, and Loy Beaver.

Notable among these collectors was Eugene Earle, whose home in New Jersey was stacked wall-to-wall with old hillbilly 78s. (His collection had been based on his long correspondence with John Edwards, an Australian collector of old-time hillbilly records, and their joint collections became the John Edwards Memorial Foundation.) On many occasions I would strap a tape recorder to the back of my Vespa motor scooter and drive across the George Washington Bridge for an evening of listening to and taping old records. It still remains a mystery to me how the selections were made, for there were more than ten thousand records available to choose from, and very few criteria upon which to make decisions. There wasn't enough time to hear them all. My choices often were based on some quirk in the title of a song, particularly if it resembled or evoked something I already knew from old folk song books or Burl Ives records, or if it was by an artist mentioned in Harry Smith's *Anthology.*

One of my best intuitive choices was to select a recording on the Challenge label (which featured a green image of a medieval knight in armor) for a performance of "Sweet Sunny South" by Da Costa Woltz's Southern Broadcasters.[32] I heard the electrifying sound of two banjos, a fiddle, and a high voice singing in the old-time way. The other side of the record was an equally exciting rendering of "Old Joe Clark." Here was old-time music that matched the intensity and drive of bluegrass. Later research indicated that the singer was Ben Jarrell, father of Tommy Jarrell. But we didn't know anything about them back in the early 1960s.[33]

Another astounding "discovery" amongst Gene Earle's collection was an unaccompanied fiddle performance of "Sally Goodin" by Eck Robertson. It was the sound that hit me first, and later discographic evidence showed that this was the first record made by a traditional American fiddler. The recording was done in 1922. Eventually Tracy Schwarz and myself drove across Texas to Amarillo to meet and record Eck Robertson at his home in 1963.

Once we had located a network of friends, collectors, folk song societies, and musicians across the country, the next step was to establish an organization that could protect, perpetuate, and help realize our ideas. In January 1961, Ralph Rinzler and myself joined with Izzy Young to create the Friends of Old Time Music, whose purpose was to present traditional musicians from around the country in their first New York City concerts.[34] The first challenge was how to assemble an audience without funds for advertising. Our first concert, in February 1961, included the Greenbriar Boys and Jean Ritchie as well as the New Lost City Ramblers. We all donated our services in order to pay for the guest artist, Roscoe Holcomb, to travel from Daisy, Kentucky. The auditorium at P.S. 41 in Greenwich Village was packed to capacity with about 400 people. We announced that membership in the FOTM was defined as attending the concert, so everyone signed up and we had a mailing list; this became standard practice.

Our next concert featured Clarence "Coo Coo Bird" Ashley with his string band of farmers from North Carolina. One of these "side" musicians was Doc Watson, who was greatly appreciated by the audience, and he and his family became our third FOTM concert. (It was here that the song "Amazing Grace" had its initial impact on a Revival audience.) Eventually the Friends of Old Time Music presented the first New York City concerts of the Stanley Brothers, Bill Monroe, Bessie Jones, Dock Boggs and Mississippi John Hurt (who shared a bill), Almeda Riddle, Hobart Smith, Joseph Spence (from the Bahamas), Gus Cannon and Furry Lewis, and Jesse Fuller. Many of the concerts were given full reviews by Robert Shelton in *The New York Times*. Often we would arrange for college concert appearances for these artists in conjunction with their New York City appearances. Most of the people who attended the concerts are still practicing musicians themselves. The research, production, and coordination of the concerts became a trial run for Ralph Rinzler, who went on to continue this kind of activity, first with the Newport Folk Festival and eventually with the Smithsonian Festival of American Folklife.

Small magazines, such as *Caravan, Gardyloo,* and *The Little Sandy Review*, as well as Izzy Young's column in *Sing Out!*, were supportive of the traditional music movement and used it as a basis for criticism of the commercial folk singers and record companies. The writings of Jon Pankake and Paul Nelson had a devastating effect on record companies such as Vanguard, in our opinion. Eventually other advocate publications emerged, such as *Frets, Bluegrass Unlimited, Old-Time Music* (from Britain), and presently *The Old-Time Herald* and the *Traditional Music Guide*. They continue to support the music to this day.

Folkways was the first company active in the folk song revival, then Elektra (Tom Paley made an early solo record for them), along with Riverside, Stinson, and many others. Folkways created the RBF label to put out reissues of old 78s,[35] Arhoolie Records followed with its Old Timey label, and County Records was next. Although it, too, was involved with reissues, County made an effort to search out the original artists and draw up new contracts for reissuing their earlier material. Part of County's initial records were "field" recordings of back-porch banjo players and fiddlers, and they eventually directed their sales at the rural audience in the Appalachians. There were plenty of bluegrass recordings on County as well.

Rounder Records started with an NEA Youth Grant to reissue 78s documenting the early history of bluegrass. Eventually similar small record companies, such as Rebel, Heritage, and Old

Homestead, evolved in the South. Evidence of the demand for out-of-print records was seen when Victor and Columbia found it financially feasible to reissue some of their early material. Musicians in the urban scene sought out Starday (from Nashville), where some of the original old-timers, Sam and Kirk McGee, were still recording, and which continued to issue some of the traditional bluegrass bands into the '70s.

It might be useful to compare in detail the way commercial folk singers and the traditional revivalists approached the music, both instrumentally and vocally. Probably the strongest precedent for the commercial folk singers was the Weavers, whose mixture of infectious projection and political optimism spilled over into the mass media before they were destroyed by the blacklist. They set a musical tone which the Kingston Trio and Peter, Paul and Mary took up a decade later. Their carefully crafted arrangements were accompanied by Fred Hellerman's intelligent and sophisticated use of the guitar. The way he played had no relation to anything heard on blues or hillbilly records, but came from the earlier urban tradition of piano arrangements for folk songs (to be performed around a piano or in a concert hall). He also incorporated elements from jazz and a nightclub style of earlier days. Likewise, Ronnie Gilbert's clear and wide-open singing was characterized by its resemblance to classical and pop styles of projection. In their own way, Mary Travers, Joan Baez, and Judy Collins continued this tradition.

By contrast, the country traditionalists starting with the NLCR, and urban blues singers such as Dave Van Ronk, Gino Foreman, Koerner, Ray and Glover, and John Hammond took their styles from old records. The blues singers moved further from any urban or suburban background. They had to get out of themselves and into an emotional, expressive, black style of singing. They took immense vocal risks, and in the process linked up with what was happening in rhythm and blues, eventually merging with rock 'n' roll, a process which continues today.

The nasal twang qualities of country singing were less taken up by the old-time string band musicians, who were more attracted to the quirky individualism which marked the pre-Nashville styles of country music. However, the forceful dictates of bluegrass singing as established by Bill Monroe were so much an integral part of that music that it was not possible to perform bluegrass in any other manner. The old-time string bands leaned heavily on the fiddle for their leading sound; the vocal styles seemed to follow. However, it became interesting to see how the nature of bluegrass singing invited a search for precedents in Appalachian ballad, gospel, and blues styles. Certain Carter Family harmonies seemed to offer an insight into bluegrass traditions (as heard clearly in their late recording of "The Girl from the Greenbriar Shore").

Besides the emphasis on the fiddle, the major factor which distinguishes the old-time string bands from the rest of the Revival is in the way they have been perpetuated. The measure of the success of the NLCR was not in money, hits, or how many records were sold, but in the continuation of the idea by people who had taken up the music. Some were not concerned with our sense of research, ethics, or moral stance; they just got deeply into the music. Although there were informal old-time string bands during the heyday of the Revival, since 1970 a serious progression of quality bands have emerged with a highly developed level of musicianship. This evolution is documented in Ray Alden's two-record anthology of the old-time music scene, *The Young Fogies*. It comes complete with personal notes and histories from the musicians, as well as a map of their distribution across the United States. It includes: the Highwoods Stringband, Alan Jabbour and the Hollow Rock String Band, Art Rosenbaum, the Fuzzy Mountain String Band, the Red Clay Ramblers, and representatives of the old-time musical congregations of fiddlers from the Lexington, Virginia scene; the Ithaca-Trumansburg, New York scene; the Berkeley, California-Colby Street scene; and the Bloomington, Indiana scene as well as individual musicians, along with recent bands like the Chicken Chokers, the Tompkins County Horseflies, and the Heart-beats.

Perhaps the greatest celebration of these bands was at the Highwoods Picnic, held at Trumansburg, New York for three or four years. This was truly a gathering of the clans, with fiddle bands converging from Virginia to New England, as well as from the Midwest. There was so much good music played in every corner of the site (along with the softball and volleyball games) that I felt, for the only time ever, as much satisfaction being there or listening as I did from actually playing the music.

Today, old-time music continues on the same informal basis, and is one of the few areas within the Revival where music is still actively played among musicians for pleasure, and not just as preparation for the stage. Still, it is welcomed at festivals and fiddle conventions nationwide, from the West Coast (Port Townsend) to Vermont. In the South, the annual Galax fiddle convention remains a mecca. The string bands have maintained their separation from bluegrass, and the Brandywine Festival is devoted solely to old-time music.

The horizons of traditional music, however, extended beyond old-time southern music. The Smithsonian Festival of American Folklife brought the issue to Congress's doorstep. The campaign for establishing an American Folklife Center in the Library of Congress was first articulated at workshops led by Archie Green, and he became the insistent proselytizer for legislation that mandated that it reflect regional traditions from every part of the nation. As the scope of traditional music broadened to include ethnic groups—the music of recent immigrants as well as of Native American cultures—the title of the center shifted from folklore and folk song to folklife (which now included crafts and cooking). The Folk Arts Program of the National Endowment for the Arts under Bess Lomax Hawes encouraged the establishment of state folk arts councils, which created jobs for state folklorists.[36] The NEA also adapted the Japanese concept of Living National Treasures to a wide range of traditional American folk artists and craftsmen via the National Heritage Fellowships.

Perhaps the most exemplary model of what was achieved in the dialogue between traditional music and the Revival can be seen in the re-emergence of Cajun music from its near demise in the early '60s. French culture in Louisiana at that time was near its lowest ebb, with the language not spoken in school and the young people not playing the local music. There was a statement at that time, "There is no such thing as an educated Cajun." But at meetings of the Newport Folk Festival Board at this time (in the early 1960s), the board, a diverse assembly of folk singers selected to represent the many facets of the Revival, was considering how best to use the substantial money generated from Newport festival attendance. Alan Lomax (who had recorded Cajun music for the Library of Congress during the '30s) together with Pete Seeger devised a revitalization program whereby traditional cultures might be explored and encouraged through an influx of funds from Newport.

The Newport board hired Ralph Rinzler to act on this program, and part of his work was to go to Louisiana and assess the situation there. He met several people within the Cajun culture who were also concerned about its decline. In conjunction with Ralph and the Newport board they created a Louisiana Folk Foundation, which put on a festival of French culture to showcase Cajun music. One of the first festivals was a celebration of harvest time in the various rural parishes. It was successful, and the word trickled out, leading to appearances by Cajun musicians at the Newport festival in 1964. Chris Strachwitz issued records of Cajun music on his Arhoolie label which were distributed in New York, Boston, and Berkeley. A concerted effort was made to "revive" the music.

The NLCR took part, with Mike Seeger singing "Parlez-Nous à Boire" in French and Tracy singing "Waltz du Bambouchard" from California to London. The idea was to get the folk song festivals interested in Cajun music, and for the Cajun musicians in Louisiana to know that their music was appreciated.[37] The results were astounding, and today Cajun music and its black counterpart, zydeco, are known throughout the United States and much of the world. Tracy Schwarz of the NLCR worked with Dewey Balfa for over a decade, producing records of how to play Cajun fiddle, doing workshops, and effectively spreading the word as well as the way. The music of younger Cajun bands such as Beausoleil is very popular in films and at festivals.

Although folk music does not enjoy the boom status and commercial appeal it once had, the structures for traditional music are now in place. This is evidenced by the proliferation of fiddle contests and bluegrass festivals, the growth of the National Folk Festival and the Smithsonian Folklife Festival, and the establishment of NEA folk arts programs and state folk arts councils. However, there are lingering perceptions about old-time string bands that have surfaced recently and that show how certain old prejudices refuse to go away. At the Clearwater Hudson River Revival Festival, Ray Alden had organized an old-time music stage which included a fiddle contest as well as a string band contest. Few old-time musicians play professionally; it remains essentially home-made music, and the contests provided opportunities for musicians to hear each other. But the Clearwater organization challenged the validity of this contest, accusing it of being white only, male-dominated, and competitive. These were values that the Hudson

River Revival did not want to encourage. They were operating from their own preconceptions rather than by examining the actual practices at the old-time music stage. Several bands consisting entirely of women had won the contest. There had been black blues performers on stage along with traditional fiddlers and bands. The fiddle competition was never prize-oriented, unless distributing ribbons, records, and guitar strings to all the participants is considered commercial. The character of these events was in the spirit of the southern fiddle conventions, and they took their standards from an old recording by Pop Stoneman and Eck Dunford, wherein the first prize is a bag of turnips. At a fiddle contest in Berkeley, California, the first prize was awarded to a band that was in Switzerland, for having the good sense not to show up. The quirky humor of the old-time music revival is better experienced than described. But the fiddle and band contests at the Hudson River Revival have been discontinued.

Currently a controversy has arisen among those who are concerned with the continuing role of traditional music. The lines seem to be drawn between those who shape directions by controlling funding on the one hand—folklorists, members of folk arts councils, National Endowment panels—and the "revival" performers on the other. The issue seems to be one of authenticity (read "purity") and whether one was born in the right place. The validity of revivalist performers has been put into question, just as the "purity" of the traditional performers has been elevated. This is more than a tempest in a teakettle. Rather, it is an aesthetic argument that has turned back upon itself. The traditionalists have been forced to examine their own criteria and validity in a way that borders on self-hatred. For an artist this is a deadly exercise, although it is the basic business of historians and critics. As Charles Seeger pointed out in "Folk Music in the Schools of a Highly Industrialized Society," drawing too tight a definition for folklore can be dangerous. He suggested instead that "folk" be seen as a process.

A few stories illustrate the dilemma. Revivalist, banjo player, collector, field recordist, record producer, and schoolteacher Ray Alden has had a close relationship with the Kimball family of southern Virginia, who had essentially stopped playing music. Ray's frequent visits and his playing music with them got things going again. They enjoy making music now with Ray and his friends. The Kimballs' musical existence today has developed in close dialogue with the Revival. Yet, when it comes to determining who performs at festivals the Kimballs are fundable, while Ray and his friends are not.

Peter Siegel ran into the same problem while writing notes for a concert of traditional music funded by folk arts councils. He was describing a young Irish fiddler and a New York revivalist fiddler, both of whom were to play.[38] Neither of them was born in the tradition. Through his interviews with them, Peter learned that both had been attracted to fiddle music; had learned the music from records, attended concerts, and approached and studied with master traditional musicians; had entered and won contests and made recordings; and now did performances. One (the Irish woman) is considered "traditional" and fundable by folk arts criteria. The other, a revivalist, is ineligible and deemed less valid.

The question this poses is not about the musicians, but about the philosophical positions of the folklore councils and panelists: their uneasy connection to scholarship and to their own "revival" training (many folklorists today also play traditional music). They have had to impose a "purer" set of values on an "impure" situation, using criteria that were developed within an isolated context. The problem has its roots in the earliest definition of "folklore," which was based on class distinctions that bordered on racism. Folklore study was a way for one class of people to look at the culture of another: an elite group defining the lower classes. More than a hundred years of usage of this concept has produced many abuses and created various monsters.

The NEA Folk Arts panelists are not ignoring folk singers. As the Revival constructed its own "star system" of traditional music, including Scruggs, Monroe, Doc Watson, and Tommy Jarrell, all of them were eventually awarded National Heritage Award status.[39] It seems clear that without the enthusiasm and support of the Revival, these folk/traditional artists would not have become so recognized. Their aesthetic positions were taken up and discussed by the revivalists who attended their college concerts and their appearances at folk festivals. Their music likewise was internalized, accepted, and performed by the revivalists. This recognition was echoed in the NEA panel's set of choices, but it was the Revival which did the initial "voting."

What is fundable as "authentic" has become itself a dynamic process, and today one of the best jokes goes like this: In earlier years the NEA Folk Arts and folk festivals would consider something as authentic only if it was played on unamplified instruments. Then it became okay if you played electric guitars, *if* you were black. Now anybody can "plug in" and still be considered authentic—but if you're black, you can also include a saxophone.

Perhaps the most endearing effect of the traditional music revival has been its impact beyond the movement. There have always been interfaces with pop music. Other influences were more subtle, but of significance. Paul Brady is an Irish musician known for his rock 'n' roll as well as his traditional Irish songs. He told me how important the NLCR records were to him in Ireland when he was getting started as a musician. They gave him the idea that he could perform his own national, traditional, "authentic" music even though he was not from within the tradition himself. The possibility exemplified by the NLCR gave him this permission. The mission was more important than the particular music.

The need for the Revival is over. The Village has become Global, and traditional music is synonymous with ethnic music. It is connected to worldwide ethnic identities and nations that refuse to go away. The continuous spread of international market economics and their dependence on consumer conformity is challenged by the strength and diversity of traditional cultures.

NOTES

[1] Charles Seeger did a record for the Library of Congress on the variants of "Barbara Allen."

[2] Although we were operating outside the defined boundaries of academia and commerce, twenty-five years later both Mike Seeger and myself received Guggenheim Fellowships, while Ralph Rinzler went on to help oversee the Smithsonian Folklife Festival as an undersecretary at the Smithsonian.

[3] Irwin Silber at *Sing Out!* viewed folk singers as a way to draw a crowd to get them to listen to the political messages.

[4] See David Whisnant's book *All That Is Native and Fine: The Politics of Culture in an American Region* (Chapel Hill: University of North Carolina Press, 1983) for more about the Whitetop Festival and John Powell.

[5] Roscoe told me that when he was young he could sing like

Dolly Parton. This issue was directly faced in Charles Seeger's essay "The Folkness of the Nonfolk and the Nonfolkness of the Folk," in his *Studies in Musicology, 1935-1975* (Berkeley: University of California Press, 1977), 335-343.

[6] Besides his recordings of ballads with five-string banjo, Clarence "Tom" Ashley also did comedy in blackface and claims to have "discovered" Roy Acuff.

[7] It also confirmed musical comparisons between Woody Guthrie's versions of songs such as "Gypsy Davy" and supposed old English versions (via Dyer-Bennet's "Raggle Taggle Gypsy-O") of the same.

[8] In 1960, the Greenbriar Boys competed at the Union Grove Old Time Fiddlers convention. In 1961, Mike Seeger, Lisa Chiera, and myself documented the convention for a Folkways record. The reporter Robert Shelton did an article on the convention for *The New York Times*. Within a few years, the convention grew in size from less than 1,000 to more than 15,000 people (including various motorcycle gangs taking over the small town of Union Grove). Old-time and bluegrass bands from New York competed. City dwellers made the trip to Union Grove every Easter, and the scene became greater than the music. As the recognition given by the Revival grew, many fiddlers' conventions in the South picked up new energy. The idea of visiting a convention became a popular activity. Within a few years, country people and urban students were meeting and playing music together from Vermont to Montana, especially in the South.

[9] Lomax has described how he "helped to get the folk Revival zooming down the line." He points to two series of twenty-six radio shows he produced in 1939 and '40, which were circulated and played in school systems across the nation. Alan asked Pete Seeger to help him with this "Columbia [Broadcasting System] School of the Air." These CBS radio programs were recorded in New York City every week. Each was an hour-long show whose purpose, according to Pete Seeger, was to relate people's culture to high culture. Alan used singers, including Pete, Joanna Colcorde, folk singers, and any "traditional" singers if they were available (he mentioned Leadbelly); Alan also sang. The format was for a performer to do a folk song; then a symphony orchestra would play an arrangement of it. The composers included Aaron Copland, Charles Seeger, Ruth Crawford Seeger, and others.

Alan also wrote and produced nationwide broadcasts (with Nicholas Ray) for the CBS Forecast Series: in 1940, "Back Where I Come From," with Woody Guthrie, Burl Ives, Josh White, and the Golden Gate Quartet; and in 1947, *Hootenanny*, with Pete Seeger, Sonny Terry, Woody Guthrie, Brownie McGhee, Hally Wood, Sidney Bechet, Cisco Houston, and others, with John Henry Faulk as host. Lomax states that his strategy was to present these musicians as "stars," because the American entertainment industry was based on a star system. He also used many of these same artists in a BBC show he wrote called "The Martins and The Coys," which was designed as anti-Nazi propaganda to be part of the war effort.

In the late '40s, besides reissuing hillbilly material for Decca and producing Cousin Emmy in a city-oriented package album, Lomax brought Burl Ives to Moe Asch's Disc label and produced an album of Hobart Smith and Texas Gladden for Disc. He had earlier recorded them for the Library of Congress.

Much research remains to be done about how Lomax fed songs to and developed repertoire for Woody Guthrie, Burl Ives, and Josh White. Possibly it happened in the course of producing these radio shows. (Such research could begin with the song "House of the Rising Sun," which was in Guthrie and White's repertoire.) Recently, Lomax noted: "In the 1960s I turned from my work as a popularizer and promoter in order to devote my energies to the taxonomy and geography of world song styles, in order to investigate what general principles underlay the whole world picture."

[10] In the late '40s, when Jean Ritchie came to New York City from Kentucky, she also worked at Henry Street Settlement. The role of the settlement houses on the Lower East Side of New York needs further examination: I know that my parents, who were first-generation immigrants from Russia, were introduced to folk singing and folk dancing at the Madison Street Settlement in the 1920s.

[11] Besides ASDG, another group called Folksay was quite serious about square dancing. Both these groups were separate from Michael Herman's International Folk Dance Movement and probably were also more consciously political. Irwin Silber belonged to Folksay. My parents, who were involved in the folk dance movement, sometimes had Margot Mayo come and teach square dancing on alternate weeks in Sunnyside, Queens, in the late

1930s.

[12] Pete Seeger recalls that when he first started singing (after dropping out of college in 1938), he could get $5 for singing at Dalton, and then at the Walden School. It was there that he first met Margot Mayo, and she invited him to join ASDG. He recalls that her intention was to introduce square dancing and to make sure that it was "done right." She was a down-to-earth person, very catholic in taste. According to Pete, she would put up with his communism, and with John Jacob Niles's anti-Semitism. Pete was nineteen years old then and met his future wife Toshi (who was sixteen) at the ASDG.

[13] Norman Studer was also director of the Little Red Schoolhouse in Greenwich Village and later was director of the Downtown Community School on East 11th Street. He and his wife, Hanna, lived in Sunnyside, Queens, where I knew of them as a child.

[14] For more on this tradition, see Simon Bronner, *Old Time Music Makers of New York State* (Syracuse: Syracuse University Press, 1987). Also see Norman Cazden's *The Abelard Folk Song Book* (New York: Abelard Schuman, 1958) for material collected at the camp.

[15] The camp had a political orientation as well, and many children of blacklisted writers and children of politically persecuted Communists were welcome at the camp.

[16] At the end of one summer I worked as a waiter at a nearby resort. Two of my co-workers were Tom Paley and Izzy Young.

[17] Kent Sidon at Oberlin College was the first to present Pete Seeger in solo concerts after the Weavers had been broken up by the blacklist in the early 1950s.

[18] The hoots went on well into the 1960s, and a second folk singing event from Yale, the Indian Neck Folk Festival, continued for many years.

[19] The reissues of hillbilly and blues records were in great contrast to what had been available on radio and records during the '40s, when on the radio, for example, were Marais and Miranda and Burl Ives. In the '50s things brightened with Oscar Brand's weekly radio show on WNYC; on records there was Dyer-Bennet, John Jacob Niles, Susan Reed, and Josh White.

[20] Years later I did a long interview with Harry Smith at the Chelsea Hotel which appeared in two issues of *Sing Out!* (April/May

and July/August 1969). Harry's original design for the cover of the *Anthology* featured an image of the celestial monochord from Robert Fludd's book on mysticism. During the folk boom that engraving was replaced by a Farm Security Administration photo of a poor farmer in overalls.

[21] This sort of decision had been made earlier by California record collectors when Columbia sold off its 14000 and 15000 series from warehouses in the Bay Area during World War II. Collectors had to choose hillbilly or blues, for no one could afford to seriously collect both. This infusion of earlier records set the stage for Harry Smith's *Anthology*. Harry lived in the Bay Area at that time.

[22] In 1962, Monroe made his first appearance outside of the country circuit, playing one weekend at the University of Chicago Folk Festival, and the next weekend in New York City for the Friends of Old Time Music. At the same time Monroe appeared on the cover of *Sing Out!*, with a lead article written by Ralph Rinzler.

[23] A year earlier Mike and Ralph had tried to make a similar record for Moe that evidently hadn't worked out. I was unaware of this. However, I had met Moe a year earlier while accompanying Guy Carawan on his first record. I spoke to Moe about some of his pre-Folkways recordings of Woody, Cisco, and Sonny Terry. I expressed how much I was excited by the spirit on those sessions. Months later, after playing music with Tom and Mike in Maryland, in the spring of 1958, I told Moe of this group, which sounded like his earlier recordings. He asked who were the musicians, and he agreed to the record without any audition.

[24] Such as *Kramer vs. Kramer* and *Places in the Heart*.

[25] The first was presented by the American Youth Hostels and organized by my brother, Mike. We shared the program with Andrew Rowan Summers. The second concert, in June, was at Mills College, presented by the Folksingers' Guild. It was notorious for gags, audience participation, tapes of Tom tuning for sale, and a guitar with a prepared neck which was supposed to break off when Tom tuned it, and which was eventually smashed and jumped upon on stage. We also did a concert in Washington, D.C., with Elizabeth Cotten and a concert for Charlie Faurot at Trinity College.

[26] In 1961, a trio of managers offered to manage us, and briefly and near-disastrously, we signed with them and their

booking agency, ITA. We also sang uptown at the sophisticated
Blue Angel in New York City. It was there that we were forced to
adopt another "format," which was a repeatable program or show.
It caused great division between us; Tom preferred to walk out
rather than do the same show twice. But we devised our own
format, in which we could substitute within our entire range of
music and still have a predictable order of some length. Our "basic
show" consisted of an opening instrumental breakdown followed
by one or two hard-driving full string band songs (such as "Battle-
ship of Maine"); then we would present a Carter Family song,
followed by two or three "solos"—usually a ballad (with Mike on
Autoharp) a banjo song, and a monologue or such. By then we
figured the audience was bored, so we'd do a furious ragtime
instrumental, a duet (later, with Tracy Schwarz, it was bluegrass
style), and a preposterous song ("Arkansas Traveler" or "There Ain't
No Bugs on Me"), and we'd end with a rousing double fiddle and
guitar song. This format stayed with us, and we could create
expanded or shortened versions. But the management didn't work
out; we got no jobs, were stuck in an exclusive contract, and almost
gave up. But a series of Seeger Family Concerts that winter saw us
through, and we legally got out of the contract and took on Manny
Greenhill as our manager for the remainder of our years performing
full-time.

   [27] Johnny Cash, who had shared the bill with us at the Ash
Grove, later caricatured our song intros when he announced "as
Mike Seeger would say" and then gave his own discography on
stage.

   [28] Other introductions offered curious perversions of aca-
demic and mythic folklore. I recall Mike introducing a song this way:
"This is an old ballad I learned from my mother when I was a child."
What he failed to mention was that his mother (Ruth Crawford
Seeger) was singing the song in order to transcribe it from a Library
of Congress record for Alan Lomax's book Folk Song U.S.A.

   Tom Paley had a fabricated song intro: "Once there was a
fella named Brown who was a Red. He used to run the ferry out
of New Lost City. After he finished running them out, he wrote this
white blues, called the 'Brown's Ferry Blues.'" At a performance in
San Francisco's Great American Music Hall I improvised this intro:
"This is a song that was recorded in the late '20s. Actually it wasn't
recorded because the musicians got lost on their way to the

recording studio." Mike chimes in, "There wasn't any studio." I returned, "This is what they would have recorded if they had gotten there. We studied the recording session ledger sheets, which are a form of scholarly discographic research, and found that they were blank for that day. But there were little marks on the paper, so we rubbed graphite into those to get an indication of what they would have sung if the pencil hadn't broke. So this is transcribed from their intentions."

[29] I will never forget my introduction to Tex Logan's Texas bluegrass fiddling, when I was asked to play backup guitar on his recording session. I could only resort to Riley Puckett's chromatic guitar runs, because at that point I was unfamiliar with the orthodoxy of the Lester Flatt G run used in bluegrass music.

[30] Mike Seeger's long involvement with traditional musicians deserves a separate study by itself. His history connects to the issues developed within the Seeger family and also was affected by his own experience during the late 50s working in TB hospitals in the Baltimore area. It was here he came in contact with displaced country people, including the family of Hazel Dickens. He also was close to the Baltimore bluegrass bars. Eventually, after the NLCR, he brought many traditional singers on concert tours with him. Seeger has continued to issue recordings of traditional musicians and has produced at least thirty such documentary records over the years.

[31] I already had had the experience of climbing around the Peruvian Andes, collecting material about weaving for my MFA thesis at Yale University in 1957, and saw the opportunity of visiting eastern Kentucky as another foray into a new world for me.

[32] Da Costa Woltz was the mayor of Galax, who organized the band.

[33] At the close of the early NLCR concerts we would invite members of the audience up to play a few tunes at the finale. In the winter of 1960, we invited Libba Cotten to share the program with us. Her presence, combined with the musicians from the audience, set the idea in motion of including traditional performers in the concerts. This was the immediate antecedent to the Friends of Old Time Music and became a significant step within the Revival.

Traditional musicians were not part of earlier folk song concerts in the '30s, '40s, and '50s. According to Pete Seeger, his father's attitude back then was that stage appearances changed the traditional performance style. For example, Aunt Molly Jackson would smile and wave at the audience during a song, and although Woody Guthrie attempted to retain his Oklahoma traditional form of presentation, Charlie felt he was putting it on for the audience. His "agenda" for folk songs was recording and documenting them accurately in the field, and then arranging them and reintroducing them into the schools in order to preserve them as living traditions. This is spelled out fully in his article "Folk Music in the Schools of a Highly Industrialized Society," in his *Studies in Musicology*, 330-334.

It should be noted that there were no traditional performers at the first Newport Folk Festival in 1959 (although bluegrass music was represented by the Stanley Brothers and Earl Scruggs).

[34] The FOTM was the popular name for the Society For Traditional Music, Inc. The board of trustees included Margot Mayo and Jean Ritchie. Besides income from concert admissions, the major source of income was royalties generated by the Simon and Schuster *Young Folk Song Book* (New York, 1963), featuring Joan Baez, Bob Dylan, Peggy Seeger, Jack Elliott, the Greenbriar Boys, and the New Lost City Ramblers. The book was dedicated to Elizabeth Cotten. We also issued a record on Folkways of performances from the concerts.

[35] This separate label was created to avoid damage to Folkways in the event of legal action owing to the issuance of material from other companies. Moe Asch's moral premise was that when an artist signs a contract with a company, his or her work is made available to the public, and that when a company lets the record go out of print, it is depriving the artist of that access, along with the concomitant income. In contrast to the major labels, Folkways never let anything go out of print.

[36] By offering potential jobs to qualified graduates with folklore degrees, the councils helped strengthen university folklore programs.

[37] In 1965, we made a tour of Europe and brought a Cajun band with us (along with Cousin Emmy, the Stanley Brothers, and Roscoe Holcomb). In 1964, I had taken CBS News to Louisiana for a program that highlighted Cajun culture, but it was cancelled because CBS executive Fred Friendly felt that "nobody would listen to thirty seconds of that music."

[38] It should be noted that the concentration and hours of

practice required to study and master traditional fiddle styles is equal in many respects to a college education. Chris Strachwitz has pointed out that someone learning fiddle puts in as many hours, or more, as a medical student. There are college graduates who have continued their intellectual and artistic commitment to their music, just as they did vis-à-vis their academic studies. Some of them are living right here in Bloomington, unnoticed by the folklorists who study here.

[39] Within the traditional music revival, echoes of the mainstream culture resurfaced, and a series of stars (or foci of attention) and preferred fiddle tunes have emerged and briefly seized the spotlight. Initially (back in the '50s), Pete Seeger was the star of traditional music (along with everything else he did), but within the Revival, Earl Scruggs emerged as the preeminent banjo player and became a dominant focus, only to be re-evaluated and replaced by Bill Monroe as the founder of bluegrass. From this emerged an old time music vs. bluegrass axis. The presence of Doc Watson moved the focus back toward a home-grown musical experience, but Doc's widespread success and ability to cash in on this tainted the issue somewhat. He accomplished the sought-after crossover between old-time and bluegrass, but among the traditionalists, the focus shifted to Tommy Jarrell, indicating yet another reordering of values, as if the pop art/pop culture/folk culture discussion was over and we were back to a sense of individual regional style as being of high value. As the Cajun revival grew, Dewey Balfa's perspective and musical commitment were greeted in much the same way. It was Tracy Schwarz (of the NLCR) who did much of the legwork to make Dewey accessible.

3 Ed Kahn

I recently attended a local fiddle contest in southern California and it brought back lots of memories. I thought of exciting festivals I had attended in Galax, Virginia, and even earlier in Asheville, North Carolina, some thirty-five years ago when Bascom Lamar Lunsford still hosted his annual event. What a world of change had taken place over these years! I asked myself how folklorists a hundred years from now will view the folk song revival of the mid-twentieth century. And I ask myself if enough time has passed for me to begin to evaluate the folk song revival with some objectivity.

Perhaps objectivity is not possible, but it is now time to reflect on the Revival within a broad historical context. For chronicling my journey through this time, my experiences as record review editor from 1963 to 1970 for *Western Folklore* under the editorship of Wayland D. Hand were important. Reviewing records forced me to examine a wide range of material for possible coverage and helped me see trends, themes, and changes as they unfolded.

When I think back to the folk song revival, I see a number of themes begging for analysis. On the one hand, the folk song revival was part of the commercial music industry. On the other hand, I see that this revival was not all that unlike earlier folk song revivals.[1] I suspect that the folklorist of the future will see that old songs gained a new lease on life while new songs entered the folk repertoire through this newly emerging tradition. Unlike any revival of the past, however, this revival involved a marriage of high technology and tradition. In essence, a study of the folk song revival is a study of the folk process. In this sense, the tools folklorists have developed over the life of their discipline are the right tools for

studying this newest chapter in the life and times of folk songs. But
the model for studying this folk process must now broaden to
include new technological and commercial considerations as well
as the more traditional concerns of the folklorist. The tools for
analyzing the impact of technology and the commercial music
industry are new to the folklorist. They were not part of the early
studies of the folk process.

In the old days, folklorists did field work with pen and
notepad. By the 1890s, the first field recordings were made on
cylinders.[2] These recordings were innovative and experimental
and ushered in a new era in folkloristic fieldwork. By the 1920s,
both commercial and noncommercial recordings were being made
on a regular basis, but the equipment was bulky and expensive. A
recording becomes a snapshot of sound. It freezes a performance
for us to analyze, appreciate, imitate, or build upon. Scholars listen
and try to make sense out of broad patterns; performers listen and
imitate or incorporate; fans listen and appreciate.

John Lomax pioneered in the use of mechanical recording
devices for the collection of American vernacular music. In 1907, he
committed the first English language folk songs to sound recordings. A host of other collectors, including Howard Odum, Robert
Winslow Gordon, and Guy B. Johnson, soon followed. The work
of both Gordon and Lomax, now joined by his son Alan, formed the
basis for the Library of Congress folk song archive.

By the mid-1950s, a romanticized picture of folk song
collecting was firmly planted in the popular imagination through the
work of the Library of Congress and the press. Borden Deal, in his
1959 novel, *The Insolent Breed*, describes a fictional folk song
collector who visits a family of rural musicians. When the family
sees a heavily loaded car approaching, they first guess it is a
bootlegger. When the collector arrives, he tells them he is making
recordings of old songs for his college and that the best of the
material will be passed on to the Library of Congress.[3] This
description conforms to the popular image of a folk song collector
and attests to the bulk and volume of early disk recording equipment. Deal's description paints a reasonably accurate composite
portrait of these early fieldworkers.

A generation of new folk music enthusiasts followed in the
mold of earlier collectors and began to comb the backwoods of the
United States and especially the South in search of folk songs.

Technology reduced the cost and bulk of sound recording equipment to the point that hundreds of enthusiasts were doing sophisticated fieldwork. Much of this material ended up on recordings and in archives as well as in personal collections.

I was a product of this revolution and began fieldwork in the spring of 1957 with a fifty-pound Magnecorder that was technically portable but far too bulky for casual work. By the mid-1960s, I had shifted over to an Ampex 600 recorder, which was smaller and lighter and captured better sound. In recording equipment, there has always been a trade-off between price and portability. As early as the 1960s, relatively lightweight machines such as the Nagra were available, but they carried price tags that put them out of reach of many amateur collectors. In succeeding years, more and more lightweight equipment of high quality became available. Folkways Records was the first commercial record company to open the way for collectors to make the fieldwork collected on these machines available to a general audience.

Traditional artists whom folk song collectors "discovered" now had the opportunity to enter into the commercial arena. Doc Watson, for instance, began his commercial success as a member of Tom Ashley's string band. When folk song collectors Ralph Rinzler and Eugene W. Earle found him in the summer of 1960, his life changed because he entered the commercial music business as a performer and recording artist. Similar stories can be told about many musicians, some of whom, like Tom Ashley, had enjoyed commercial success through the record industry in years past and some of whom made their way onto wax for the first time as a result of the efforts of fieldworkers armed with newly available inexpensive recording equipment.

The folk song revival can be recognized as one locus wherein the folk process meets the industrial complex. Musicians, once they leave the ranks of amateurs, inevitably move into the world of business. Gradually the musician—whether a traditional or revival artist—comes into close contact with managers, bookers, publishers, record company executives, and a host of other businessmen, including lawyers and agents. While some musicians may choose to stay clear of commercial interests, the vast majority of the best musicians are drawn into this alien world if they have any interest in attaining either part-time or full-time professional musicianship. In turn, the Revival, to the extent that it was commercially motivated and driven, forced the music in new directions.

The record reviewer inevitably makes judgments about the music that he reviews. As a record review editor in the 1960s, I was fascinated by the Revival for a number of reasons. I saw it stimulating and expanding the market for traditional musicians. Additionally, I have always been interested as a folklorist in the folk process. I admittedly made judgment calls as I decided what to review and what to leave aside. Time often proves the folklorist wrong. In any case, it proved me wrong. Looking back, I would prefer to have taken a wider view than I did in the 1960s and to have let time show whether I was then too inclusive.

Charles Seeger's 1948 *Journal of American Folklore* review of four 78 RPM albums (*Listen to Our Story, Mountain Frolic, Sod Buster Ballads*, and *Deep Sea Chanteys and Whaling Ballads*) inaugurated record reviewing in an academic journal.[4] Interestingly, he chose to review two albums of commercial reissues of early hillbilly records originally marketed to the same rural audience from which the music came; the records, in this repackaged format, were now redirected to an urban audience. We label his second pair of records early folk song revival recordings even though the Revival had not yet begun. (I tend to date the folk song revival's key years as the decade during which the Kingston Trio recorded—from 1958 through 1967.)

In a sense, all four albums Seeger discussed were part of and highlighted two different facets of the folk song revival. The Revival not only stimulated new interest in genuine traditional music, but also fostered new recordings of traditional and quasi-traditional material. Two of the albums in Seeger's review, as we have seen, are early examples of traditional vernacular recordings repackaged and marketed to a new, urban audience; along with the recordings came a sing-along booklet. The other two albums are clearly pre-Revival recordings that set the stage for the folk song revival, still a decade away. In any case, the record companies directed all four of these albums to the same non-folk urban audience. The Revival did more to popularize traditional songs to this largely urban audience than any promotion that any record company executive ever dreamed up. The movement eventually spread through the urban centers back to the rural base.

Since well before the beginning of the recording industry, the term "folk music" has had a distinctly different meaning for the public at large and for the folklorist. Neither the general public nor the music industry embraced the folklorist's notion that folk music meant traditional music performed in a traditional style. Over the years, the record industry's notion of just what folk music does mean has changed, but never has it corresponded with the definition of the folklorist. I recently went into a large record store that specialized in close-out items. The store offered a huge section labeled folk music. As I thumbed through the offerings, I was struck by the fact that not one single recording even approached what I, as a folklorist, would call folk music. The music industry has long regarded folk music as a style of performance or a kind of song that has little, if anything, to do with authenticity or tradition. It still does not matter to the record executive if any or all of the material the "folk artist" offers is of recent vintage. Quite the contrary, record companies remain in the business of making money, and new compositions are preferable to the old ones because they offer more lucrative possibilities. Copyright is simply not as profitable with traditional material as with new compositions. It does not matter if the style presented represents traditions established during the folk song revival rather than traditional folk song styles.

From time to time, however, some folklorists found that they were able to work with the industry. For one thing, record company staffers read record reviews and looked for the stamp of approval that intellectual appreciation brought. The industry wanted to feel itself progressive in the best sense of the word and did not want to appear closed-minded. Hence, some company executives listened to folklorists. For example, Kenneth Goldstein was early able to get work as a record producer. Much of his material stands out for embodying the highest standards of quality and scholarship. He was able to work with the industry and get approval to present, through recordings, literally hundreds of artists and thousands of songs. But in the long run, Goldstein selected an academic career. His timing for moving into the academic world coincided with the Revival moving into high gear and embracing a kind of music that he did not wish to produce.

Other academics also had a profound influence on the folk song revival. Ralph Rinzler, for instance, had a huge influence on the career of Bill Monroe. Single-handedly, Rinzler directed Monroe's music to an urban audience, where he found a new kind of appreciation. Likewise, Flatt and Scruggs, Mac Wiseman, and a

host of other bluegrass musicians found an eager audience in the
cities and on college campuses.

I remember seeing Flatt and Scruggs perform in a rural
drive-in theater in Kentucky in the early '60s and seeing them
perform not too many years later at the Ash Grove in Los Angeles.
The contrast startled me. In the Kentucky setting, the Flatt and
Scruggs band performed from the roof of the concession stand of
the drive-in. The sound was delivered through a common public
address system and the lighting provided by floodlights. The
audience listened to familiar music in a familiar setting. The fans felt
relaxed and free to wander around during the performance. The
show was peppered with rural humor, and a particularly apprecia-
tive audience response to one musical number prompted Flatt and
Scruggs to play a few more bars of the same song.

In contrast, when they played in Los Angeles, Flatt and
Scruggs appeared on a stage well lit by focused spotlights. The
sound system provided the audience with the best acoustics. The
audience seemed reverential—you could hear a pin drop—as they
listened to music essentially outside their own tradition. The
coffeehouse setting seemed concert-like even though the audience
could buy alcoholic and nonalcoholic drinks. Flatt and Scruggs
played the same music in both settings, but by the time I heard
them in Los Angeles, they had tailored their show for an urban
audience. They had toned down their rural humor, and an encore
at the end of the show consisting of new numbers replaced the
practice I had seen in Kentucky of repeating a few bars of an
appreciated number. Flatt and Scruggs had added a new style of
presentation for a new audience while maintaining their old style for
their old audience.

Gradually their repertoire shifted to meet what they per-
ceived to be the tastes of their new urban audience. They came to
understand that their city audience had a new respect for more
traditional sounds and songs. The enthusiastic urban audience saw
them as preserving an older musical heritage into which they were
weaving their own unique strands before passing it along to a new
generation. The work of academic folklorists influenced these
changes, since folklorists often maintained active contact with
traditional rural performing artists and helped bring a new pride and
respect to purveyors of older musical styles and songs.

The folklorist also had a similar influence on the record

producers themselves. Small companies throughout the South came to realize that a vast new audience existed for the same music they had been selling for years. They needed only to redirect their promotional efforts. Folklorists became part of the stable of resources on which many of the most successful record producers relied.

Nevertheless, many folklorists who had contact with the record industry found a sharp conflict between their own aesthetics and the popular aesthetic. While much good came from the folk song revival—university folklore programs, for instance, received a new generation of young scholars interested in folk song and balladry—much baggage accumulated that the folklorists did not like. It proved difficult to accept the commercialization of traditional music, the dilution of traditional songs and styles, and the growth in popularity of a new music called folk music that had little or nothing to do with previous academic definitions.

At the same time, folk song scholars lost objectivity. We know that the collector influences the informant, but we overlook how extensively the scholar is affected by close contact with the performer and the industry that envelops the music. What had once been obscure now became mainstream. The broad acceptance of this music played a role in coloring the objectivity of the folk song scholar. Scholars now were in contact with bookers and agents as they planned and participated in folk song festivals and concert appearances. The days of scholarly isolation had ended.

Gradually, a movement began toward the merging of performance and scholarship as more and more young scholars also performed. Performance increases insight. Much as an art historian gains insight by dabbling in painting, folk song scholars increased their perception by participating in performance. But at the same time, they became a part of the process. Many of the best workers in the field came from a generation of folk song enthusiasts who began their careers as performers and gradually became well-rounded folklorists. Examples abound, but we can cite Alan Jabbour, Joe Hickerson, Richard Bauman, Ellen Stekert, and Roger Abrahams as representative of this phenomenon.

Charles Seeger, in a particularly insightful and often over-looked article in *Grove's Dictionary of Music and Musicians*, lists four stages of acculturation that well describe what happened in the folk song revival: hostility, satirization, admiration, and adoption.[5]

A record reviewer is positioned to see examples of each of these stages, and the folk song revival abounds in examples of Revival performances stuck in one or more of them. I am sure that some musicians evolved through each of these stages. However, Seeger's description illustrates the development of the folk song revival itself.

The record company's A and R (artists and repertoire) man found himself at the nexus of this phenomenon. He ultimately had to decide which songs and artists he wanted to record. The A and R man had to juggle his personal preferences, the tastes of his artists, and the industry's values. The composite of these resulted in the released records, each reflecting a unique blend of these forces.

Urban revival performers fall into two broad classes. The first group, the traditionalists, emulated earlier field and commercial recordings. One of the great differences between these revival artists and their traditional counterparts lies in the circumstance that the revival artists drew on a much wider range of repertoire and style than most of the traditional artists, who were largely regional in their approach to the music.

The second class of revival artist consisted of modernists, who consciously introduced new material as well as non-folk styles of performance. This new repertoire often became much more relevant to these musicians than older material far removed culturally and stylistically from their musical and life experiences. Modern artists who disregarded traditional styles could look back on a long history of non-folk performers who enjoyed the melodies and texts of folk music while abhorring the sound and style of traditional music. Operatic singers like Leonard Warren and early folk song figures like John Jacob Niles established the pedigree of this tradition.

We need to look at the merging of traditions which the folk song revival encouraged. On the business level, record executives like Kenneth Goldstein fully participated in laying the foundations of the Revival within the record industry. Goldstein influenced other record producers and established trends. He, however, never tried to make it into the mainstream of the commercial folk song revival. I suspect that even if he had tried he would not have succeeded, as it was far from his interests and tastes. Recording executives who have strong preferences in material and style are seldom able to shift radically, although they often grow within a framework.

On the musical level, we find abundant examples of traditions merging. Bill Keith, a Boston banjo picker, became one of the most influential banjo players in bluegrass circles through his association with Earl Scruggs and a stint with Bill Monroe. Ralph Rinzler assisted in this union. City and country traditions flowed together as mass media and the folk song revival brought common interests to the fore. It is interesting to listen to recent recordings by the children of Grandpa Jones, a commercial Nashville musician who always reflected his strong love of traditional music.[6] Clearly, they were as much influenced by the folk song revival as by their father's strong commitment to traditional styles.

Eventually, the merging of traditions results in the emergence of something new. Synthesis ultimately and inevitably gives birth to something different. In the case of the folk song revival, the merging of traditions eventually gave birth to a new form of popular music. My initial mention of folk music as having a different meaning for the commercial music industry and for the folklorist signifies the development of something new. The Kingston Trio and Peter, Paul and Mary created new sounds, not re-creations of something old. Similarly, Bob Dylan, while having roots in the folk song revival, has gone on to create something quite unique and firmly rooted in popular music.

I move to a brief discussion of the relationship between the study of vernacular music and the study of the folk song revival. We now see that the issues facing the study of the folk song revival bear more similarity to the study of vernacular music than folklorists might once have thought—or rather wanted to admit. Scholars will need to identify the similarities and study the differences.

One big difference stems from the role money played in the process. In the early days of recording vernacular music, money was much less a consideration than it became in the heyday of the Revival. Early rural artists who committed their performances to wax did so out of pride and personal reward rather than for monetary considerations. While a few artists made a good deal of money, none of the early artists made the kind of money gained by the Kingston Trio, or even by the Weavers a decade earlier. Rural musicians, for the most part, experimented with a new medium and had little expectation of making it big. With few exceptions, even successful rural artists had to rely on personal appearances or outside employment in order to make ends meet. The Revival opened the possibility of really making a living from traditional and quasi-traditional music. Even some of the resurrected old-time artists who enjoyed success on the folk music circuit admitted that they made much more money during the Revival than they ever did during their initial careers in r.usic.

In order to study commercially recorded vernacular music, we had to modify our old ways of thinking. Once it became clear that the commercial recording industry had documented traditional informants, scholars turned to the broad repertoire represented by the industry. First, the folklorist became interested in traditional material captured on commercial recordings. Next, folklorists began to study the performers themselves. In time, scholars began to document the folk process and widen the area of inquiry to include the role the industry itself played in the process. It was a simple leap to become interested in new songs created in response to commercial demands. The evidence clearly indicates that songs with commercial origins entered tradition through initial dissemination on recordings. One well-known example is Blind Andy Jenkins' composition "The Death of Floyd Collins."

The Reverend Andrew Jenkins was a well-known songwriter in Atlanta at the beginning of hillbilly music's golden era—roughly from 1923 until the beginning of the Second World War. In 1925, the story of Floyd Collins, a young Kentuckian trapped in a sandstone cave near Mammoth Cave, Kentucky, captivated America. From January 30 until February 16, the country waited anxiously as a rescue party tried to free Collins. When they finally reached him, he was dead. In April 1925, record producer Polk C. Brockman wired Andy Jenkins and told him to write a song about the event. Jenkins' composition quickly entered into tradition and has been widely recovered by folk song collectors.[7]

To study the folk song revival in the decades ahead, it will be necessary to modify our way of thinking. We can start with a conservative definition of folk song, but we also will have to consider everything that this study touches on: tune, text, context, biography, and means of transmission, as well as other influences that will come to light. If we study all of these facets, we will have a huge area of interest. And when case studies of ballads become fashionable again, no researcher will exclude Revival recordings regardless of how far removed from tradition the style of performance. Folklorists will need to examine the record and include all evidence that gives clues as to the transmission and change of material. Over time, the folklorist has moved from a model which analyzed only oral transmission of anonymous material that seemed to come from folk origins to a broader study of folk process which includes all of the forces and influences that play a role in the process. Material comes from all kinds of sources and finds an acceptance and life of its own among traditional singers. No one can deny that a clear understanding of the folk song revival is essential to an understanding of the contemporary folk process.

The Revival drew from and provided an audience for traditional material and styles. The broadened Revival audience assimilated the material to varying degrees and reinterpreted the material into new styles. We know that numerous popular groups grew out of the folk song revival and illustrate this point. We can examine the work of groups like the Byrds and their offshoots, the Eagles and the Flying Burrito Brothers. All three groups drew heavily from traditional country music styles; they synthesized country music and their folk song revival roots. But they were products of the folk song revival, not of mainstream country music. The Revival served as a conduit for styles to re-emerge in popular music.

Likewise, traditional revival musicians often served to introduce new audiences to older musical styles. An audience would discover new music through the performance of folk song revival artists. In time, many members of this audience would look into the roots of the music that attracted them. Similarly, reinterpreted music of the Revival often whetted the appetite of individuals who then, through the experience of the Revival, became familiar with music that had formerly been unknown or inaccessible.

The Revival also served as a conduit for music to filter back to the folk. I remember doing fieldwork in Atlanta one summer in the early 1960s with Archie Green. We heard a southern youth singing in a coffeehouse and beating out "Columbus Stockade Blues" as much like the Kingston Trio as he could manage. We had just come from visiting Tom Darby and Jimmie Tarlton, who had made the first recording of that song. When we asked the singer why he was singing the song in Manhattan/Hollywood style when the song originated only a few miles away, he replied that he did not want to be a "redneck." This illustrates a number of things. First, he was not interested, at that time, in a traditional rendition of the song, for complex sociocultural reasons. Secondly, that song would not have entered his repertoire had it not been for a commercial, sanitized version coming directly from the Revival. Finally, we glimpse from this illustration the complexity of the folk process that moved this song a hundred miles over a thirty-five-year period. The song had traveled thousands of miles in order to make this short leap. It had to find its way, through a complex transmission pattern, from the hills of Alabama back to Atlanta. If the history of this transmission could be documented, it would reveal much about patterns of folk song transmission and illustrate a fascinating phenomenon.

A final example concerns the Autoharp style of Mother Maybelle Carter. Maybelle began playing the Autoharp early in her career with her daughters, Helen, June, and Anita. Somewhere along the way, she found that it was inconvenient to hold the instrument on her lap or play it on a table when she performed into a microphone. Hence, she devised a method of holding the instrument against her chest. This technique has now become almost universal, but it came to rural performers largely through the Revival. Although Maybelle had been performing this way for years, it was not until Mike Seeger and other Revival artists adopted this instrument and style that her technique really spread.

I began this chapter by recalling a recent fiddle contest in southern California. My thoughts led me to appreciate the vitality of the folk song revival and note its many and subtle influences. On that warm Sunday in Santa Barbara, hundreds of people played traditional instruments, sang traditional songs, imitated traditional styles and demonstrated that they had incorporated this material into their musical lives. Is this a continuation of the folk process? Do these performers represent a new generation of traditional singers? By conventional standards, it is doubtful that a single one of these musicians could qualify as traditional. Nevertheless, when any of the songs or ballads performed that day are studied, it will be necessary to point out that the material enjoyed a renewed popularity through the Revival.

Folk song is in many ways like language. When a person grows up speaking a non-English tongue and comes to the United States, no matter how well the person learns English, he or she is still not considered a native speaker. Linguists will still insist that English is not the speaker's mother tongue regardless of his or her level of proficiency. Similarly, even though these singers have mastered the idiom to perfection, they are not traditional folk singers. The real test will be to see if these people pass on this musical culture to a new generation who incorporate it into their lives, much as a second-generation English speaker does with the language. Scholarly work on the folk song revival has just begun and offers a unique opportunity to document a phenomenon of cultural appeal reflecting an important chapter in the social history of folk and popular music.[8]

NOTES

[1] For a discussion of earlier folk song revivals, see Richard Blaustein, "Rethinking Folk Revivalism: Grass-Roots Preservation and Folk Romanticism," in Neil V. Rosenberg, ed., *Transforming Tradition* (Urbana: University of Illinois Press, 1993), 258-274.

[2] Joseph C. Hickerson, "American Folksong: Some Comments on the History of Its Collection and Archiving," in George McCue, ed., *Music in American Society, 1776-1976: From Puritan Hymn to Synthesizer* (New Brunswick, NJ: Transaction Books, 1977), 107-117.

[3] Borden Deal, *The Insolent Breed* (New York: Scribner, 1959), 183-219.

[4] *Journal of American Folklore*, vol. 61 (April 1948), 215-218.

[5] Charles Seeger, "Folk Music: U.S.A." in *Grove's Dictionary of Music and Musicians*, 5th ed., Eric Blom, ed. (New York: St. Martin's Press, 1954), vol. 3, 387-398.

[6] For a deeper understanding of Grandpa Jones and his relationship to traditional folk songs and styles, see Louis M. Jones with Charles Wolfe, *Everybody's Grandpa* (Knoxville: University of Tennessee Press, 1984).

[7] See Malcolm Laws, *Native American Balladry*, rev. ed. (Philadelphia: American Folklore Society, 1964), 51, 223-224, for a bibliography of collected versions of "The Death of Floyd Collins" as well as details of Polk Brockman's and Andrew Jenkins' roles in the birth of this ballad.

[8] I owe thanks to a number of individuals who have given me leads and discussed various issues raised in this chapter. I particularly want to acknowledge the help of Norm Cohen, Ronald D. Cohen, Archie Green, Joe Hickerson, and Margaret Moore.

4 Neil V. Rosenberg

I think one impression that's really strong for me after two days of talking with and listening to the others at this conference is the New York-centric aspect of much of what I've heard. As someone who was born on the Pacific Coast and in fact had never been east of the Great Plains until the age of eighteen, I have a different perspective. I remember the shock I felt when I first went to Oberlin College in 1957 and discovered all these people from New York who thought that they were at the center of the universe. There are still some who feel that way, I know.

Recently, I've been editing a book of essays called *Transforming Tradition*.[1] These essays are about aspects of the folk song revival by folklorists, ethnomusicologists, and others, most of whom came up in the folk song revival—people like Bruce Jackson, Ellen Stekert, Archie Green, Burt Feintuch, and a number of others. In one of the essays Bob Cantwell was writing about "Tom Dooley," and I thought it was a good essay, but I asked him if he knew where Dave Guard had really learned "Tom Dooley," and had anybody ever asked Dave Guard? And he said no and proceeded to track Dave Guard down (this was a couple of years ago) and ask him where he learned "Tom Dooley." Now it may be that the recording by Roger Sprung and the Folksay Trio is the source of the performance. But that's not where Dave Guard learned "Tom Dooley." He learned it at a hootenanny in San Francisco. And in fact that song was being sung around the Bay Area by all kinds of people, including myself and my other teenage friends.

There was a lively scene in the Bay Area when I was a teenager. That's where I got acquainted with folk music. I remember being taken by my parents to the hungry i and hearing the Gateway Singers when I was seventeen years old, and playing

Saturday nights on KPFA on a program called *The Midnight Special*. So folk music was alive and there was a lively Bay Area scene, which I could talk about just as well as the Bloomington scene. It was through one of my schoolmates in the Bay Area scene, Rita Weill, that I learned about the Oberlin College folk scene and the Folksmiths,[2] a factor in my decision to go to Oberlin, where there was another scene that brought people who were interested in folk music in the late '50s from various parts of the country—from New York especially, but also from almost every other part of the country. And it was through someone I met there, classmate Mike Lipsky, that I came to New York City and met Izzy Young for the first time. So these connections were in place in my life very early on.

I came to Bloomington in 1961. I'd finished an undergraduate degree at Oberlin, and I came to study folklore. By this time, in my early 20s, I'd become particularly interested in bluegrass music. I was playing it. I was interested in knowing more about it. But I think that what's important to me now about that time is that being interested in bluegrass was part of a larger interest in folk music, and I think most of us at that time thought of folk music as something that was very eclectic. It was a point of view that I would say was assimilationist. We saw folk music as a sort of a broad texture, a mosaic, that included many different facets, and we were interested in one way or another in all of them. My interest in bluegrass didn't mean that I couldn't be interested in blues, and in singer-songwriters, and in all other kinds of things that I thought had some relationship to this music.

When I decided to come here and study folklore, it was because I really did want to try to figure out what folklore was and what this stuff was that was called folk music. And this was long before we had "artistic communication in small groups."[3] All of us were trying to figure out what the heck this was; that was the intellectual side of it for me. And I spent the next few years attempting to unravel it.

One of the disappointments of coming to Bloomington as a folklore student was the discovery that there wasn't much sympathy for our interest in studying folk music. We weren't encouraged to go on and follow the study of folk music here very frequently. It was difficult to do so because of the politics of the discipline and the department.[4]

At the same time there was a lot of activity here on campus, and there had been activity for some ten years. Bruce Buckley had been here, Joe Hickerson, Ellen Stekert; all of these people studying folklore, but also performing, conducting a radio show and so on. And in 1962 a club was formed, the Indiana University Folk Song Club.

It was founded in the fall of 1962, and it was built upon a scene that was already happening. There was a local coffeehouse called the Phase Three. There were radio shows. There were people performing around at hootenannies, and there was in general a lot of interest of various sorts. The club started with these aims: "to promote interest and participation in folk music activity at Indiana University, and to encourage the appreciation of folklore and its studies." I'm reading from the constitution. The club's activities were both recreational and educational, including folk sings, lectures, symposia, films, concerts, and instructional workshops.

The club, I think, typified what came to be called the folk song revival. We didn't call it the folk song revival at that time. But there was a revivalistic aspect to it, I mean in the sense of a religious revival. There was a real sense here of evangelical preaching of the message that this music was the kind of music that people ought to be involved in. So that's the revival angle that I think needs to be included if you think about this as a revival. A revival of a music that people *believed* in. Even though people might differ about what it was they believed. But that's like lots of religious phenomena.

At any rate, there was enough enthusiasm to start this club. And I read through the newsletter which flourished from 1962 to 1966, and I found that very soon the club had the second largest membership on campus, had all kinds of committees, was doing things. It was arranging exchange concerts with another club at the University of Illinois. It set in motion a series of workshops, which went on for about five years, that taught guitar, banjo, and various other instruments. And the club in general flourished. It flourished in this activity to the point that the university kicked it off campus because it was making money from the workshops. The guitar workshops were being held in the student union. When the university bureaucrats in charge of regulating student clubs heard about this they said that a club is not supposed to make money, so you must hold these things someplace else. We moved into the Phase Three coffeehouse.

Similar kinds of things occurred, conflicts that are now

interesting to me. In the first season, the club came very close—closer and closer as the end of the season approached—to losing money. The student affairs people had another rule, that clubs could not go in the red over the year. They had to break even every year. So the club was getting more and more in the hole. And so they tried something that folk song clubs everywhere did, which was to bring in somebody popular to make a lot of money in order to bankroll the club so they could bring in the less popular people that the leaders of the club felt were more interesting and deserved to be heard.

In our case, we attempted through Manny Greenhill to bring in Joan Baez. Joan Baez agreed to come, and to make the most of this we tried to get a large auditorium. And the university said, "No, that's only for our concert series. We won't let a club have that auditorium." And of course there was no other place we could have her perform, realistically. Then the university turned around and tried to book her themselves and she wouldn't come. Greenhill wouldn't book her through anybody but our club. There were editorials in the *Daily Student* and a lot of heat and light—or smoke, really, and not so much light. And a good deal of conflict.

And actually what happened at the end of that year, and I guess this sort of illustrates the drift of things as far as I was concerned, was that they lost a lot of money on a bluegrass concert, the Country Gentlemen, and in fact everyone who was a member of the board of the club had to pay a few dollars at the end of the year to cover the cost of the debt. At the same time I'd gotten into a situation where I was acting as the agent for the Country Gentlemen and got ten percent on that concert, and I resigned from the board.

Well, what was happening here is that as the years moved on in the '60s, more and more people got deeply involved in this music and became involved in it professionally. I, for example, was hired to manage Bill Monroe's Brown County Jamboree in Bean Blossom, Indiana. And I suddenly saw bluegrass not only as a form of folk art, but also as a commercial music which had definite business considerations. I began to become a bit more pragmatic about this aspect of things. And also, I feel, in my own thinking I began to drift away from the folk song club.

That's not to say that the club didn't flourish between 1963 and 1965. It had a particularly large number of people involved in its newsletter, which published all kinds of interesting material. It brought people like DocWatson, Glenn Ohrlin, Gary Davis, the New Lost City Ramblers, Frank Proffitt, and Pete Steele to campus. Many well-known performers appeared here in the early '60s. And I read those names off and think of the names of people appearing in New York. I don't see that there's a lot of difference, maybe a time lag of a year or so. But in fact these people were touring to groups like ours in many parts of the United States at this time. We felt, I think, that they each represented some aspect of folk music that it was worth making people better acquainted with. And we had enough of a constituency, the club, that we could do this, that people would come and see these artists.

Now what happened? It all seems to have fallen apart, as I look at the newsletter, after about 1965. Things suddenly started to go downhill. And it's an interesting kind of problem in history as to why this happened. A number of things took place. First of all, politics. Student involvement in the political scene here in the early '60s was pretty limited, especially on the Left. But by the mid-'60s you had the SDS (Students for a Democratic Society) and the Vietnam crisis, and a lot of people who'd been very much involved with folk music suddenly became very much involved in the SDS and in the anti-war movement. And that drew energy away from the interest in folk song and the folk song club, so that the organization suffered at that point.

At the same time you had the Beatles, the Byrds, and so on. All of a sudden rock 'n' roll was acceptable to intellectuals and college students. And that was another kind of a drain in another direction--artistic, that is. Some of the best performers who had been involved in the club's activities suddenly got electric guitars and formed bands, and they were off in another direction that at that time didn't really fall under the rubric of folk music.

I think also that other things more idiosyncratic explain some changes in the club. People have talked a lot about politics during this conference and haven't mentioned what Hank Bradley, who has written a wonderful little book called *Counterfeiting, Stealing and Cultural Plundering: A Manual for Applied Ethnomusicologists* (Seattle: Mill Gulch Music, 1989), calls "the gonad factor"—that is to say, most of the people involved in this were young people who were doing what folklorists quaintly call courtship. All kinds of intrigues and personal affairs shaped the institution of the folk song club.

As well, drugs suddenly became popular on campus, and that also had an effect on what was happening in the world of folk song. You had people not only going into the SDS and playing rock 'n' roll, but also just dropping out and getting stoned. And so by 1967 the club had disappeared. I was its last faculty adviser. I was a member of the staff of the Folklore Institute for a couple of years, from 1966 to 1968. By that time there were just not many bodies around to keep the club going.

Now that's not to say that the interest in folk music completely disappeared. In fact, many of the people who were here during that period are still involved in one way or another in folk music. But they no longer needed a club. They no longer needed an institution, just as at some point they really no longer needed Greenwich Village. The interest in and the knowledge about this stuff became so widespread by the end of the '60s that it formed its own networks. And there was a tendency for people to be much less eclectic and assimilationist and to be more particularistic about their music. And I'm an example. I got interested in bluegrass, and much more in bluegrass than anything else. Other people followed blues, old-time music, Irish music and so on. So there was a tendency for the interests to fragment as the numbers of interested people got larger.

So *that* folk song revival—what I call the "great boom," starting in the late '50s and going to about 1965—it's not that it failed or fell apart so much as that it really succeeded. It was a revival that converted a lot of people, brought them into the fold, and then they followed and created their own little sects. Some of these sects have become very successful and still exist. And in part they exist because the local scenes were never completely local. They tended to be centered around colleges, universities, urban intellectual ghettos like North Beach and Greenwich Village and Berkeley and various other places. And so people moved from one place to another and networks were constantly being renewed. We have to remember that we're dealing here with an intellectual community, and a middle-class community, that focused upon working-class music; it created its own middle-class music in response to and drawing from and embellishing upon working-class music.

And just one final little example from the very early part of my own experience: I remember going to see a movie double feature in 1956 that paired *Tobacco Road* and *Grapes of Wrath*, at a theater in Berkeley, and coming away from that being very impressed with the plight of these poor, poor white farmers and working-class people and the Okies and so on, and then being at a party a few nights later and getting into a big fight with someone who was going to sing a song that I considered an Okie song and not a folk song. My own consciousness about these issues was a very abstract one. Similarly, I was very interested in Leadbelly and Jesse Fuller and some of the other African-American performers from the San Francisco Bay area whom I'd heard in concert and whose records I owned. But I found it very difficult to talk about music with the many African-American students who were in my own high school in Berkeley. There was a real social gap. We didn't visit their homes, they didn't visit our homes. So while we were very conscious of and supportive of this music, it wasn't until I moved to Bloomington and started working at Bean Blossom and was forced to be an apprentice to country musicians, to participate in working relationships with people like Bill Monroe, Birch Monroe, and many other local musicians, and to go to local jam sessions, that I started to actually become conscious of working-class music and see how it was different from my conceptions of music that had been shaped in the middle-class intellectual milieu of the Revival with its national networks.

NOTES

[1] Subtitled *Folk Music Revivals Examined*, this volume was published in 1993 by the University of Illinois Press.

[2] Knowing I had applied to Oberlin, she drew my attention to a notice in her *Sing Out!* (vol.7, no.1 [Spring 1957], 34) about the Folksmiths, eight Oberlin students who spent the summer of that year performing in children's camps.

[3] I'm referring here to the now-classic definition of folklore set forth by Dan Ben-Amos (who started in the IU Folklore program at the same time as I) in his "Toward a Definition of Folklore in Context," *Journal of American Folklore*, vol. 84 (January-March 1971), 3-15.

[4] I've touched on these matters in my *Bluegrass: A History* (Urbana: University of Illinois Press, 1985), 4-5. See also Ellen

Stekert, "Autobiography of a Woman Folklorist," *Journal of American Folklore*, vol. 100 (October-December 1987), 579-585.

5 Dave Samuelson

Every so often I go through my record collection to weed out albums that I'll probably never play again. In 1968, I selectively axed many of my folk revival recordings, most of which I bought five years earlier while attending high school. My tastes had changed since then, thanks to my exposure to outstanding musicians at the University of Chicago Folk Festival and a brief involvement with the Campus Folksong Club at the University of Illinois in Champaign. Other collectors renewed my long-dormant interests in ragtime, traditional jazz, and early rock 'n' roll. While I hung onto records by some revivalists whose work still appealed to me, my primary musical interests were focused on old-time music, bluegrass, western swing, prewar jazz, postwar country music, and rockabilly. So when a former college roommate offered me $30 for all of my Kingston Trio albums, I sold them with little hesitation. And why not? I just couldn't see ever having the slightest desire to listen to any pop folk groups from the early sixties.

About three years later, I spotted a sealed, stereo copy of *String Along with the Kingston Trio* in a "3 for $5.00" record bin at a Chicago department store. Remembering it as one of the trio's better albums, I stuck it under my arm along with two budget-priced country music reissues. So, how did this album sound to me after years of intense listening to the Stanley Brothers, Charlie Poole, Milton Brown, Bill Monroe, and Django Reinhardt? I'm a little embarrassed to admit that I enjoyed it as much as I ever did. In fact, it rekindled my interest in the Kingston Trio. Over the next few years I bought back most of the trio's albums.

After reading countless essays in *Sing Out!* and other publications on commercialism and the folk revival, I had accepted the concept that what was traditional was to be valued and what was commercial was to be discarded. Quality and purity were synonymous. My record collecting friends reinforced this philosophy by steering me away from anything even moderately commercial. "Avoid the Delmore Brothers' and Lonnie Johnson's postwar King recordings," they told me. "They're junk." As a result of this thinking, I closed my ears to some of the best music the Delmores and Johnson ever made.

Sure, the Kingston Trio tailored its music, act, and visual identity for commercial appeal. But then again, so did most of the musicians I was listening to at the time. For example, Jimmie Rodgers carefully cultivated a romantic persona during the '20s as "The Singing Brakeman." In reality, he was a shrewd show business professional whose marketing genius equalled and possibly surpassed his talents as a performer. That hardly diminishes Rodgers' artistry, although it helps explain his continuing mystique and the enduring popularity of his recordings.

Arguments about who is traditional and who is commercial are nothing new. Few folk music scholars of the late twenties and early thirties paid serious attention to the white rural artists recorded by Polk Brockman, Ralph Peer, Frank Walker, and other pioneering country music producers. A popular string band like Charlie Poole and the North Carolina Ramblers tended to be dismissed as nothing more than commercial hillbilly music. After Folkways released Harry Smith's three-volume *Anthology of American Folk Music* in 1952, these string bands took on a different perspective. To many listeners—particularly urban musicians in the folk revival—artists like Poole reflected an authentic musical tradition. Few fans of the Smith anthology recognized that Poole and his contemporaries were actually participants in an earlier folk revival that was triggered by Vernon Dalhart's 1924 hit record "The Wreck of the Old 97"/"The Prisoner's Song."

We cannot always single out any artist as purely traditional while dismissing another as entirely commercial. The actual boundaries are rarely that distinct, and they appear to be getting fuzzier with time. In 1993, the Kingston Trio joined the gospel group Mighty Clouds of Joy, West Virginia singer Hazel Dickens, bluegrass patriarch Bill Monroe, and others for the ninth annual "Roots of American Music Festival," part of New York City's month-long "Lincoln Center Out-of-Doors" series.

Finding the Kingston Trio at a roots music festival is

somewhat ironic. To many purists, the group symbolizes virtually every commercial excess associated with the popular folk music revival. Trio members Dave Guard, Nick Reynolds, and Bob Shane never intended to educate or enlighten people about folk music. They always considered themselves entertainers. However, we cannot deny the group's appeal or its residual effect on popular culture. How many of today's blues, bluegrass, and old-time music scholars and musicians attribute their lifelong interest in vernacular music to early exposure to the Kingston Trio? How many influential rock performers from the late sixties learned to play guitar after first hearing the trio's early records?

In retrospect, we now see that Poole and the Kingston Trio share more similarities than differences. Both were professional entertainers with self-contained acts that combined hit records with new songs, comedy material, and physical humor. Kinney Rorrer's biography *Rambling Blues: The Life & Songs of Charlie Poole* presents Poole as a charismatic master showman, fully aware of his talents and abilities. "Many times, as the fiddles played a furious breakdown, Charlie would do cartwheels across the stage," Rorrer wrote. "His favorite stunt was to take a running start across the stage, make a flying leap over a chair and land on his hands—and then do a clog dance with them." The Kingston Trio also placed considerable emphasis on developing an entertaining act. "We would do every job with a clipboard, and I would say we choreographed every song," manager Frank Werber told Paul Surratt. "Every move was planned, every line . . . and the character of the show was developed in seven months of three and four shows a night, six nights a week, and a session after each show—football/ basketball team style."[1]

Both Poole and trio leader Guard were knowledgeable about traditional music, and both freely drew ideas and songs from popular, nontraditional sources. If anything, Poole was a traditional performer interested in commercial urban music; Guard was a commercial urban performer interested in traditional music. Research by Rorrer and others confirms that much of Poole's recorded repertoire came from printed, nontraditional sources. Vaudeville tunes and sentimental songs from the turn of the century account for about 72 percent of his vocal recordings for Columbia; the remaining 28 percent were rearranged or adapted traditional pieces. By contrast, about 57 percent of the original Kingston Trio's recorded repertoire consisted of new or previously published compositions; the remaining 43 percent were rearranged or adapted traditional pieces.[2]

Musically, Poole was fascinated by the intricate classical/ ragtime banjo style associated with early recording artists Vess Ossman and Fred Van Eps. Poole became fairly adept at playing in this nontraditional urban style; he later recorded several instrumentals from Van Eps' repertoire. Poole's musical tastes were fairly broad; Charlie Poole, Jr., told Eugene Earle and Archie Green that his father listened to Al Jolson, Rudy Vallee, Blind Blake, and Fritz Kreisler.

Growing up in Honolulu, Dave Guard and Bob Shane assimilated the fluid rhythms of traditional Hawaiian musicians; both credited slack-key guitar master Gabby Pahinui as an inspiration. "Our music definitely had Hawaiian overtones to it, even on the things that weren't Hawaiian at all," Shane told William J. Bush. One of the most striking pieces in the Kingston Trio's early repertoire was "Lei Pakalana," a Samuel Omar composition popularized in Hawaii during the late 1940s by Richard Kahui's Quartette. The trio sang it in the original Hawaiian, respectfully retaining the flowing rhythms and emphatic pauses of Kahui's original Bell recording. If anything, "Lei Pakalana" reveals them as native interpreters—not commercial popularizers—of traditional material.[3]

Both Poole and the trio were popular recording artists on major labels. Poole was one of the better-selling performers in Columbia's 15000 series of "Old Familiar Tunes"; his early records sold between 15,000 and 102,000 copies at a time when sales of 5,000 copies were considered good and anything over 20,000 was a hit. By comparison, the Kingston Trio's early Capitol albums each sold between 200,000 and almost one million copies—as many as their labelmate Frank Sinatra and considerably more than Nat King Cole, Dean Martin, and Judy Garland usually sold.[4]

Poole and the Kingston Trio shared one song in common, "Frankie and Johnny (You'll Miss Me in the Days to Come)," a 1911 composition tailored for vaudeville by the Leighton Brothers and Ren Shields. On September 18, 1926, Poole recorded this song for Columbia under the title "Leaving Home." Poole's source is unknown, but a 1923 revival of the song generated new recordings by Isham Jones and others. The Kingston Trio recorded it on January 12, 1961, for Capitol under the title "You're Gonna Miss Me." Trio leader Dave Guard learned the song from the New Lost City

Ramblers—John Cohen, Tom Paley, and Mike Seeger—whose 1960 Folkways recording closely approximated Poole's original version.[5]

Thirty-four years separate Poole's "Leaving Home" from the Kingston Trio's "You're Gonna Miss Me." Just as many years now distance us from the trio's recording. From today's viewpoint, Poole's record retains the same mystique that it exerted on the Ramblers and old-time music enthusiasts, collectors, and performers three decades ago. Its durability was verified in 1993 when the song was reissued on two separate compact discs. One was a Columbia/Sony collection of prewar white country blues; the other was an expanded compilation of County Records' initial Charlie Poole and the North Carolina Ramblers reissue from 1965.

The Kingston Trio's version seems likely to endure as well. The years have not dimmed its appeal and youthful vitality. It appeared on compact disc in January 1992 on *Make Way/Goin' Places*. Although Capitol deleted this collection in the spring of 1994, the song is being considered for a proposed Kingston Trio boxed set. Part of the reason for its timelessness can be credited to the trio's exclusive use of acoustic stringed instruments. Another reason is Guard's deceptively simple vocal and instrumental arrangement, which is relatively free from the pretentiousness that dates many pop/folk performances of the era.[6]

In some ways "You're Gonna Miss Me" is reminiscent of traditional bluegrass. Shane lays a rhythmic foundation using the same bass-heavy Martin D-28 guitar favored by bluegrass guitarists. Guard alternates his banjo style between a three-finger roll and a strum. Reynolds fills the bluegrass mandolinist's role by slapping chords on the offbeat, using a Martin tenor guitar capoed high up on the neck. The band's driving rhythm was exceptionally tight, freeing bassist David "Buck" Wheat to explore the fingerboard of his instrument. Arguably, this record captures much of the spirit of early Bill Monroe, Lester Flatt and Earl Scruggs, the Stanley Brothers, and other bluegrass pioneers—a spirit that's often lacking in today's contemporary bluegrass bands.

The trio's performance of "You're Gonna Miss Me" is straightforward, enthusiastic and respectful of the song. By contrast, Poole's live performances of "Leaving Home" reflected a vaudevillian's flair, according to Rorer: "When he reached the line in which Frankie fires the gun five times into Johnny, Poole stopped playing for a second and snapped his fingers five times in rapid succession against the banjo head, giving a gunshot effect."[7]

My intent is not to build up the Kingston Trio at the expense of the legendary North Carolina songster, but to place both of them in the proper context. While they each represent different eras and cultures, they share an important similarity: Both were popular entertainers who built successful careers through folk-based music. They created vaild, enduring forms of musical expression that deserve to be preserved, evaluated and appreciated.

Poole's world is almost gone. Living memories of the man and his environment are disappearing; only his recordings remain indelible. Fortunately, many details of Poole's life, music, and context have been studied and preserved by foresighted collectors and scholars like Kinney Rorrer, John Cohen, Mike Seeger, Eugene Earle, Archie Green, Ed Kahn, Richard Nevins, David Freeman, and Janet Kerr. Inevitably, the Kingston Trio's world and environment will be gone, too. It's not difficult to imagine future historians eagerly scanning on-line databases for any references, articles, dissertations, and unpublished material relating to the trio and their pop/folk contemporaries of the late 1950s and early 1960s.

Fortunately, academic attitudes toward the folk revival are beginning to change, but research lags far behind the accomplishments made in jazz, blues, country, ethnic, and rock music scholarship. Many aspects of the Revival still remain undocumented. Historians have not completely unravelled the convoluted history of the Almanac Singers. A balanced, comprehensive biography and analytical study of the Weavers is long overdue. The stories of important, influential revivalists like Erik Darling, Bob Gibson, Tom Glazer, Ernie (Sheldon) Lieberman, and others basically remain untold. We also need to know more about the entrepreneurs who promoted concerts, managed artists, and launched folk clubs and record labels. Relevant recordings need to be collected, indexed, and dated for publication in a comprehensive folk revival discography. We need to locate and preserve relevant film footage, broadcast kinescopes, and videotapes. Many of the key figures who nurtured this movement are well into their retirement years. We need to act quickly if we want to capture and preserve their insights into their backgrounds, sources, ideals, and ambitions.

NOTES

[1] Kinney Rorrer, *Rambling Blues: The Life & Songs of Charlie Poole* (London: Old Time Music, 1982), 48; Paul Surratt, "The Frank Werber Interview," in Benjamin Blake, Jack Rubeck and Allan Shaw, *The Kingston Trio on Record* (Naperville: Kingston Korner, Inc., 1986), 18-19.

[2] "Transcripts: Interview with Charlie Poole, Jr.," *JEMF Newsletter*, vol. 1, no. 3 (June 1966), 34.

[3] William J. Bush, "The Kingston Trio," *Frets*, vol. 6, no. 6 (June 1984), 27; "Lei Pakalana," by Richard Kahui's Quartette appears on Bell 500. I'm unaware of any earlier recordings of this song, nor am I aware of any LP or CD reissues of Kahui's record. The original Kingston Trio never commercially recorded "Lei Pakalana." While searching the Capitol vaults in the mid-'80s, Kingston Trio researchers Steve Fiott and Allan Shaw discovered a privately made tape of the song from a 1958 San Francisco night club appearance. It was released in 1986 on *Stereo Concert Plus!* (Folk Era FE2037CD). In early 1966, after John Stewart replaced Dave Guard in the group, Bob Shane and Nick Reynolds recorded the song on *Children of Morning* (Decca DL4758/DL74758), which is currently unavailable on compact disc.

[4] Rorrer, *Rambling Blues*, 31; Blake et al., *The Kingston Trio on Record*, 29-48.

[5] Three folk-based recordings of the Leighton Brothers and Ren Shields' "Frankie and Johnny (You'll Miss Me in the Days to Come)" have been available on compact disc. Charlie Poole's "Leaving Home," originally on Columbia 15116-D, is best heard on *Charlie Poole and the North Carolina Ramblers* (County CD-3501). The New Lost City Ramblers' 1959 recreation, originally on Folkways FA2397, now appears on *The New Lost City Ramblers: The Early Years* (Smithsonian/Folkways CD-40036). The Kingston Trio's "You're Gonna Miss Me," originally on Capitol 4536 and T/ST 1564, appeared on *Make Way/Goin' Places* (Capitol CDP 796836-2).

[6] This does not mean the Kingston Trio never succumbed to excess. Purists justifiably winced when the trio's Capitol recording of an old North Carolina murder ballad became a fluke number-one hit in November 1958. Guard's arrangement of "Tom Dooley" was overdramatic, to be sure; the group would later parody its excesses on stage.

[7] Rorrer, *Rambling Blues*, 35.

'THE ONLY MONTHLY IN THE
FOLK MUSIC FIELD'

no. 12

THE LITTLE SANDY REVIEW

30¢

LITTLE SANDY REVIEW

3220 Park Avenue South
Minneapolis 7, Minnesota

The FOLK RECORD MONTHLY

For complete record
reviews and listings
each and every month
of the year — plus
the best in "free-
wheeling iconoclasm"
and "rapier-like
thrusts," subscribe
to the now-famous
LSR. $3.00 yearly.

EDITED BY JON PANKAKE & PAUL NELSON

```
*****************************
Name _____
Address _____
City _____
State _____
Enclosed please find three
dollars for 12 issues.
*****************************
```

Folk Magazines

SING OUT!

Vol. 2, No. 11   May 1952   25¢

TO PAUL ROBESON

They don't let us sing our songs, Robeson,
Eagle singer, Negro brother,
They don't want us to sing our songs.

They are scared, Robeson,
Scared of the dawn and of seeing,
Scared of hearing and touching.

They are scared of loving,
They are scared of the seed, the earth,
The running water and the memory
    of a friend's hand
Asking no discount, no commission,
    no interest,
A hand which has never paused like
    a bird in their hands.

They are scared, Negro brother,
Our songs scare them, Robeson.

                –Nazim Hikmet–

6   Irwin Silber

The title for this section is "Folk Magazines," but I'll confine myself to the magazines I know something about. These are the *People's Songs* bulletin (1946-49) and *Sing Out!* I want to discuss *Sing Out!* in two parts: the magazine published by People's Artists in the 1950s; and the one put out after my association with Moe Asch, Folkways Records, and Oak Publications in the 1960s up to 1967, when I resigned as its editor.

Today, in the language common to the folk song revival, it is customary to speak of these as folk song magazines. But even though, mostly at Moe Asch's urging, we called the 1960s *Sing Out!* "The Folk Song Magazine," none of these were really folk song magazines. They were, however, significant to what, in our shorthand, we now call the folk revival.

What was unique about these magazines? My guess is that most people would say "their politics." And there's a lot to be said for that answer. But in my view, the key to understanding the uniqueness of these magazines is that they were *song* magazines.

Now that might seem to be belaboring the obvious. But in 1946, when the *People's Songs* bulletin began publication, there were no song magazines. There were occasional publications of the lyrics to top forty hits, some of which appeared more or less regularly. There were also songbooks and sheet music—but that's all. No song magazines. That's the reason *People's Songs* got started.

Of course, I don't mean to beg the question of politics. The songs which appeared in the pages of the *People's Songs* bulletin had a particular political bent. And I will discuss this at some length shortly. But implicit in putting out a magazine consisting principally of songs is the belief that an audience wants these songs—not just the words but also the tunes and guitar chords to go with them. Again, this may seem self-evident, but it supposed that there existed across the country a body of people who played guitars, fiddles, banjos, and pianos and who were receptive to these particular kinds of songs and wanted to get them on a regular basis.

What was the nature of this phenomenon that enabled Pete Seeger to convince a bunch of folks to throw themselves into this unprecedented enterprise? It was the fact that a certain kind of topical-political music had begun to take hold in the country—not just among several hundred or even a few thousand musicians, but for a significantly larger audience who identified with those songs and wanted to hear them and, thanks largely to Pete, sing along with them. Before the war (World War II), the Almanac Singers had tapped into that potential audience, in the process initiating a culture/propaganda revolution whose musical and political fallout would resonate for the next half-century. It stayed alive during the war as folk-based win-the-war ballads, and songs became part of the war's ideological arsenal. And it picked up again after the war, but this time with a vastly expanded audience. I was both part of that audience and involved in the creative side of it. I was a director of the American Folksay Group in New York, and the music generated by this folk-cum-political explosion was our culture. The people who wrote and sang these songs were our culture heroes. We wanted the songs they wrote and sang, and there were many others like us.

This was soon demonstrated by People's Songs' success in its first year. In broader cultural terms, its growth was not spectacular. That would happen later in the early '60s when Sing Out!'s circulation would soar into the tens of thousands. But who could have imagined that after a year, 2,000 people would subscribe to a monthly song magazine mostly to get Left-oriented topical-political songs? (There weren't that many articles, and except for Lee Hays's acerbic columns, they weren't that scintillating. Nor did we have much in the way of record reviews. It was the songs—getting hold of them, and fast.)

So that's the first thing to keep in mind. These magazines distributed songs. Second, of course, is the political outlook which informed them. As one can imagine, I've given this question a lot of thought. And even when I was inclined to put it out of my mind and get on with new projects, people like Dick Reuss—and he wasn't the only one—would come around to pick at what was left of my brain in order to find out what went on in those days. One of the ironies of this process is that occasionally I run across a view which goes something like this: How come, in putting out the *People's Songs* bulletin or *Sing Out!*, you chose to make them so political? Now this question is really impossible to answer because, when I think about it, it wasn't really a matter of choice. It's impossible to imagine these magazines and the various other activities associated with them outside of their politics.

Now I hope that Izzy (Young) was kidding—although I can't always tell—when he suggested that what we were doing was some kind of Communist conspiracy.

[Young interjects: I'm serious.]

Well, that would make Pete Seeger the arch-conspirator who started People's Songs and I guess I'm elected chief plotter—along with Betty Sanders, Ernie Lieberman, and Bob Wolfe—of the People's Artists/*Sing Out!* conspiracy.

Now this all sounds fairly ridiculous today, but the charge of Communist conspiracy actually hung heavy over the Revival throughout the '50s and into the '60s. Think of how many of us were hauled before the House Un-American Activities Committee in the effort to establish how, when, and under what circumstances the Communist Party ordered us to cloak its multifarious subversions with the patina of American folk music. Think, too, of all those books, ranging from *Rhythm, Riots, and Revolution* to Denisoff's *Great Day Coming*, which perpetuated this myth while cashing in on it.

I do not mean to simplify what is indeed a highly complex reality. Certainly there was a connection between the People's Songs-*Sing Out!* continuum and Left-wing politics. And some of us were Communist Party members—at least for a while. And there were times when we indulged in the fiction that there was a greater distance between the two than there really was—but that was also a self-defensive function in those times of witch-hunts and black-lists. On the other hand, to collapse that distinction—as though the political folk music of the '40s and '50s was simply the creation of the Communists—is absurd. Those who would try to understand the folk revival and situate it in a broader sociopolitical reality must be prepared to deal with the complexities not only of the Revival but of American communism as well.

When I say that People's Songs and *Sing Out!* were unimaginable without the politics, I am speaking, in the first place, about what motivated those of us who had the most to do with these undertakings. In my case, it was the same motivation that brought me into the Young Communist League and, later on, the Communist Party. But our interest in folk music as well as folk-based political music was more a reflection of the motion and energy of the times than of "party orders." (If the truth be known, the Communist Party did not really take our activity all that seriously. But that's a subject for another discussion.) Our "success," such as it was, we owed to the fact that we were in tune with a larger social reality. We were the products of currents sent in motion by the Great Depression, the New Deal, the victories of industrial unionism and the black migration out of the South.

But let me risk a broader generalization. Much of our political mythology could be found in the pages of Carl Sandburg's *The People, Yes* and was later captured in that phrase which became Henry Wallace's theme, "the century of the common man." It was a pompous phrase, of course. But, in my opinion, it also touched a certain truth about the twentieth century; namely, that in this century, the masses of people, the "great unwashed," whatever cliché one wants to employ, became—more than ever before—the subject rather than the object of history. I think this was a consequence of the Industrial Revolution, the decline of agriculture as the motor of economic life, the urbanization of society, the breakup of the colonial system, and similar phenomena. In the industrialized world, mass trade unions and parties came into being. Socialism and communism—largely intellectual pursuits in the nineteenth century—spawned self-generating movements. (Both the Socialist Party of Eugene Debs and the Industrial Workers of the World, after all, predated communism.) The colonial world was wracked by the impact of mass national liberation movements. As a result, the indigenous popular expression of what Alan Lomax, in his foreword to *The People's Song Book,* called, in one of the less fortunate phrases of the time, "the little people," assumed a cultural-historical significance it had not previously enjoyed.

Somewhere in that cauldron, it seems to me, one finds the roots of what we now call the folk revival. Indeed, one cannot really understand the revival without situating it within that much broader social process. And in that sense, we all touched a chord.

The Revival began long before the Almanac Singers and People's Songs. It began before the Left took it up, when the Communist movement's music was still characterized by the European mass chorus tradition and when Maxim Gorky could still contemptuously dismiss jazz as "fat man's music." It bubbled up in the attempts by the Lomaxes to rescue folk music from the suffocating grip of academia. It surfaced in the efforts by many pioneers to call attention to the fact that there was a living musical tradition—especially among southern blacks and white mountain folk—which went largely unnoticed by the cultural arbiters of the times.

In the early '30s, you could see the process in the WPA folklore projects, which in seeking to preserve the legacy, had implicitly begun to popularize it. This was research which broke out of the confines the earlier academic folklorists had imposed. It saw the music—as well as all the other expressions of popular art—as part of a living culture, not as museum pieces. And, of course, this living culture was constantly reproducing itself and giving voice to the new circumstances its progenitors encountered as their previous isolation gave way to the inexorable march of socialization.

No one personified this process more than Woody Guthrie. Contrary to the mythology, Woody was a highly conscious artist/intellectual. One only has to read through his non-song poetry and personal musings to sense his awareness of the complexities confronting the contemporary artist. But Woody never concerned himself with the one topic which seems to have consumed several generations of professional folklorists: Is it a folk song? Perhaps he thought about it once in a while as a point of intellectual curiosity, but clearly it was not a question which ever assumed any importance, although some people may recall the delightfully trenchant piece on the subject he wrote for an early *Sing Out!* For Woody, both the tradition and the new expression were part of what he was. Nor was he the only one. There were also folks like Aunt Molly Jackson, Florence Reese, and so many others whose songs encompassed the wrenching disruptions which twentieth-century capitalism had imposed on their traditional circumstances.

A similar process with even broader cultural and social ramifications was taking place in African-American culture. Here one thinks especially of great artists like Big Bill Broonzy, steeped in the Mississippi blues tradition and then writing and singing for transplanted southern blacks in the Chicago ghetto. Big Bill likewise casually dismissed the "But-is-it-a-folk-song?" debate.

I think that's the way most of us associated with People's Songs and *Sing Out!* felt. From time to time the "Is-it-really-a-folk-song?" controversy would erupt in our pages. But at least for me—and I'm sure for most of the others—we didn't really care that much. And frankly, I still don't. Perhaps that categorization of folk/non-folk has some use academically, though I tend to think it has done more harm than good even in those terms. But for those of us at People's Songs and *Sing Out!* trying to make our work part of a living cultural and political process, it was simply irrelevant. One can see that just by going through the pages of these magazines. It was our strength and, for many people, our vulnerability.

What should also be kept in mind is that, for us, politics was not simply a set of ideas that existed in our heads. It had to do with actual tensions and interactions of encountered life. It became fashionable in later years to lampoon the upper-middle-class folk singers donning jeans to incite college audiences to "roll the union on." But in the 1930s and '40s there really was a mass union audience for the kinds of music we felt we were promoting. I remember in 1947 going along with Pete and Woody to a meeting of the National Maritime Union where 5,000 seamen were debating whether to go out on strike. There was some grumbling when Pete and Woody were introduced, because passions were running high and the music was looked at as an unnecessary interruption of the meeting's "real business." But the NMU leaders who had brought Pete and Woody there knew what they were doing. They were trying to build up fervor for the coming strike and evoke a sense of solidarity among the workers. And they succeeded. One doesn't get to see and hear moments like that too often these days—once in a while, maybe, like during the Watsonville strike of largely Chicano food processing workers. Even back in the '40s, such meetings were the exception rather than the rule. But I wish that those who have heard these songs only at concerts could feel the electricity generated when several thousand workers, each identifying completely with every last syllable, thunder that "if the boss gets in the way, we're gonna roll it over him."

What the Almanacs and People's Songs were able to demonstrate was not that singing these songs would suddenly infuse the labor movement with militancy, but that such singing could capture the already existing militancy and give it focus and energy. This was the intersection with a world that actually existed outside the concert hall or the living room or the turntable. And that's why it's so ironic to hear people talk of the Communist conspiracy and the Communist plan to do all this as though popular movements can be brought to life by "outside agitation."

The Communists were certainly a part of this intersection, principally because they were part of the union movement. John L. Lewis once said, "I don't trust the Communists, but they're the best organizers I have." I imagine the feeling was mutual. But if Lewis felt the Communists were doing the CIO's work, by the same token, the CIO was the actualization of every Communist's dream. There it was, the old Socialist Party of Debs and the industrial unionism of the IWW rolled together in one, finally finding visible expression in a mass movement of militant trade unionists organized along industrial lines. If you were a Communist, wouldn't you just jump right into the middle of that? Well, of course, they did. It's easy enough to poke fun at now; and those of us who were part of all that will do so with a mixture of bemused wryness and pride. But it was real.

Another element in this equation was the anti-racist movement. The role of the Communists in that process has been written about extensively. One only has to recall the famous case of the Scottsboro Boys, in which the Communist Party braved the terrors of white Alabama justice to make this frame-up a national (and international) *cause célèbre* to appreciate the extent to which the Communists were able to establish their political credibility in black communities both north and south. And remember, this took place at a time when support for a federal anti-lynching law was considered to be a sign of extreme radicalism.

The cultural side of this political intersection was just as significant. The Left was identified with interracialism. Its cultural events, summer camps, etc., were consciously integrated. Café Society, a Greenwich Village night club owned and operated by a Communist, became the principal venue for performers like Josh White, Billie Holiday, and others. Unlike most night clubs in New York—to say nothing of the rest of the country—its policy was to welcome mixed audiences. In 1938, it was the Communist-run magazine *New Masses* which sponsored the historic "From Spirituals to Swing" Carnegie Hall concert at which many great southern black artists first appeared before northern audiences. And then there was Paul Robeson, whose enormous gifts and towering presence added an indigenous legitimacy to the intersection of politics, art, and the Left's sense that it was on the cutting edge of the struggle for racial equality.

In the late 1930s and in the '40s, that energy also assumed an international expression in the form of anti-fascism, beginning with the Spanish Civil War and culminating in World War II.

These then were the ideological tendencies out of which People's Songs and Sing Out! were born: an America based on the celebration of "working people" and the "common man"; the trade union movement and the hope that it would be the driving force for a "better" America; a commitment to racial equality; anti-fascism; and a sense that communism as we knew it was a political and spiritual force in that process.

And it was because these ideas had a resonance in a large enough section of society that People's Songs had an initial social base for its activity. I would identify three main elements in that base: first, the unions, especially the Left-led unions in the CIO, whose membership at the time numbered in the millions; second, a left-liberal constituency most directly associated with the New Deal and the Democratic Party of Franklin Roosevelt, which found its culmination in the 1948 Henry Wallace campaign; and finally, the institutions of the Left.

Keep in mind that this was a period in which the Communist Party itself was an organization of significant size and influence. It was at the peak of its membership—in the ninety to one hundred thousand range—and it could rightfully claim influence among several million others in a network of constituencies. So this was a sizable base.

Well, I mentioned that I would belabor the obvious, but I think all this needs to be said in order to cut through a lot of the nonsense that is frequently associated with this topic and to understand that these magazines, which played such a seminal role in the folk revival, were not imaginable in any other form.

None of this was a secret at the time. Still, I can't help but be amazed at the horror with which the academic folklore establishment reacted to it. Even then, I used to wonder why they cared that much. The People's Songs bulletin didn't claim to be a folk music magazine. We didn't invade the sacred halls of academia or try to take over the American Folklore Society. In fact, in my naiveté, I thought they would welcome our attempts to popularize folk music, thereby promoting what I assumed were our shared values. Well, apparently I knew little about folklore studies. I didn't even know that in those circles "popularizing" was considered an unnatural act. In reflecting back on it now, however, I think I have a better appreciation of their rage. First, I think they were furious that some of the most distinguished names in American folklore— Lomax, Seeger, Botkin—associated themselves with People's Songs and legitimated it. Second, I think they found it especially galling that the term "folk" inevitably got attached to our activity. As a result, People's Songs threatened the monopoly that the academic folklorists had established for themselves as the ultimate arbiters of what was legitimate and illegitimate use of the category "folk."

But they weren't the only folks we rubbed the wrong way. We also drew the fire of those who, unsympathetic to our political objectives, attacked us on "aesthetic" grounds. I was especially reminded of this by Pete Seeger who, just a few days before I left California to come to this conference, called me to suggest that I look up the review of *The People's Song Book* written by Stanley Edgar Hyman back in 1948. Well, thanks to the UC-Berkeley Library I found it, and following are some excerpts from it.

"Much of the book's content," he wrote, "is humorless and pastoral in the worst sense, and some of it is plain trash. The People's Songs group seems oblivious to the most obvious fact in the extensive history of protest folk song: that there are two traditions, one hermetic and symbolic, the other directly militant; that the songs effective in terms of social action have more often than not tended to be the former, from the medieval 'Cutty Wren' to the Negro spirituals and chain-gang songs, and that troops are rather more apt to be inspired by something like 'Yankee Doodle' than by a tear-jerking hymn about the nobility of their cause."

I have often wondered what got people like Stanley Edgar Hyman so worked up. After all, he was neither the first nor the last to tell us, in effect, "It's not what you say, it's the way that you say it." Well, I think I've finally figured it out. First, in most cases, they really were objecting to *what* we were saying and not just the way we said it. By and large, the songs Hyman likes are "complaint" songs; and many are quite moving and beautiful. But for a variety of reasons—often because of the circumstances under which they

were sung—they are not "and-here's-what-we're-gonna-do-about-
it" songs. Sure, troops in the American Revolution sang "Yankee
Doodle." But how about those who, almost one hundred years
later, marched off to war singing "John Brown's Body" and "The
Battle Hymn of the Republic" and "Battle Cry of Freedom"? Or the
troops who fought in class wars singing "Solidarity Forever," "Hold
the Fort," and "Which Side Are You On?" Plenty of "noble cause"
rhetoric in those songs, but who would want to argue that they
weren't popular among the embattled?

But Hyman's vitriol rises out of another prejudice. Namely,
that there is something inherently suspect about "protest songs"
written by those who may not themselves be the direct victims of
the oppression being protested. In a way, it's the old "outside
agitator" red herring. The abolitionists heard it, as did the Wobblies,
long before we latter-day lefties were attacked on the same
grounds.

Of course, we were well aware of the fact that not every
song we put into print was a gem of poetry or a model of subtlety.
Some of them were as crude as they could be. But even if a song
was only good for one strike or one meeting or one moment that
would agitate people and inspire them in a struggle, we felt it had
served its purpose. After all, we weren't writing these songs for
history or as contributions to great literature, but in order to deal
with real political battles. If a handful lasted beyond the immediate
circumstances which produced them—and I think songs like "Joe
Hill," "The Hammer Song," "Banks of Marble," "Union Maid," and
a few others have—so much the better.

At the same time, many of us felt that what we were doing
served a larger purpose than any immediate cause or issue.
Certainly it's the way I felt. I never believed that our songs, by
themselves, were going to change the world. But I saw them as a
conscious part of that larger purpose. I believed that, as Lenin had
said, we were living in an age of revolution and that songs would
help that revolution spread and ultimately win. Of course, that was
always a romantic notion and, in light of recent events, wildly out
of touch with reality. But at the time, it didn't seem that way.

A big part of the problem of the Marxist movement, it
seems to me now in retrospect, was that it held on to Lenin's
assessment that capitalism was in its death throes and the international proletariat was little more than a heartbeat away from

revolution far longer than could possibly be justified by events in the real world. I think this contributed to the sectarianism which has been all too characteristic of much of the Left. And it also spilled over into the activity of People's Songs and *Sing Out!*

Now I want to say a few things about the People's Artists/ *Sing Out!* part of this phenomenon. Let me start with something David Dunaway [a conference participant] said earlier when he noted that Pete Seeger and the Weavers were the first singers to be investigated for sedition or subversion in the United States. Let's not forget that Paul Robeson had been under investigation—and more—even before then. And that the attacks on him—as at Peekskill—as well as the blacklisting of a man who was arguably the country's foremost singer had reached an unmatched frenzy.

I mention this because just as People's Songs was inconceivable without Pete and Woody and Lee Hays, so *Sing Out!* and People's Artists were inconceivable without Paul Robeson. In this continuum from People's Songs to *Sing Out!*, Paul Robeson is the commanding figure of the 1950s. It was Robeson who delivered the keynote speech at the founding meeting of People's Artists in 1949. People's Artists was the producer of the Peekskill concerts. The foreword to *Lift Every Voice!*, "The Second People's Song Book," is by Paul Robeson. Go through the pages of *Sing Out!* in those years, and you will be struck by the extent to which Robeson appears there. There is no way to comprehend the emotional and ideological underpinning of People's Artists and *Sing Out!* without the Paul Robeson context. Paul symbolized so much for us: the new motion stirring in the black community, which was to shortly mature into the mass civil rights movement; the Left and Communist movements' potential for developing a mass social base; the persecution of those trying years and the spirit of resistance which a few of us tried to keep alive. Most particularly, he was, for us, the quintessential role model of the committed artist.

I will never forget a letter we received back in 1949 from the Ku Klux Klan of Westchester County. It thanked us for our activities, the Peekskill concert in particular, saying that this had enabled them to recruit hundreds of new members. The reason, they said, was that "people in Westchester Country really don't like Negroes and especially they've got no use for red niggers like the kind that you're promoting. And so we thank you for all of your efforts on our behalf."

Maybe the biggest difference between *Sing Out!* and People's Songs was this. People's Songs came along at a time when the Left still had a lot of political initiative, when it could still make things happen. It had a measure of mass influence. As it turns out, the Left was at the tail end of a roll, but of course we didn't know that at the time. *Sing Out!*, on the other hand, came along when the Left was on the defensive, and throughout the decade of the 50s, that was the climate that pervaded our work.

If "Roll the Union On" was, in some ways, the musical symbol of People's Songs, the words of "The Hammer Song"—"I'd sing out danger, I'd sing out a warning"—characterized *Sing Out!* In fact, as you can see, that's where the name *Sing Out!* came from. (The song itself, as you collectors know, appeared on the very first page of the very first issue of *Sing Out!*) Our overtly political songs dealt with political repression ("In Contempt"), the Cold War, the Korean War, the Rosenbergs. And after a couple of years, even these were in short supply. Partly in response to the charge that we were "un-American," we instituted a regular feature in *Sing Out!* that we called "Heritage, U.S.A.," which tried to show how songs of protest were an indelible part of the American cultural legacy.

But those of you trying to understand *Sing Out!* in the 1950s won't get an accurate picture if you confine yourselves to the magazine's pages. People's Artists was much more than that. It was, first of all, a booking agency not just for political singers but for blacklisted performers. We found work for actors either driven out of Hollywood or blocked from getting there—people like Morris Carnovsky, Howard Da Silva, Lloyd Gough and Herschel Bernardi. The People's Artists hootenannies—we put on three or four every year—maintained a Left public presence during those years when, aside from trials and witch-hunts, much of the Left had been made invisible. We also issued some records, including what was the first ever recording of a live folk concert, and published several books and pamphlets.

This period began to wind down in late 1955. A U.S.-Soviet summit, the first in a decade, signified a "thaw" in the Cold War, while the exposure of Senator McCarthy in his battle with the Army helped foster a similar thaw in the climate of domestic repression. A sign of the changing times was the reappearance of the Weavers in their now legendary Carnegie Hall concert of December 1955. Many previously blacklisted performers were able to obtain work

once again—although not in Hollywood—so that the booking
agency function of People's Artists declined drastically. At the same
time, there was less call for "Left" musicians, since public events on
the Left were few and far between. As a result, People's Artists
dissolved itself in 1957.

A small group of us—principally myself, Jerry Silverman,
Walter Raim, and Ed Badeaux, with help and advice from Pete, Earl
Robinson, and Anne Wayne—continued putting out *Sing Out!* But
it was rough going. We could barely meet our printing and postage
bills; paying anyone a salary was out of the question. I got a job
writing for the *Daily Worker,* but that paper folded in the midst of
(and due to) the internecine political struggle which had broken out
in the Communist Party following Khrushchev's revelations about
Stalin. Next I got a job as a copywriter at Avon Books for several
months, but I was then called before the House Un-American
Activities Committee (in June 1958). Although I wasn't fired, the
handwriting was on the wall, and I decided that I had better find
some employment where my history would not constantly hang
over my head.

It was at that point that I decided to convince Moe Asch to
give me a job. The timing was perfect. The first outcroppings of
what would later be called the "folk boom" were already being felt.
Previously, Harry Belafonte had scored some popular success with
his calypso songs. In early 1956, Merle Travis's "Sixteen Tons"
swept the country, revealing not only a hunger for a folk music
sound but the legitimacy of songs of substance and even protest.
This was unimaginable two years earlier. Then the Tarriers had a
commercial hit with an adaptation of the Georgia Sea Island song
first popularized by Pete, "Pay Me My Money Down."[1] This was
also when "This Land Is Your Land" and "Rock Island Line" became
pop hits. The return of the Weavers likewise paved the way for other
folk-singing groups. In addition to the Tarriers, there were the
Gateway Singers, the Kingston Trio, and others. By early 1959, the
phenomenon was so widespread that *Sing Out!* carried an article
on "Commercialism and the Folk Song Revival."[2]

Although still in its early stages, the "folk boom" was also
being felt by Folkways, so that when I approached Moe about a job,
he was also feeling the need to expand. And I was, in many ways,
exactly the right person. Aside from my affinity for what Folkways
was doing, my particular skills were well suited to take over major

areas of work. Within months, I had assumed responsibility for
coordinating the physical production of Folkways, directed an
immensely successful major sales promotion effort, and begun a
complete rewrite of the Folkways catalog. Moe Asch, as many
people know, was not an easy person to get along with. His life
work is an incredible cultural and intellectual monument, but he
was also an irascible small-scale capitalist of the old school. (I
sometimes think that he never could have succeeded otherwise.)
Similarly, as many people also know, I was (and, to a certain extent,
still am) quite opinionated on almost everything and not bashful
about making those opinions known. So we had a stormy
relationship.

But the point of all this is that my relationship with Moe
Asch was the beginning of Sing Out!'s next phase. I had told Moe
that a condition of my going to work for Folkways was that I would
continue to put out Sing Out! and that I would have a certain
amount of space available to me for that purpose. Moe's response
took me by surprise. He wanted to become a "partner" in Sing Out!,
with the understanding that he would have no say in editorial policy
but would concentrate on the business end. I had never before
thought of Sing Out! as a "commercial" entity. But it was obvious
that its days as a publication with a base of support in the organized
Left were gone. The "new" Sing Out! could and did retain much of
the political/ideological outlook which had characterized it up until
then; but it would also have to operate on the basis of business
logic. So I agreed, but in order to assure the magazine's independence from any change of heart on Moe's part—or, for that matter,
on mine—we agreed that we would each own 45 percent of the
stock while Pete Seeger would hold the other 10 percent. Moe
bought his share of Sing Out! for $2,500, all of which was used to
recapitalize it. And I must say that in the years that followed, Moe
held to his part of the agreement. There were some heated
discussions about editorial policy, but there was never any suggestion that he would try to exercise power over the magazine's
contents. (I think there were times when some of the other editors
wished that he would.)

Thus began the next period of Sing Out! Unlike the People's
Songs bulletin or the earlier Sing Out!, it is not so easy to sum up
the magazine's character during this time. Inevitably it was defined
by the folk music explosion of the early to mid-60s. Not surpris-

ingly, all the dichotomies of that phenomenon were to be found in *Sing Out!* as well. We took plenty of shots at what we regarded as the exploitative nature of the revival, but as part of the Folkways-Oak-*Sing Out!* cartel, we benefited enormously from the huge market that the boom engendered. The old debates—pure vs. popular, politics vs. tradition—were a constant. But there was also the pull of New Left-Old Left conflict. The mass audience and big bucks of the revival left their imprint, but *Sing Out!* also promoted do-it-yourself folk music. Thanks largely to John Cohen, we became much more open to old-time music and to artists in the white country tradition. At the same time, our anti-war outlook came up against the fact that musical support for the Vietnam War was found principally among professional country artists. Whereas the anti-racist songs we published in the '50s came principally from progressive-minded white songwriters, the southern Freedom Song movement inundated our pages in the '60s. And then there were the innumerable Bob Dylan controversies. As a result, though our general political bent was unmistakable, *Sing Out!* was characterized by an agreed-upon but increasingly tenuous eclecticism. In time, this became increasingly difficult to sustain.

In a sense, I became the magazine's biggest problem. The deepening political polarization in the country—reflected in both the urban black explosions and the mass antiwar movement—had a profound effect on me. I began to look at and judge the revival not simply by its self-image but by the availability of its institutions and resources to what I regarded as the defining political and moral questions of that time. My growing alienation came to a head at the Newport Folk Festival in the summer of 1967. Fairly or not, I reacted against what I felt was a climate of self-congratulation and "business as usual" at a moment when Newark was (literally) in flames and the reign of death in Vietnam was intensifying. Out of that alienation grew the notion that it was my job to blow the whistle on what I saw as a retreat from if not a betrayal of what I regarded as the genuine *Sing Out!* legacy.

When I gave vent to those feelings in an article about Newport (*Sing Out!*, vol. 17, no. 5), Pete Seeger became furious with me. And when I drafted a proposal to reorient *Sing Out!* toward greater social relevancy, most of my fellow editors erupted and demanded my ouster. One can hardly blame them. However legitimate my feelings may have seemed to me in the context of the time, good sense should have told me that my proposal was thoroughly quixotic.

In retrospect, I think I was probably inviting a confrontation in preparation for what turned out to be my imminent departure from the West Forty-seventh Street "folk" combine. Three months later I resigned as editor of *Sing Out!*, but, in an effort to assure some continuity, remained part of a reconstituted editorial board. In April 1968 I resigned from the board as well. I also arranged for the sale of Oak Publications (the company Moe Asch and I had jointly started in 1960), thereby making my departure from the "folk scene" complete. Subsequently, Barbara Dane and I put out *The Vietnam Songbook* and started Paredon Records, which specialized in music of political protest and national liberation movements. But these projects were largely peripheral to the post-boom folk scene. Most of my work from 1968 until the end of the '70s was with *The Guardian*, where I became movie reviewer, political columnist, and after a few years, Executive Editor.

Concerning the next *Sing Out!*, the one that emerged after my departure, someone else, of course, will have to figure out its place in the history of the revival.

NOTES

[1] This song, oddly enough, led me to my job at Avon Books. The new lyric, called "Cindy," was written by Bob Nemiroff and Bert D'Lugoff. Bob was married to Lorraine Hansberry, who for several years had worked at the *Sing Out!* office. He was working at Avon Books, but when "Cindy" became a hit, Bob decided to leave Avon and get into songwriting, publishing, and producing. Before leaving, however, he recommended me for the interview at Avon, which led to my getting his former job.

[2] The author of this article, ironically, was Ronald Radosh, who in later years became one of the early converts to vitriolic anti-communism.

7 Jon Pankake

It appears that nobody knows anything about me. A friend recently called my attention to the *Down Home Music* catalog, which contained a reference to me as "the legendary Jon Pankake." I would like to refute that, and to demonstrate that I am indeed documentary.

A little over thirty years ago, when Paul Nelson and I were undergraduate students at the University of Minnesota, we started a magazine called *The Little Sandy Review*, in which we reviewed folk music records. As with most small entrepreneurial efforts, it didn't last long. We published it for about four years, about thirty issues, at which point Barry Hansen took it over. We started with nothing and grew to be very, very small. Our press run was about 300 copies, of which about 200 went to subscribers and 100 went to bookstores. At the time we never dreamed we would be even a footnote in the history of the folk music revival, so thirty years later to discuss *The Little Sandy Review* is amazing to me. This is certainly the second weirdest thing that's happened to me in my connection with folk music, the weirdest being my appearances on worldwide live radio before three and a half million listeners of *A Prairie Home Companion* as "the masked folk singer, the singer as anonymous as the material he sings." That still takes the cake. But coming here and learning that people are still mad about the bad reviews they received in *The Little Sandy* thirty years ago is just weird.

I want to talk about folk music journalism and to point out that *The Little Sandy Review* did bring into the revival several strains of popular journalism of which people may be unaware.

The Little Sandy comes out of a 1950s subjournalistic tradition called the "fanzine." The fanzine was an early version of what we would now call "desktop publishing"—that is, self-publishing made possible by a technology. In the 1950s that technology was the mimeograph machine. For a few pennies you could write your profound thoughts on as many sheets as you wanted to pay for, ditto up copies, and send them into the world—and that's basically what fanzines did. Our technology was one of the best: a high speed Gestetner mimeograph machine which Paul used after hours in the place where he worked, which was, not coincidentally, the regional distributor of Folkways Records.

Several characteristics define the fanzine. It is always the product of one or two voices. That is, the fanzine speaks in a personal voice—like getting a letter from someone. It has no institutional voice in the manner of professional magazines, in which the magazine's voice is filtered through a publisher, a publication policy, an editorial board, a senior editor, assistant editors, and numerous writers. The fanzine bypasses all of that. It is essentially a letter from one or two people to its readers—whoever is willing to read it.

The second characteristic of the fanzine is that it has very little to do with money; it isn't a commercial enterprise. Fanzines in the 1950s typically charged very little for a subscription. I think we began by charging $3.00 for twelve issues. Other fanzines asked only for postage stamps. Some were happy to put you on their mailing list and you received it free. We paid for *The Little Sandy* out of our pockets, so while we didn't intend to make any money, we needed to keep it cheap. That was our philosophy: a fanzine, a cheap way of publishing.

As such, we fanzines had no commerce. We didn't sell advertising. We printed ads in *The Little Sandy*, but they were fakes—we just put them in ourselves. If we found a record we thought was particularly good and we wanted to promote it in our tiny way, we would give it an ad. Paul loved to fool around with graphics, so we advertised, but for no income.

The defining characteristic of the fanzine as a form of journalism, however, is that it conveys a strong point of view on a topic of interest to the publisher. "Fanzine" is, of course, a portmanteau word—a shortening of "fanatic's magazine." It is published by a writer who feels very strongly about a subject and who then expresses those feelings. Fanzines are not rational, considered, analytical, or objective; they don't document, but rather tell you what they like and what they don't like, and that is their point. We used to see fanzines about chess, for example, in which chess fanatics would reprint newspaper accounts of famous chess matches and reanalyze the moves. We saw quite a few fanzines devoted to science fiction. These would review the new Isaac Asimov books, or publish letters hotly debating the profundity of the science in the new Philip K. Dick novel; and there would be original poems and stories written by the publishers. Science fiction was a major fanzine topic, but there were record collectors' fanzines in the 1950s also. We saw several devoted to vintage phonograph records, jazz and blues discs. There were a few devoted to old hillbilly records which we liked—Lou Deneumoustier and Joe Nicholas published them. Since *The Little Sandy* was about folk music records, I suppose we most resembled Nicholas's *Disc Collector*.

The fanzine has a very Manichean view of the world. There is no middle ground. Mike Seeger got to the heart of it very early when he used to call us "The Little Sanity Review"—Mike recognized that we were a fanatic's magazine, fanatic about our likes and dislikes in folk music.

People remember the bad reviews that we gave to records we didn't like, records we raked over the coals. Oddly enough, no one seems to remember that we were just as fanatic and excessive on the other side, on records that we praised. I wish some people had been as critical about our praise as they were about our negative points of view. I think we gushed embarrassingly about, for example, Peggy Seeger, or Shirley Elizabeth Collins, or Jeannie Redpath, or the New Lost City Ramblers. But it's the bad reviews that people remember.

I thought it interesting that in discussing our bad reviews [during the conference], Lee Haring and Barry Hansen both invoked the metaphor of vitriol, or "vitriolic reviews." As a former teacher of literature, I would have circled that word on their papers and asked if that were really an appropriately chosen metaphor. A passage of literary "vitriol" would be vitriolic to everyone who reads it—a piece of literary vitriol offends everyone. Jonathan Swift's "A Modest Proposal" is an example of literary vitriol—it offends everyone who reads it. It was intended to do so.

However, a piece of literature that makes the subject of the writing uncomfortable, but makes other people who read it laugh—

that is called humor. It may not be nice, but a lot of humor is not
nice. Thomas Hobbes defined humor as the delight we take in the
misfortunes of our fellow man. There is often an edge to humor.
We thought we were being funny rather than vitriolic, frankly.
Readers laughed like crazy at *The Little Sandy*, and many thought
we were the humor magazine of the revival. And readers egged us
on terribly—some told us they looked forward to the bad reviews.
They didn't care about the crap we were writing about Jean
Redpath, but they wanted to see what we would say about the new
Limeliters album. They laughed at it; it was humor to them.

I suspect we thought of ourselves as using humor to deflate
humbug in the way that Mark Twain says humor is to be used—
Blow the humbug away with laughter. We certainly weren't Mark
Twains by any means—we weren't good enough—and perhaps
there was no humbug in the folk revival. Perhaps everything was
straight and honest and true and sincere. If there was no humbug,
then we were really off the mark, weren't we?—shooting at
something that wasn't there. But if there *was* humbug, maybe we
were the only ones targeting it. We could certainly have done a
better job of it. The actor Edmund Gwenn is supposed to have said
on his deathbed that "dying is easy; comedy is hard." So if we didn't
pull it off all the time, well, we were only twenty years old. We were
having fun trying something hard.

We certainly weren't considering the personal circumstances of performers whose records we ridiculed. Somebody
goes commercial because he needs money for his wife and kids—
that wasn't a consideration, for otherwise we would have had to
give positive reviews to everyone. We went with how we felt
listening to the record.

Fanzines are generally only tenuously connected to the real
world. The fanzine lives in its own little fantasy world—we were like
that, too. I don't think we were connected with what was "going on"
in the music scene—we just bought the records. We weren't
political in the way that *People's Songs* and *Sing Out!* were—
actively working toward a political end. Paul and I were just not
political. We were vaguely liberal in that we favored integration and
peace on earth and labor unions, but we did not demonstrate or
work in any movement. Our politics were probably Marxist in the
Groucho sense. I recall that Paul and I cast our first presidential
votes for John Kennedy not because we really thought he was that

much better than Richard Nixon, but because we were entranced with Jackie. We knew that if JFK were elected, we would see Jackie in the newsreels for the next four years. We were into Jackie iconography even before Andy Warhol. Nor were we folk music performers. We had nothing to do with the performance scene, so if we gave a bad review to a singer we didn't have to worry that we'd be sharing the green room with him in Bloomington a month later. Or that our manager wouldn't be able to get gigs for us if we were critical of other performers.

We also had nothing to do with the recording industry—promoting, producing records—and we didn't have to worry if a review said something bad about a Columbia Records product that that might cause Columbia to pull their advertising budget. Hey, no advertising budget!

In March 1960, I went to New York to personally deliver the first shipment of *Little Sandy Reviews* to the Folklore Center. We had corresponded with Izzy Young before that, and he had agreed to carry the magazine sight unseen. When I brought it into the store, Izzy read the first few pages, looked at me, and said, "This is a thing to get free records, right?" Wrong, it wasn't. We never got a free review copy of a record—we didn't want free records. We bought every record that we reviewed in *The Little Sandy*, with a couple of exceptions where an artist gave us a copy. We did not want to be beholden to record companies. We didn't want to have someone give us a free record only to have us nail it right to the barn door. We would have felt bad about that. So we bought our records—that gave us a free hand to pan them if we felt they weren't good.

We likewise had no connection to the academic study of folklore. Neither Paul nor I had ever taken an ethnography or anthropology or musicology class. When we began taking an interest in folk music, we looked into the *Journal of American Folklore* and found most of it boring and confusing. And that was even before Theory. We stayed in our own world.

As Izzy said, we were even geographically isolated out there in flyover land—geographically remote from places like the Ash Grove and the Village. To use a current word, we were marginalized. And we loved being marginalized. We liked the distance from the center that gave us the freedom inherent in the fanzine medium to say anything we wanted. We weren't responsible to anyone for anything, and we had fun with that freedom from responsibility. We found it exhilarating to be twenty years old and in love with writing and to fall in love with folk music and just have a blast putting those two loves together.

The year before we began *The Little Sandy*, we had talked with Pete Seeger about it and had asked Pete's advice about publishing a folk music record review magazine. Pete said, "Hey, it's a free country. You can print anything you want in America." We followed Pete's advice.

Paul and I were certainly capable of other kinds of writing than that which we did for *The Little Sandy*. We eventually wrote for *Sing Out!* and for other magazines in which we didn't use the fanzine persona. I currently review records for *The Old-Time Herald* and I don't write as I did for *The Little Sandy*, which always remained true to its nature as a fanzine.

The aesthetic and style of *The Little Sandy Review* constitute another kind of popular journalism that we transplanted into that little corner of the folk scene we occupied. That is the aesthetic and style of movie reviewing. In the late 1950s, Paul and I were equally "fanatic" about movies as we were about folk music, and we were educating ourselves in film history, both informally and academically. In my sophomore year in college, I saw over 300 theatrically exhibited movies—much to the detriment of my grades. Paul and I were also studying film aesthetics and history at the University of Minnesota under George Amberg. Years later, when we were trying to reconstruct for ourselves how it was that we started *The Little Sandy Review*, we seemed to remember that there was a point at which we weren't sure whether we wanted to write about movies or about folk music. Maybe we flipped a coin and folk music won—or lost, as the case may be. Whether or not we actually flipped a coin, we believed that *The Little Sandy* could as well have been a movie fanzine as a folk music fanzine.

In our excitement about movies, we were discovering that we could distinguish between two classes of movies. One kind was purely "product"—made for the market. Some of these were exquisitely made and enjoyable, such as Cecil B. DeMille's films. Others were vulgar or inept. But we could identify another class of movie, one in which the films had an intellectual complexity and emotional commitment, an aesthetic integrity, that made them quite different viewing experiences. We discovered, for example, that John Wayne westerns directed by Howard Hawks or John Ford were tremendously better than Wayne westerns directed by Henry Hathaway or Andrew McLaglen. We were puzzled by people who professed to be unable to see this difference. We felt that a movie like John Ford's *The Searchers* was too fabulous a movie to be dismissed as a "John Wayne western." We wanted to learn why and what it was that made *The Searchers* so qualitatively different from other John Wayne movies.

In melodramas we discovered directors like Phil Carlson and Douglas Sirk, who made gripping and unforgettable films compared with those flabbier ones directed by Mark Robson or Daniel Mann that were sometimes bigger-budgeted movies but that struck us as being only product.

We were bright undergraduates on the verge of discovering for ourselves a cultural insight that had, of course, already been discovered by far brighter and more experienced scholars of whom we hadn't heard. In our case, these scholars were the *politique des auteurs* film theorists first published in *Cahiers du Cinéma* in Paris in the mid-1950s. Paul and I had never heard of the "auteur theory," whose tenets we were independently discovering, but we were to read of it avidly during the years of *The Little Sandy* as it became popularized by New York writers such as Peter Bogdanovich and Andrew Sarris. The auteur theory even came to have its own fanzine in those years, Jonas Mekas's *Film Culture,* published in New York.

What Paul and I tried to do—and this is the secret of *The Little Sandy Review*—was to make the same distinction in folk music records that we had learned to make in movies. That is, to distinguish, in a market of consumer products, those artifacts that were just "product"—out to make a buck, to entertain, some slickly and some ineptly—from those that had intellectual value, integrity, commitment, emotional depth, meaning. We wanted to be the auteurists of folk music. We tried to do this in the pages of *The Little Sandy Review*—to distinguish those records that invoked passion in us from those that were mere product.

As amateurs, we lacked a vocabulary and a conceptual framework to make clear those qualities for which we felt a record should be purchased and cherished. These qualities we found not only in the reissues and documentary recordings of authentics such as Dock Boggs, but also in the performances of some city perform-ers. We may even have been fumbling our way toward some definition of performance style which we lacked the technical ability to describe.

The writing style of *The Little Sandy* we lifted from movie writing. In the late 1950s, *The New Yorker* employed a movie reviewer named John McCartan, a very good writer whom we tried to emulate. McCartan was an acid, intellectual reviewer—we loved to see him take a big, bloated, pretentious Hollywood movie and flay it right on the pages of *The New Yorker*. We loved that; we wanted to do that, too.

Barry also revealed a writer's secret: Invective is easier to write than praise. To sound original and knowledgeable in invective is easier. Unless it's awfully well done, praise tends to sound hollow and conventional. So McCartan's pans were an inspiration. Also, Malcolm Muggeridge and Dwight MacDonald were writing in *Esquire* in those years. We loved their curmudgeonly prose, and emulated that—twenty-year-old curmudgeons!

We were also influenced by a magazine called *Films in Review*, which, though published professionally as the organ of the National Board of Review, was little better than a fanzine. Its editor, Henry Hart, had a bombastic writing style that colored not only his own signed articles but those that appeared above every other byline in the magazine. We believed that Hart wrote the whole magazine himself using pseudonyms, so we also used pseudonyms in *The Little Sandy*. When we'd get tired of writing under our own names, we'd invent some—but the style was always the same, just as in *Films in Review*.

As I look back on *The Little Sandy*, I don't think of it as journalism. My definition of journalism would be writing that is engaged with the issues of the day, with real life. Horace Greeley called newspapers "the daybooks of history," which provides a very good definition of journalism. Anyone studying the folk music revival will not find the daybook of the revival in the pages of *The Little Sandy Review*. We were too far out, too hermetic, too arcane, to serve the function of journalism.

I think *The Little Sandy Review* was fiction. If I were to reread it now, I would read it as a novel, a novel in thirty chapters, published periodically like Dickens' novels, a novel about two fictitious characters named Pankake and Nelson who were obsessed with folk music records at a particular time in history when one could have suffered no more fascinating an obsession. Like all fiction, this novel does portray something about its time.

I think that more than any other writing of that time, *The Little Sandy* portrayed the absurdity of the folk music revival. I use "absurdity" not in its pejorative sense but in an honorific sense, in the way half-educated intellectuals of the 1950s who had a nodding acquaintance with existentialism and the theater of the absurd used the word to describe stimulating and delicious incongruities that we found ourselves living. It was absurd that city people drenched in popular culture—movies, pop music—would embrace rural and oral tradition. That's an absurd leap. Paul and I went in the space of one year from listening to Peggy Lee to falling utterly in love with the singing of Vera Hall. We loved Vera Hall so much, and she was so alien to us in life experience—and time, and place, and anything else you can name—that she could just as well have been from Mars. But we loved her records and we loved her voice, and doing so was an astonishing experience. It was absurd.

It was absurd for people like us and others who were formally educated to embrace naive culture. Paul was an English major at the University of Minnesota and I was a Western Civilization major. During the day we would attend classes and read and write about Montaigne and Marcus Aurelius and St. Augustine and Faulkner and Melville (those now discredited writers of the canon). And then we would come home from classes and put Furry Lewis or Gus Cannon's Jug Stompers on the phonograph, and find them as interesting and aesthetically satisfying as Faulkner and Melville—and it was absurd. How could this be happening to us?

It was absurd during the folk revival for urban liberals to become so enamored of a people and a culture whose politics they would find repugnant when exposed to them. I recall in 1965 when J. E. Mainer brought his band from North Carolina to Minneapolis to perform at the Guthrie Theatre as part of a folk music festival we had been asked to book (a series in which, since we seldom got out of Minneapolis, we brought the best of the revival musicians to us). On the day of his concert, J. E. came to me a bit upset. The band wanted to perform a skit during the concert that evening and they had forgotten their makeup. He described the skit, which the band performed in drag and in blackface—a farce entitled "Sambo Sues Eliza For Divorce." There was, of course, a budding folklorist within me that wanted to see this performance of purely racist entertainment before it passed into history forever, but unlike *The Little*

Sandy Review, this concert series had an obligation to the community. I found myself in the absurd position of trying to convince J. E. Mainer that there was no black greasepaint or burnt cork within *miles* of Minneapolis, and that the show would have to go on without the skit. I felt like a character in a Samuel Beckett play.

Absurd. How absurd it was for two country boys from rural Minnesota to publish a magazine, each issue of which we personally assembled on a Ping-Pong table in Tony Glover's basement, and then to have that magazine read approvingly by Alan Lomax and mentioned in *Time*'s think piece on the folk revival. Do things like this happen in real life?

And how absurd it is, thirty years later, to be discussing all of this. This is the most delicious absurdity of all.

8 Barry Hansen

"**H**aywire Mac" McClintock, the early twentieth century folk singer who wrote and popularized the songs "Hallelujah, I'm a Bum!" and "The Big Rock Candy Mountain," among many others, loved to brag about the different jobs that he'd had in his life. He was a mule skinner in the Philippines, a ranch foreman in Nevada, organizer for the IWW, roadhouse owner in California, railroad worker just about everywhere there were tracks, sheepherder, cowboy, newspaper reporter, painter, actor, writer, hobo, and radio and recording artist, probably a precursor of the folk revival, and all that. Well, I have not had as strenuous a life as he did, by any means, but I have done a lot of different things. I've been a roadie for rock groups in the '60s; usher, emcee and light man at the Ash Grove in Los Angeles; audiotape editor; dubbing engineer for reissues of old 78s; record producer; radio show producer, educational radio station manager, and host of several radio programs—including one called *The Doctor Demento Show*, with mad music and crazy comedy, that's run for some twenty years now with 185 stations; host of several TV specials; VJ on a home video compilation; collaborator on some computer software having to do with the history of records; and from time to time a record critic for various publications, which is I guess why I'm here.

All those occupations have one thing in common. I've always been a guy who loved music. There's always music in my head. But due to a lack of manual dexterity and the lack of a suitably diligent attitude toward rehearsal, I really can't sing or play a note. I don't believe the handful of records on which I attempt to sing and/or play piano are any kind of convincing evidence to the contrary. Now if I were growing up in the 1990s, when thanks to synthesizers and sampling and drum machines one now no longer needs manual dexterity or long hours of practice to become a professional musician, things might have turned out very differently. But in the '50s and '60s I had to find other outlets besides performance for all my musical drives.

My record collecting goes back to my childhood. My father was an amateur musician and a music lover, mostly classical, though he did go to hear Leadbelly in concert and bought a Leadbelly album the next day. But he had all these records and played the phonograph all the time. The phonograph was really my main source of musical input. He started to get me to take piano lessons at a very early age, but it was hard for me to keep at them because after, you know, slaving away trying to pick out something that Mozart wrote when he was six and never getting anywhere, I could walk over to the phonograph and put on this magic disk, and voilà! Toscanini. So I became really addicted to the phonograph at a very early age, and it really goes from there. All different kinds of records, just whatever came along I'd develop a passion for.

My first career move came when I was a junior in high school, which is when my first record reviews were published. Considering the meaning of the word "sophomoric" it might have been more appropriate if I'd gotten into record criticism as a sophomore, but I was in fact a junior. The year was 1958 when I decided I knew a lot about how records should be made and would put some of that in print. I developed a taste for the contemporary Chicago blues of the time: Muddy Waters, Little Walter, Jimmy Reed, and so forth. These people were all putting out new 45 RPM singles of their latest songs every so often. I tried very had to instill this taste in my classmates at my 99-1/2 percent white high school but never made more than two or three real converts. However, I was getting A's in English composition, and when a jazz record collectors' magazine called *Record Research* (that my mother had given me a subscription to for my birthday) ran a letter to the editor suggesting that they do reviews of current Chicago blues 45s, I eagerly volunteered.

As it turned out, I was the only volunteer. I mean, this magazine really appealed much more to devotees of Bix Beiderbecke and Red Nichols, for whom jazz music really stopped around 1935; but anyway, they offered me some space, so for the next couple of years *Record Research* ran a few of my one-paragraph reviews of the latest blues releases in almost every issue. Later they started a spinoff called *Blues Research*, and I was in that instead. Perhaps for laughs or whatever I'll read you one of the earnest reviews that appeared in my very first column, which was a then brand-new coupling by Bo Diddley that I gave a score of 81 to on one side and 76 on the other. They were entitled "Hey Bo Diddley" and "Mona." "Mona" was much later covered by the Rolling Stones, but that was far in the future when I wrote this:

> This singer has achieved just about the perfect combination of rock 'n' roll and southern blues influences. The top side is an uptempo number on which he tells about his farm on which he has some women. A band with a strong backbeat and a vocal group chanting "Hey Bo Diddley" accompany him through this burst of energy which lasts two minutes and nine seconds. On the other side he sings a primitive chant to a syncopated backing in a high and quavering voice. This is also a burst of energy, picking up speed as the record goes on. If you like a noisy record, buy this.

I don't know what I meant by that last sentence. I could have been referring to the surface noise, but I think it was my general impression, or I couldn't think of a better way to conclude this masterpiece. But it was not too bad for a sixteen-year-old novice.

My main stylistic influences were the capsule reviews of new pop singles that appeared in *Downbeat* and *Billboard* at the time. It certainly wasn't the *Journal of American Folklore*, which I had never heard of. And there wasn't really anything else that I could look to for inspiration. There were no books about postwar blues at that time, or for that matter about any blues, outside of John Lomax's book about Leadbelly and whatever passing references you might encounter in the jazz literature. There weren't any periodicals, except for a pulp magazine called *Rhythm and Blues* that was mainly song lyrics and ads for cosmetics. And I certainly couldn't read anything about Muddy Waters in the *Minneapolis Tribune*. Except for *The New York Times*, most of the U.S. daily press did not cover pop music or country or rhythm and blues very much at all, except as a social phenomenon. The music seemed beneath criticism at that time.

In 1959, I was off to Reed College in Portland, Oregon. I stayed in touch with one of the few other young, white, blues fans I'd known in Minneapolis; in fact, we met when the proprietor of the

one store in downtown Minneapolis that really made an effort to
stock R & B records saw us both in the store at the same time and
introduced us. He, unlike me, was a good musician, a harmonica
player, and his name was Dave Glover; that was before he changed
his name to Tony Satan, and then Tony "Little Sun" Glover, under
which name he made a number of records and did some fine
writing. Anyway, when I came home for Christmas 1959 it was
Tony who said, "Barry, you gotta go to the Ten O'Clock Scholar,"
which was a fifty-seat coffeehouse near the University of Minnesota
campus: "You gotta go and hear Dylan." Bob Dylan. So I did. That
was during the year or so that Dylan was at the University of
Minnesota, before he went on to New York. He wasn't writing too
many songs yet, but I certainly remember his style as being very
different from anything else I'd ever heard on records or live. Not
totally traditional, but definitely nothing like the commercial folk
singers who had recorded at that time. For a while thereafter, I
thought I'd been much impressed by someone named Bob D-i-l-
l-o-n, since the Ten O'Clock Scholar did not have a marquee, but I
was impressed.

I got a letter from Tony in 1960 saying some new friends
of his at the university had started a little monthly magazine devoted
mainly to reviews of new recordings of folk music. And those
friends were, as it happened, Paul Nelson and Jon Pankake. And the
magazine was *The Little Sandy Review*. Well, I came home for the
summer and hung out with Paul and Jon a little bit, and we talked
a little bit and so I began reviewing blues LPs and a few other LPs
with *The Little Sandy Review* issue number 4 in 1960. I'd learned
a little more about blues by then. Sam Charters' book *The Country
Blues* had come out, and Tony and Paul and Jon had introduced
me to some other sources, such as the Folkways *Anthology of
American Folk Music*, those six LPs. So here I am in issue number
4, where this is the last paragraph of about a 500-word review of
Robert Pete Williams' first album:

> Here is a near miracle of recording—a singer who has
> developed to a fabulous level of artistry in an all-Negro
> environment completely free of any reason or desire to
> "refine" for a sophisticated "folkum market" ["folkum" was
> a word that Paul Nelson and Jon Pankake taught me],
> recorded with all the fidelity and care of the best recording

Israel G. Young in Folklore Center, Greenwich Village, *ca.* 1958
(Photo by Billy Faier, Ronald D. Cohen Collection)

Frank Hamilton and Billy Faier in Folklore Center, *ca.* 1958
(Courtesy of Billy Faier, Ronald D. Cohen Collection)

Gateway Singers (L-R Travis Edmonson, Elmerlee Thomas, Lou Gottlieb, Jerry Walter), *ca.*1956 (Courtesy of Lou Gottlieb, Ronald D. Cohen Collection)

Roy Berkeley and Dave Van Ronk, Folksingers Guild concert, Greenwich Village, ca. November 1957 (Photo by Photo-Sound Assoc., courtesy of Aaron Rennert)

(L-R) Ralph Rinzler, Ellen Kossoy, Woody Guthrie, Irene Kossoy, Oscar Brand, Greenwich Village, 1959 (Photo by Photo-Sound Assoc., courtesy of Aaron Rennert)

Israel G. Young and Rev. Gary Davis, New York City, ca. 1959 (Photo by Photo-Sound Assoc., courtesy of Aaron Rennert)

(Top) Folksinging in Washington Square, 1959 (Photo by Photo-Sound Assoc., courtesy of Aaron Rennert)
(Bottom) Roger Sprung (banjo), John Cohen (guitar), Mike Seeger (mandolin), Washington Square, *ca.* 1958 (Photo by Photo-Sound Assoc., courtesy of Aaron Rennert)

(Top) Israel G. Young in New York City, 1960s (Photo by Roy Berkeley, courtesy of Roy Berkeley)
(Bottom) Bob Dylan and Joan Baez, Newport Folk Festival, 1964 (Photo by Roy Berkeley, courtesy of Roy Berkeley)

(L-R) Guy Carawan, Fannie Lou Hamer, Bernice Johnson Reagon, Len Chandler, Newport Folk Festival, 1965 (Photo by Joe Alper, courtesy of Jackie Gibson Alper)

(Top) New Lost City Ramblers (Tracy Schwarz, Mike Seeger, John Cohen),
Newport Folk Festival, 1965 (Photo by Joe Alper, courtesy of Jackie Gibson
Alper)
(Bottom) (L-R) "Spider" John Koerner, Tony "Little Sun" Glover, Dave
"Snaker" Ray, Newport Folk Festival, 1964 (Photo by Joe Alper, courtesy
of Jackie Gibson Alper)

Hunter College Concert, January 28, 1966 (L-R Pete Seeger, Doc Watson, John Cohen, Tracy Schwarz, Mike Seeger, Ralph Rinzler, Frank Warner, Jean Ritchie, Caroline Paton, Sandy Paton) (Photo by Roy Berkeley, courtesy of Roy Berkeley)

(Top) Mississippi John Hurt, The Gaslight, Greenwich Village (Photo by Roy Berkeley, courtesy of Roy Berkeley)
(Bottom) Doc Watson, The Gaslight, Greenwich Village (Photo by Roy Berkeley, courtesy of Roy Berkeley)

(Top) Mimi Fariña and Bob Gibson, Bloomington, Indiana, May 16, 1991
(Photo by Rich Remsberg, courtesy of Rich Remsberg)
(Bottom) Len Chandler, Indiana University, Bloomington, Indiana, May 17,
1991 (Photo by Rich Remsberg, courtesy of Rich Remsberg)

(L-R) Dick Weissman, Lou Gottlieb, Bob Gibson, Dave Samuelson, Indiana University, Bloomington, Indiana, May 17, 1991(Photo by Rich Remsberg, courtesy of Rich Remsberg)

(L-R) Jon Pankake, Irwin Silber, Izzy Young, Indiana University, Bloomington, Indiana, May 18, 1991 (Photo by Rich Remsberg, courtesy of Rich Remsberg)

(Top) (L-R) Neil Rosenberg and Roy Berkeley, Indiana University, Bloomington, Indiana, May 18, 1991 (Photo by Anne Koehler, Ronald D. Cohen Collection)
(Bottom) Doctor Demento, Indiana University, Bloomington, Indiana, May 17, 1991 (Photo by Rich Remsberg, courtesy of Rich Remsberg)

techniques. The cornerstones of Negro music on LP—
Lightning Hopkins on Folkways, Leadbelly on Stinson
SLP51, Sonny and Brownie on Fantasy, and John Lee
Hooker on Audio Lab—can now welcome another—Robert Pete Williams on Folk-Lyric.

During the next five years a total of thirty issues of *The Little Sandy Review* came out. The issues gradually became bigger and more professional looking. But as the issues became more classy looking and had more stuff in them and more nice photographs, they also became less frequent. Especially after Paul Nelson moved to New York and went to work for *Sing Out! The Little Sandy Review* never had more than 300 subscribers, if that many. But it was hailed by many as the real conscience of the folk music revival and certainly gained an influence at the time and over the years, far greater than what you might think from how small its list of subscribers really was. I think that issue number 30 might have been distributed to a few more than 300 people through being stocked in the Folklore Center and some of the other stores that sold instruments around the country. But really it was only just a very few people that ever bought that magazine at the time that it came out.
    While some people hailed it as the conscience of the folk music revival, it was not a unanimous opinion by any means. The editors and myself as well considered ourselves traditionalists; we tried not to think of ourselves as dogmatic purists but undoubtedly came across that way to some. People like the Kingston Trio and Harry Belafonte came in for a lot of abuse, and so did a lot of other people who made what has certainly turned out to be, in retrospect, very worthwhile music; but anybody who in any way tried to pass themselves off as a traditionalist but in our opinion, perhaps, was not quite as pure a traditionalist as we seemed to think he was passing himself off as—there were a lot like that at the time—was likely to come in for a little abuse and sarcasm from *The Little Sandy Review*. Even Folkways Records sometimes received a few brickbats from us, deserved or not. To some people *The Little Sandy* is best remembered as an early champion of the work of Bob Dylan, and indeed his first album got one of the longest and most ecstatic reviews that the magazine ever ran, in issue 22, 1962. But the editors roundly panned his second album, *The Freewheelin'*

Bob Dylan, which they called "a flat tire." I don't know whether Jon
or Paul Nelson wrote this piece, because they signed them "The
Editors" together—it was kind of like John Lennon and Paul
McCartney; one of them would generally write the song, but they
would sign it Lennon and McCartney. But anyway, they wrote
things like:

> As a songwriter, he has become melodramatic and maud-
> lin, lacking all Guthriesque economy; his melodies bear
> more relation now to popular music than folk music. As a
> performer, he is at times affected and pretentious, although
> his harmonica technique has greatly improved. The main
> trouble now seems to be that he has no foundation or base
> for his songs; they seem to float vaguely above the ground
> in amorphous hazes; the talent is still apparent, but all the
> parts and working mechanisms seem to have broken
> down or gone out of control. Like Chaplin's feeding
> machine in *Modern Times*, the functions have gotten all
> mixed up, and the result is a mess.

Well, I quote that not in any way to put Jon Pankake and Paul Nelson
in some kind of hall of shame alongside the people who gave
Beethoven bad reviews when he was alive, but to show, one, that
The Little Sandy Review could be very eloquent, and two, that it
would go after anybody that they felt needed going after. There
were a lot of sacred cows around in those days, and the editors of
The Little Sandy Review and myself as a writer and contributor
certainly did not practice the Hindu attitude toward sacred cows.
    I could also be vitriolic at times. I was addressing a few
people who I thought had the same passion for traditional folk
music as I did. And I was also addressing myself, in a broader
sense, to people who were maybe on the edge, people who had
heard a little bit of more commercial stuff whom I wanted to get
interested in the kind of music that I loved—like perhaps somebody
who had heard some Josh White, and I would rather have them
listen to Robert Pete Williams. And so I was trying to convince them
in my writing that Josh White was BS, and that Robert Pete Williams
was much more worth listening to. In the process I probably
heaped it on Josh White a little thicker than in retrospect I should
have, but I was young, I was sophomoric, and that was the way that
my mind operated at the time. And so that's how the vitriol came

out. I would probably not write like that today, but at the time we felt that we were in a war, and our words were our weapons.

I continued to review records regularly for *The Little Sandy* until Paul and Jon's last issue, which was issue number 30, published in 1965. By that time I was listed as the Los Angeles editor. I was at UCLA, having enrolled in the master's degree program under professor D. K. Wilgus, an inspiration in a great many ways. Meanwhile, I got involved with the Ash Grove in Los Angeles, where I heard and met many of the same great traditional performers I'd been writing about. I also got exposed to the folk-rock movement and started to gravitate a bit to the rock side of folk-rock.

I still wrote the odd record review for *The Little Sandy Review*, but when no issues appeared for a year, I asked Jon Pankake about it and he talked with Paul, and the next thing I knew I was the sole editor and proprietor of *The Little Sandy Review*. And I put out two issues in 1966, with hand-drawn covers, which contained some good stuff, if I may say so. The late Alan Wilson of the Canned Heat blues band, the same guys that I was roadie for, wrote a brilliant and learned two-part analysis of Robert Pete Williams' music, for instance. But the long-suffering readers were not overly delighted with my emphasis on such newfound heroes as Paul Butterfield, Frank Zappa, and the Beatles, and I found I didn't have the time or temperament to put out a magazine on a regular schedule, especially when it started to run out of money. So I turned it over to some people with a more traditionalist outlook, who put out, I believe, one more issue, and that was the story of *The Little Sandy Review*. In retrospect I kind of wish I'd kept on with it, even in the direction it was going—if only because I had a chance to get in on the ground floor of the phenomenon of rock journalism, which was just beginning to exist in 1967, and in the years since then has provided a large number of writers, good, bad and mediocre, with varying degrees of fame and fortune. In fact, Paul Nelson, one of the founders of *The Little Sandy*, went on to become a rock writer of some distinction. As it was, I did write some record reviews for *Rolling Stone*, which, starting in the fall of 1967, became the most prominent vehicle for rock journalism. I got sidetracked writing a book for them, which was an unmanageable project for all concerned.

I wound up making a living more with my mouth than with my typewriter, on the radio. The first radio show I ever had was under the auspices of the John Edwards Memorial Foundation, which was set up primarily to study commercial country music, and I did a show for them under Ed Kahn's supervision and the other people who ran the JEMF. But I became a writer. I did a good deal of writing for *Hit Parader* after *The Little Sandy*—*Hit Parader* got a fair amount of circulation—and for *Rolling Stone*. And the people who ran the local underground FM rock station, back in the days when those were flourishing in the late '60s and early '70s, heard about that. One of them came to a party at my house, saw my record collection, I played some of my zingers for him, and he said, "You ought to bring these down to the radio station." And I'd always been, I'd always wanted to be a disk jockey. I tried to get a job as a disk jockey as early as 1963. But in those days you needed a big booming voice and I didn't quite have that, but by 1970 radio had changed and I was offered a gig playing the most obscure oldies I could think of at this underground radio station. I quickly found that the funny stuff got the biggest response. One of the other disk jockeys at the station named me Doctor Demento after a joke that he heard years ago in which Doctor Demento was portrayed as a mad scientist, and I was off and running.

I still write now and then. But not many record reviews. There came a point, after I'd done a number of reviews for *Rolling Stone*, around eleven years after that first Bo Diddley item for *Record Research*, when I somehow began finding it a little bit distasteful to have myself out there in print trying to tell Otis Spann he was not playing the piano correctly, considering that I could hardly have done it one one-hundredth as well myself. Now I know a lot of other non-musicians who have had no qualms at all about doing that sort of thing, but I couldn't help feeling that way. On the other hand, I cannot argue for a minute that record reviewing does not serve a valid purpose. I guess record reviews in a way started to become important the day that the local record store took out those little booths where you used to (in my childhood days) be able to try out all the new records before you bought them. In some stores you could get a real musical education that way. And now that hearing new music on the radio is such a hit-or-miss proposition there's every reason to have a print medium where you can read some hopefully qualified person's opinion on whether a given recording is worth your money. Especially now that we're talking $14.99 or more for a compact disc, rather than just five bucks or less for an LP, like the way it was in the '60s. With records, or I should say CDs, and cassettes today, often the only real question is Are they entertaining enough to be worth the money?

But as I reread those old *Little Sandy Reviews* from the '60s I'm constantly reminded that reviewing a record in the '60s, especially a record devoted to any kind of folk music, almost always involved a lot more than money. It was a lot more than just "Is this entertaining? Is this worth $3.98?" There were so many other issues that you got involved in whenever you were talking about folk music. Of course there was politics. Now that was about the only controversial aspect of folk music in the '60s that *The Little Sandy Review* did not get much involved with. I think just for me, I can speak for myself, that I was just a lot more interested in the music itself. And there was more than enough controversy involved in just the music, even if you didn't talk about world affairs or civil rights, or the other necessary and burning issues of the day.

I think that everybody involved in the folk revival of the '60s shared the basic assumption that traditional folk music, black and white, was pure gold. And that we were all on a mighty mission to get more Americans to appreciate that beauty. Of course, some were in it for what we consider to be noble and altruistic motives and others were in it, frankly, to get some of that gold and put it in their bank accounts. And there were so many shades in between, from the scholar who felt that the only folk music really worth considering was a Child ballad sung by somebody who had never been near a radio or a phonograph, to the concert promoter who was just interested in putting fannies in those theater seats. Well, the people who ran *The Little Sandy*, and myself as well, certainly irritated a few people.

Many times reading the old *Little Sandy*s, the letters section is the most fascinating part nowadays. There was the time that I accused Folkways Records of putting overdubs on a Leadbelly album. And Moe Asch wrote to me indignantly and strenuously denied having done that. As far as I'm concerned, the letter from Moe Asch was pretty much an issue restricted to that one album and I accepted his statement, and he was other than that very supportive to us. The feedback did one thing for me: It made me realize that perhaps I'd stepped over the line a little bit sometimes in terms of turning my negative reviews of records into personal attacks. And it made me realize after a while that perhaps that was not the best way to go about it. And it may have eventually led to my decision to retire from the world of record reviewing and find what I considered to be a more friendly way of promoting music that I liked. There were many more complex issues that inspired contentious letters from Manny Solomon at Vanguard Records, from John Greenway, from Cynthia Gooding, and of course from lay readers of many ideological stripes.

I decided to get into something a little less controversial, and be a record critic only in the sense that if I like records and think that my audience will like them I put them on my radio show, and if I don't like them I don't. And so that's the extent of my record criticism these days. I don't know if I should have gotten out of criticism or not, but I told you the way I felt about it at the time. But anyway, I'm very happy doing what I do now, and in the same way I'm proud of some of the feathers I might have ruffled as part of *The Little Sandy Review*.

I've been doing *The Doctor Demento Show* for over twenty years now. Certainly it has only limited relevance to the folk revival or any other kind of folk music, though I have proudly played the records of many people who are here in this room: Bob Gibson, Lou Gottlieb, and more. Len Chandler, of course, some of your songs. Folk music has contributed a lot to the big fabric of music that I present on the show. One thing I say about *The Doctor Demento Show* is if you don't like one record, the next one's gonna be a whole lot different.

When I wrote for *The Little Sandy*, I saw my audience as somebody who had heard a certain amount of folk music (they certainly wouldn't be buying this obscure little publication if they hadn't). But somebody who, I thought, perhaps I could improve their taste a little bit. That was what I thought at the time that I was writing for *The Little Sandy*. And at the time that I wrote for other publications such as *Rolling Stone* later on, I was either trying to tell the world about somebody that I liked a whole lot, or perhaps trying to say, this is something that you might be tempted to spend your money on and perhaps shouldn't. You should buy something else instead. That's kind of what I saw as my purpose.

Performance
Stories

THE
NATIONAL
TOPICAL
SONG
MAGAZINE

BROADSIDE #48

JULY 20
1964
Price
50¢

Broadside
1962
WORK FOR
PEACE
JAMES
MEREDITH
EMMETT TILL
1963
MASTERS of
WAR
LITTLE BOXES
VIETNAM
MEDGAR EVERS
J.F.K.
1964
HAZARD, KY.
MISSISSIPPI
TIMES
ARE
CHANGIN'

IN THIS ISSUE

SONGS BY
RICHARD FARIÑA
LEN CHANDLER
PHIL OCHS
MALVINA REYNOLDS
ROGER K. LEIB
PEGGY SEEGER
JOHN BRUNNER
JENES COTTRELL

A R T I C L E S

THE ART OF BOB DYLAN'S "HATTIE
CARROLL" --- BY PHIL OCHS

TOPICAL SONGS IN THE STREETS OF
NEW YORK -- BY JULIUS LESTER

HOMAGE TO ERIC ANDERSEN

U.C. FOLK FESTIVAL

9 Len Chandler

I started taking piano lessons when I was eight years old. And then when I was fourteen years old I went to school and told them I wanted to play in the school band, they gave me the only box that was left; that's how I started playing oboe. I had an 8" by 10" fingering chart; that was my instruction on the oboe for the next four years. I really loved to play the oboe, because not many people did. And so you got special treatment and special positions, and you got to play, not because you played so great but because there were so few players. By the time I was a senior in high school I was playing in the Akron University Orchestra. By the time I was a senior at Akron University I was playing in the Akron Symphony Orchestra.

My days would be very, very weird. Jon Pankake was talking about the absurdity in his life, about how the different influences can impact on you. I don't think it was absurd myself. I think it was very logical. It was very logical for me to spend mornings in the university sight-reading Handel with a French-horn player because my English horn was also in "F" and so we could sight-read things together. And to spend the afternoon practicing a tone poem by Norodom Sihanouk, the crown prince of Cambodia; then spend the early evening with my introduction to folk music, which was Norman Luboff's eight-part chorale arrangements of "Shenandoah"; and then try to catch this great-looking girl and dance to B. B. King and Little Richard and Howlin' Wolf and Little Willie John. So that's the way a day in my life was, and it felt perfectly normal to me. Then after I left the dance, I'd get to go by Howard Street, where I would be able to catch my dad playing a late set. He was a saxophone player, a jazz player who, when all the jazz jobs dried up, he was in there honkin', playing R & B. Maybe I would be able to catch a ride home with him.

In my high school somebody wanted my group, a quartet that used to sing things like "Walking in a Winter Wonderland," to sing a commercial for one of their dances, but the parody they'd written sucked. So I wrote another song for them, because I wouldn't sing what they had given me. That song stopped everybody who heard it on our little intercom radio station, and it got a great response. The dance was full, so I became the commercial jingle writer for the school. Everybody who had any kind of event to promote commissioned me to write a song, put the music together and produce it and put it on the school's radio.

I started playing the ukelele, and that was because nobody could hear the oboe on the band bus. I got a banjo-ukelele, because that was louder still. In college, I wrote twenty-three songs for a musical that got a great big splash in the newspapers. It was the first original musical that the school had produced in twenty-five years. So that got me a lot of positive strokes and positive feedback. I got asked to write a couple of songs for plays that were being produced at the university. And one was a play called *Rainmaker*, and I said, "Well, I'd like to try to do that." An English professor said, "We need somebody to write a song, sing it, and play the guitar." So I said, "Well, when does it have to be done?" He said, "Well, the production is in a month." I said, "I'd like to try that." So I took the banjo-mandolin that I had inherited and traded it for a Stella guitar, wrote the song, auditioned on the guitar, and got the part. When the reviews came out my picture was in the paper, and it said, "Singer Steals Show at Akron U. Production." So I said, "Hmm, this is getting interesting."

This professor, Walter Lehrman, who was from the Greenwich Village scene in New York, had heard the things that I had written for this production. He came up to me in the cafeteria and said, "How's your mamma?" For some people who might not be aware, that's the introduction to a game called the dirty dozens that young black boys play. It's a series of elaborate insults to your mother. They're rhymed and metered and sometimes they're very complex and always filthy. I mean little things like: "I saw your mother on the corner of Seventh Avenue and Kelly with a mattress tied to her back calling curb service." That wasn't rhymed. Or, "I screwed your mamma on the top of a piano. Baby came out singing 'Old Susannah.'" Stuff like that, but some of them would be longer and much more vulgar.

So this guy came up to me and said, "Well, look, I've heard your songs, and I really like the way you're writing, but I think that you've only been listening to the radio and I have an enormous collection of wonderful records that I'd like to put at your disposal. However, there is something that I need from you. I'm doing my doctoral thesis on the dirty dozens, and as a white man, if I go up and ask some kids to say some to me they'd go tell their mother, or they'd think I'm some freak or something; anyway it doesn't work. So if you want to trade me dirty dozens, my record collection is available to you." I immediately spewed about half an hour of dozens on him and made this deal, and for the first time I got to hear Leadbelly, Furry Lewis, Lonnie Johnson, Mississippi John Hurt, Lightnin' Hopkins, Son House, and then also Cisco Houston and a lot of the pickers and players that I soon came to love.

I was getting drafted into the Army at that time. And I decided that since I was a virtuoso instrumentalist I could go to any branch of the service and get into a band. Not because I was so good, but because there were so few oboe players that were going to be joining things like the Marine Corps. So I wanted to join the Marine Corps, because they had the prettiest uniforms and they were supposed to be the baddest. A friend of mine grabbed me and said, "Don't do it, don't do it." And he spent the whole afternoon telling me about how horrible the Marine Corps was and how stupid they were and how crazy, and it just made me want to do it more. I joined the Marine Corps because it only had a two-year enlistment. If I had joined anything else it would have been four years. Since I wanted to go to graduate school and I wanted to see the world, it was a great choice. I joined the Marine Corps; they ripped my knee up in about six months in a physical training exercise, then gave me a medical discharge, which put me a year and a half ahead of my program.

I came back to Akron, and there was a contest for all advanced instrumentalists in Ohio. I had been in the Marine Corps for six months, my lips were like rubber, I had no chops at all, and I got a job as a substitute teacher and then I practiced from the time I got up in the morning, except when I was teaching, until I went to bed at night. I'd get up and brush my teeth and I'd practice until I had to go to school. I took my oboe reed and put it in a shot glass of water on top of a piano, then I'd teach a class. When there was a fifteen-minute break when they were changing classes, I'd practice the oboe. So I won the contest. The contest took place behind a screen. The judges couldn't see you. The screen was arranged by my allies so the judges could not discriminate. And so the only thing that they had was your number. I played a Handel sonata and a piece by Wayne Barlow called "The Winters Past," an orchestral work based on two old folk songs, "Black Is the Color of My True Love's Hair," the old version, and "Wayfaring Stranger." After I won, Walter Lehrman, the professor, said, "I'm going to be driving to New York, my wife doesn't drive. You need to go to New York. You can share the driving with me. You *need* to go to the Village in New York. You want to go?" I said, "Sure."

I went and got a job working in the elevator at Columbia University, enrolled in Columbia graduate school, and walked down to MacDougal Street and walked into this place called the "Izzy Young Folklore Center," where I saw Dave Van Ronk playing the guitar. It was the first time that I ever saw finger picking. I had gotten a job teaching at Saint Barnabas House, which was a shelter for neglected children on Mulberry Street, and I had ten kids under my care while I was going to graduate school. I took them to Washington Square Park to roller-skate every Sunday and saw the players singing folk songs around the fountain. With a little theory background, I soon figured out how to play about eight or ten chords and learned about fifty songs. I started playing in the Square. This guy named Hugh Romney, who later became Wavy Gravy, saw me playing on the circle, near the pool that never had water in it, in the Square and said, "Look, we're going to play in Hartford, Connecticut, a couple of nights, you want to go? You can have a third of the money that we collect from the door." I said sure. Hugh said, "Kind of dress down. Don't dress like that, you know, with that button-down shirt and stuff. Dress down, man. We're supposed to be beatniks, man." And so I said, "I don't have anything like that." And he said, "Just dress down, dress real, real, real casual." So I wore this nice pair of black pants and a red shirt. That wasn't it. But they let me play anyway.

And after that they invited me to join them singing at the Gaslight between the poets, and the poets were Hugh Romney and John Brent and other people who would come in. It is my recollection that in the Village that was the only coffeehouse at that moment, I'm talking 1958, that had live entertainment: the poets, and I was singing American folk songs in between. A person came

Len Chandler

131

in one night and was being very rude, he was heckling and drunk. And he was heckling the poets, and they had to struggle to keep their focus and continue doing what they were doing. This was still early in '58 and I'm still trying to decipher the mysteries of finger picking. I had trapped a couple of guys in the park and had asked them to write these finger patterns, and I was still borrowing guitars until somebody said, "Why don't you buy your own damn guitar?" So I took out forty dollars and I said, "I'll buy that one." And he sold it to me. So, back to this heckler at the Gaslight. When my turn came I started doing some things that I knew were constructed so I would have some space to think. When he started bothering me, I would take everything that he said and I would throw it back at him and have the audience howling. When I came off the stage he said, "That was very good, I'd like to hire you." And I told him to go, well Izzy said it, "fuck himself." And so he left and about two hours later he came back with a two hundred dollar check and he said, "Here's two hundred dollars and if you call blah, blah, blah airlines there will be a round-trip ticket waiting for you." And he gave me his card, his name was John Pivell, he was the vice president of a television station in Detroit. And he said, "If you're here on this date you have a job singing on my new television show."

I went there and I sang two songs a night five days a week and I got a job at a little coffeehouse and said, "Hmm, maybe this is it." Because I really didn't want to teach school at that moment anyway. And so I got this job there and really became immersed in the folk scene. Every night I would be playing to two or three hundred people and then I would split from there at 11 o'clock and drive to the television station to do two songs and then come back to the Cup of Socrates. I would go to the library in the daytime to do research, because I liked to have new songs all the time. So I would learn maybe two songs a day at least and sing those new songs in my performance that night.

I was increasing my repertoire very rapidly. I would find the best pickers and pick their brains and teach them what I knew and try and figure out what they were doing. Hugh Romney had said to me, "No, no, get rid of that red shirt, put on these black jeans, that's very hip, and put on this work shirt. That's a really good look for you. These black boots. That's nice. Tie this kerchief around your neck, that's it. That's it, right, that's good." That's what I wore on the television station in Detroit and at the coffeehouse playing.

When I came back to New York about four months later there was a new club across the street from the Gaslight called the Commons; right down the street from that was a club called the Café Wha?; around the corner from that there was a club called the Bizarre. On Bleecker Street there was a club called the Cock and Bull, and there was the Village Gate; this whole thing had started by the time I came back to New York. There was a heated little folk music scene happening in the Village, and they all had on my costume. They all had on work shirts and black Levis. The Café Bizarre was really crazy, it was really bizarre. People had on wild, wild costumes that make the green hair and all that look like nothing now. And Café Wha? was really a snake pit, but it was very exciting because tourists were coming down in droves. You would have to walk in the street on Saturday night to get to see the rest of the players, because the sidewalk was so crowded. Everybody let you come in free, so you would listen to all the performers and there was a real feeling of camaraderie and mutual support.

But what was happening was the stagecraft stuff was starting to develop. People would say things to you like, "You know, like your timing, man, when you were in the middle of that song, you moved and you released them by moving your guitar, so they started laughing before the big laugh was on, and by the time you were saying the big laugh people were laughing and they missed it"; or, "You didn't hold them at the end of the song; you could have held them"; or, "You got into some funny position on the stage because when you started to go, you crossed your right leg over your left and turned your back to half the audience. You should have moved off with your left leg and not turned your back on the crowd." We would talk to each other and critique our sets. And so it would be very, very interesting. I started to get hired to go out of town, to go to other places, play other gigs.

When we were playing at the Gaslight there was no real applause. The Gaslight was dug out of a basement and there were air shafts that went up into the upper apartments. When people applauded after your performance it would disturb the tenants at 11 or 12 o'clock at night. So you couldn't applaud, you could only snap your fingers after a performance for years until they cemented up the air shafts. Also there was this riff that the owner John Mitchell was blowing on everybody, saying, "We cannot pay you because it is against the law. You have to have an entertainment license.

And they won't give me an entertainment license, and for me to pay you I would have to have an entertainment license or they would close the club. " So we would hire, for ten percent of what they collected, somebody to pass—it wasn't passing the hat, she held a cornucopia at the door, a woven basket, that's how we would make our money. Well, it was really exploitative and I really got pissed when I saw Mitchell counting his money. He had just broken a thousand dollars and I was only making like eighteen or twenty dollars. So I finally started getting jobs going out of town and making $150 to $250 and when I started to come back to the Gaslight I started to demand more money. Well, they decided they wouldn't pay me any more money.

I quit and I got a job teaching, going around as a substitute at these day care centers. But I'd go back every night and do guest sets. And I would try to be as outrageous as I could on my guest set. I'd try to kill on my guest set. I'd come in to do a guest set and just have the audience all screaming, and I'd make them get on the chairs to sing choruses and stuff. The Gaslight had two front doors, you could walk in one door and out this other door. I'd get the people all in a line walking around outside and back in the other door following me around singing the song. And then when I finished my song I would announce, "In about fifteen minutes I'm going to do another set at Café Wha?" And then they'd all leave. And so finally I got to negotiate a more favorable deal.

I was playing in Saratoga Springs, New York, at the Café Lena, and was staying with Jackie and Joe Alper when I wrote my first topical song. Up until this time we're talking about singing American folk songs. And the reason they appealed to me was the goose pimples. I don't care what the music is. I got goose pimples when I was working in the library, where I got a job when I was fourteen. And it taught me so much, I learned so much from that job. There were these two big black muscle builders. These were *big* guys, and they had on shades and were listening to this music in the library. The music section was mine. They had earphones on, and this one guy turned to this other and said, "Damn, man, this is better than a shot of dope." I couldn't wait to get to hear what they were listening to. And it was Béla Bartók playing Bartók on the piano. I got goose pimples from that. I got goose pimples when I first found "Shakespeare in Harlem" by Langston Hughes, I got goose pimples the first time I saw the works of Picasso, all these things that I found in the library.

I woke up one day when I was at Café Lena and went to buy the paper, as was my habit, and I saw two photographs in both the *Mirror* and the *Daily News*. There was a woman lifting a blanket to look at the body of a child, and then another woman facing the sky with her hands over her eyes. And so I studied that paper and I said, "I will write about this," and I worked on it all day and did it as my first encore that night. It was a long song, and I had to work to get it committed to memory. But I'm going to tell you the first two verses of this song. It says:

December the 15 of '61, yes that was just today.
Yes I bought the morning paper just to see what it would say.
The story on the front page struck my heart with woe.
I saw two women standing by a dead child in the snow.
One woman lifted a blanket to see a dead child's face.
One boot, some books, some Christmas cards were
scattered around the place.
The other woman hid her eyes because she couldn't bear to see.
More stories in the centerfold, see photos on page three.

And when I finished the song I thought that I had really blown it. I thought I had really offended people, because they sat there. They just looked at me. I said, "Thank you." I took my instrument and left the stage. I went into my dressing room and took off my shirt. I wiped myself. I put on another shirt. I put my guitar away, and then the applause started at some high feverish pitch that I had not heard until that time. The applause went on and on. I just sat in the dressing room and listened for a while, then went back to the stage to take a bow. I stood there for a long time, and they just kept clapping. I said to myself, "Hmm, I think I'm on to something."

Very soon after that I met Tom Paxton at the Gaslight. He was still in the Army and he was playing a nylon-string guitar and he was coming in on weekends. He said, "There's a demonstration in front of Woolworth's because they won't serve black people in several different towns." They would serve them in New York, but they were doing a sympathetic-type demonstration. And Tom Paxton was the first person I ever saw sing a song he had just made up on a picket line. It was, "What's a Matter, Mister Woolworth." So that was very impressive to me, and we started working from there.

Then everybody started. Right around that time it seemed like everybody started adding these new songs to their repertoire. Dylan had just come to town, and he was singing all traditional material. The first song that I recall him having written was a song that said, "Hey ho hey, Leadbelly. Hey ho hey, Leadbelly. Hey ho hey, Leadbelly, I just want to sing your name. Hey, hey, hey, Woody Guthrie. Hey, hey," you know, and so forth. That was one of Dylan's first songs.

Right about that time I got invited by the New Jersey Symphony to participate in a series of children's concerts. The theme of the children's concert was concert music which had thematic material that had been drawn from American folk music. My job was to be the folk singer and to go out and sing the folk material, and they would do the concert work. I had the rare opportunity of seeing my life at that moment come full circle, because I had come to New York on the basis of having won this scholarship by playing Wayne Barlow's "The Winters Past," which was based on "Black Is the Color of My True Love's Hair" and "Wayfaring Stranger." Now I got to go and sing these songs and have the New Jersey Symphony play them. I kind of blew the oboe player's mind, though, because I brought my reed and I walked up to him and said, "What kind of instrument is that?" He said, "This is an oboe." I said, "Yeah, yeah, but I was asking, what kind of oboe?" And he said, "A Lore." I said, "You mind if I look at it?" He said, "You know about oboes?" I said, "A little." So I put my reed in and played his solo. It blew him away.

About that time I started to write. I went to some conferences at Columbia where people who were just coming back from the Freedom Rides were giving lectures to the students. I was really moved by the personal stories that they told. And I had been reading, as everybody in the country had, reading the papers and looking at the newsreels about all of the things that were taking place. I started writing songs that were my comments on all of these events. I didn't know it at the time, I just wrote like I was feeling, but as I was later to learn, most of my songs at that time were relatively abstract. I mean, I would write the songs like "Secret Songs of Old." I would write the songs like "Keep On Keeping On" and "To Be a Man," and those kinds of songs had relatively abstract imagery all the way through. They weren't just banging home, well, this is wrong and we have to do something about it, that type of thing.

I got invited to participate in a conference of freedom song singers that took place in Atlanta, Georgia, in May 1964. This was a very pivotal experience for me because it brought me to the South for my first time (with the exception of my brief stay in the Marine Corps, and I was not off the base, so that wasn't important to me). It brought me for the first time in contact with people who were totally involved in the freedom movement. These were singers from Albany, Georgia and from Mississippi, and people like Charles Sherrod and Bernice Reagon and Cordell Reagon. I was really afraid at this conference, because there I was, this little ex-oboe player from Ohio, singing songs full of these abstract literary allusions, and these people are blasting the walls down with this gospel, knock-dead stuff. I wondered, "What are they going to think of me? Are they going to hate me?" I did some of my songs, and as I was saying thank you, and had started back to my seat this little grey-haired lady stopped me and said, "Could you sing that 'Keep On Keeping On' song one more time for me?" So I figured it was okay.

These guys kind of adopted me. I guess that inherently they knew that for me to do what I wanted to do my experiences would have to be expanded. Cordell told me, "Hey, man, you better call up your wife and tell her you're not coming home now because you're going to Nashville with me, 'cause things are really going down out there." He took me to Nashville and got me arrested about four or five times in about a week, and that was real important because the songs that you make up and you sing in jail and all those things really had an incredible impact on me. When I got back to the North I'm singing all these songs, and I think I can excite everybody like I'm excited about this stuff. And club owners are saying, "What?" I went to Detroit, and I had just gotten back from the freedom movement in the South and I had just written some really good songs down there. And I had learned these other great songs. I had taken traditional songs and written some additional verses. For "Which Side Are You On?" I would have verses like:

Come all you bourgeois black men, with all your excess fat.
A few days on the picket line will sure get rid of that.
Come all you high-tone college girls, pronounce your final 'g's,
But don't you forget your grandma, she's still scrubbing on her knees.
Come all you Northern liberals, take a Klansman out to lunch,

But when you dine instead of wine you should serve non-violent punch.
Which side are you on? Which side are you on?

I was at Herbie Cohen's club, called the Raven, in Detroit. I started singing some of these songs, but I would intersperse them with comedy stuff and love songs and other things that I had written. Obviously people were having a good time, because I'd have them singing at the top of their lungs. After I did that set, he came up and he said, "You can't do that." He said, "People come in here to have a good time! When they left today they were thinking!!"

I started submitting a lot of songs to *Broadside*, because sometimes what got me off the most were topical songs. I really loved the impact that would be made on people when they would hear something that you had just written right out of the news, about something that happened today. There were three young girls, like eleven, ten, thirteen, maybe even younger, who were killed in a church bombing in Alabama, and there was a meeting on the steps of the Federal Building in New York. I wrote a song for that demonstration, and the song says:

You've got to go downtown,
Go downtown today.
Put your body on the line with a picket sign
Till the wagons come and take you away.

I would write songs like that and mimeograph three hundred copies and pass them out and have everybody singing with me. I finally got a record contract with Columbia Records. John Hammond was irate because the Green Berets song was out and was a hit. And he said, "Why don't you write something to counter that?" I said, "I did." And so I played it for him, and it said:

Things are in a jam down in Vietnam.
The people down there don't dig Uncle Sam.
A rule by the people just can't be wrong.
They say the people down there are the Vietcong.
Well you're wrong, Sam, scram, don't you know you better get gone.
"Well," he said, "Thank you, thank you very much" and split. And

you know, I never heard any more from him about that.

There were situations like the March on Washington. I had gotten my left hand injured in an accident and things were really cut up, and it was about six months or so before I could play. I had to put on very light strings and I couldn't feel my fingers on my left had, so I could only tell what strings I was pressing down by looking. Dylan and Joan Baez played side-by-side with me while we did things like the song "Which Side Are You On?" and also a song I wrote called "Move On Over or We'll Move On Over You." And we did that at the March on Washington before Dr. Martin Luther King made his famous speech.

I want to mention "Move On Over" because it was based on "John Brown's Body." That melody later became the "Battle Hymn of the Republic," and it became "Solidarity Forever." It was used in the Bonus March on Washington, another version was written for that. And so a bunch of New York radicals were going to go to Harper's Ferry for the hundredth anniversary of John Brown's raid there. And of course I had to write a special version for that. And its opening lines say:

Mine eyes have seen injustice in each city, town and state
Your jails are filled with black men and your courts are white with hate
And with every bid for freedom someone whispers to us, "wait"
But, the movements movin' on.
Move on over or we'll move on over you
Move on over or we'll move on over you
Move on over or we'll move on over you
For the movement's moving on.
I declare my independence from the fool and from the knave
I declare my independence from the coward and the slave
I declare that I will fight for right and fear no jail nor grave
And, the movements movin' on.

That song became widely sung throughout the movement, in a lot of places, in the more militant sections like in Student Nonviolent Coordinating Committee (SNCC), which was always pushing King and the Southern Christian Leadership Conference forward. That song was done as a rallying cry, because it was a much better marching song and the words were quite militant.

I'm talking about these experiences from my life rather than just talking about songwriting in general because what I would like to address myself to is the response to specific events and how the call of that event can put you into emergency gear and how you can create things that are useful for that moment. Some are good songs, and some are maybe only worth the paper they were printed on and are for that day and maybe only to get people excited, to galvanize emotions for that moment. If you are crafty enough and successful enough you can create a hook that reaches out of the song and grabs you or that you can reach into the song and grab onto. The hook is like the commercial for the song. The hook insinuates itself into your consciousness and will have you repeating it whether you like the song or don't, if you have crafted a slick enough hook. You can have people go around singing, "Move on over or we'll move on over you," that's slick, you know. It's just like, if you can have people singing, "Get gone, Sam, scram, don't you know you better get gone," that's good. So that's why I would write songs for specific events like that.

During the 1965 Selma to Montgomery march I was one of the people along with Pete Seeger and a lot of people from the South who marched every step of the way for the fifty miles that the journey took. While we were marching, some old military guys started to say things like, "Left, left, left, right," and I said, "Wait a minute, wait a minute. Hold it. We've been left out, left back, left behind so much. Let's put the emphasis on the other foot. Today let's be right." So I started singing:

Pick 'em up and lay 'em down
Right! Right!
All the way to Selma town
Right! Right!
Did the rain come down
Right! Right!
Well I thought I would drown
Right! Right!
I've been walking so long
Right! Right!
I've put blisters on the street
Right! Right!
Well Lord, I got the Freedom fever

Right! Right!
And it settled in my feet
Right! Right!

A guy was walking along, had been walking all the way, and he had
only one leg. And his name was Jim Letherer, and he said, "Len,
make up a verse about me." And so after a little while I said:

Jim Letherer's leg got left
Right! Right!
But he's still in the fight
Right! Right!
Been walking day and night
Right! Right!
Jim's left leg is all right
Right! Right!

After the march was over, going back to Selma, my crew
that I was riding with came to a place where all the spotlights were
on and all the police were out, and they pulled us over and they said
that we had failed to dim our bright lights and they fined us all the
money that we had. We paid them on the spot, and then they let
us go. I went to the Dexter Avenue Baptist Church, where I found
out Viola Liuzzo had been shot to death. And I locked myself in the
toilet in that church and wrote a song that was called "Murder on the
Roads of Alabama" that said things like:

Oh it's murder on the road in Alabama.
Oh it's murder on the road in Alabama.
If you're fighting for what's right,
If you're black or if you're white,
You're a target in the night in Alabama.
There's a man behind the guns in Alabama.
There's a man behind the guns of Alabama.
There's a man behind the guns,
Kills for hate, for fear, for fun,
And George Wallace is top gun of Alabama.
There's a movement on the road in Alabama.
There's a movement on the road in Alabama.
Black man, white man, Christian, Jew,

We've got to keep on marching through,
Oh the tyrant days are few in Alabama.

Stuff like that. When the documentary on King was done, those two songs were used because they had been so widely sung and the creators of that documentary thought that they were folk songs. Luckily, Harold Leventhal didn't think so, because I had copyrighted them and published them in *Sing Out!*

Today I find political songs wherever I am. My organization is called the Los Angeles Songwriter's Showcase and we hear a lot of songs, most of them for the commercial music market. But I frequently hear, maybe because people know I like them, outrageously crafted songs, and I also have been a participant in the Freedom Song Network, which has yearly, if not bi-yearly seminars. Some people are putting together great topical songs. But probably what is happening is that sometimes we have to create the venues for them. Yes, places for them to be heard and appreciated. Previously we had the proliferation of topical songs supported by *Broadside* magazine and its editors, Sis Cunningham and Gordon Friesen. We have to continue to create places for them to be heard.

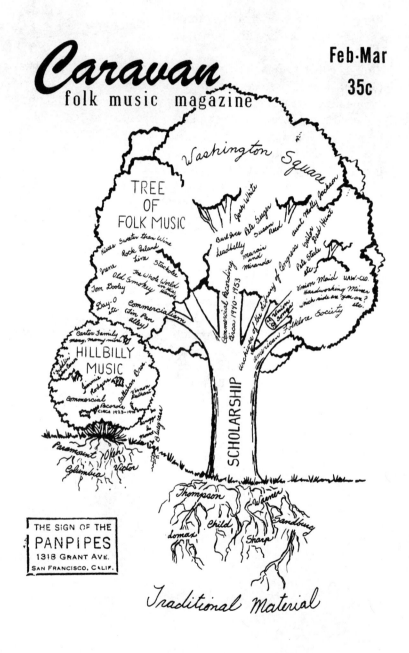

Caravan
folk music magazine

Feb-Mar
35c

TREE
OF
FOLK MUSIC

Washington Square

TREE OF FOLK MUSIC

Kisses Sweeter than Wine
Rock Island Line
Irene   Stackolee
        The Whole World
Old Smokey in His Hands
Tom Dooley
Day-O   Commercialism
etc.   (Tin Pan Alley)

Burl Ives Pete Seeger
Leadbelly   Susan Reed
        Marais
        and
        Miranda

aunt Molly Jackson
            Guy
    Pete Steele Bud Hunt
    Union Maid UAW-CIO
    Hardworking Miner
which side are you on?
        etc.

Commercial Recording
Since 1910-1953

Gun White

Archives of the Library of Congress

Union Songs

American Folklore Society

HILLBILLY
MUSIC

Carter Family
many, many more
Jimmie
Rodgers
Callahan Bros.
Vernon Dalhart
Commercial
Records
CIRCA 1923-1941

Bluegrass

SCHOLARSHIP

Paramount   Okeh
Columbia   Victor

THE SIGN OF THE
PANPIPES
1318 GRANT AVE.
SAN FRANCISCO, CALIF.

Thompson
    Child   Warner
Lomax   Sandburg
        Sharp

Traditional Material

10 Lou Gottlieb

I'd like to put three names or perhaps four out as the morphogenetic pillars of this zeitgeist. The first one is Pete Seeger. The second one is Paul Campbell. Very good, you know where that's going to lead. The next one is Elvis Presley. And the last is Joe McCarthy, Senator Joe McCarthy. I think somewhere in there we can find the forces which shaped the '50s lump of dough in a pan. While baking it fills up the pan and then makes a rounded dome on top. What shapes that dome on top? A morphogenetic field.

I am delighted to have this opportunity to address a group of people who share my interest in a musical sociological phenomenon that enabled me to retire at age 40. I'm donating the $12,000 fee plus travel and accommodations that I get for participating in this conference to EIFSBP, that's Euthanasia for Indigent Five-String Banjo Pickers. I also heard there was an epidemic of teenage gerontophilia in Bloomington. I want to check that out. I brought a few bottles of vintage Madeira for that purpose. All right. When I was discharged from the armed forces in 1946 I came back to Los Angeles and it was a wonderful place to be. Bebop was the *dernier cri*, the latest thing. Dizzy Gillespie and Charlie Parker were playing on Vine Street, Art Tatum was playing on Hollywood Boulevard, Erroll Garner was at the Suzy-Q, Boyd Rayburn had a wonderful band with tremendous arrangements by George Handy. Anyway, it was really a wonderful time. With Nat Cole, Nat "King" Cole, as my model, I formed a jazz trio called the Lou Edwards Trio, because I tried Mahalia Gottlieb, Blind Lemon Gottlieb, it didn't work, see? So I decided Lou Edwards would be the thing. The only thing is that I drove by the club where it said "Lou Edwards Trio" and I wondered, "Who could that be?" So I finally returned to Lou

Gottlieb. At any rate, the only folk songs I can remember having
known by the time I got out of the Army in 1946 were "Little Brown
Jug." Then I liked Maxine Sullivan. She sang "Loch Lomond." I
loved that. And we had a record at home that my father bought.
"The Song of the Volga Boatman."

I decided to go back to school—my father decided I should
go back to school. I went back to school the first summer session
at UCLA in 1946 and met a full professor in the German Department, a famous ballad scholar by the name of Sigurd Hustvedt. He
was a wonderful man, and he instituted a little concert series
Wednesday afternoons. He brought John Jacob Niles. He was
sensational. Thin, Mephistophelian, intense. The first thing he did
was sing some children's songs a capella. Heart melted. Goose
bumps all over. If we're not talking about goose bumps we may as
well disband this conference right now, because music is the great
goose bump hunt. Then he sang "The Maid Freed from the
Gallows." And I was electrified. He then had a piano player come
up and play some of his accompaniments that he sang to. Those
accompaniments are superb. Believe me, they are superb. Simple,
eloquent. Just try writing a keyboard accompaniment for [sings] "If
I had a ribbon bow to bind my hair." It's very difficult. His are
perfect.

Anyway, I had moved in with my dad and my stepmother,
who was a Com-symp. The *Daily People's World* used to come to
the house every day, with an article in it by Woody Guthrie, and/or
Mario "Boots" Casetta. Someplace in there I heard that the *Daily
People's World* was having a fund raiser, and guess who was
playing? Pete Seeger. And Josh White. I don't remember anything
about that concert except that Pete had his GI shoes on. A little later
that year Burl Ives got a hit on "Blue Tail Fly." So my introduction
came from the three venues from which it was available: the
academy, the left wing, and that once-in-a-while folk hit that
occasionally came along, like Glenn Miller's "Little Brown Jug."
Maxine Sullivan got a big hit on "Loch Lomond." She did, by the
way, also record "If I Had a Ribbon Bow." Anyway, I learned the
"Blue Tail Fly," but I never did it with my trio. People didn't dig it.
It was considered kind of corny. But I loved it.

By the way, the idea of including folk songs in a recital was
nothing new. I mean, Niles certainly didn't invent that. Everybody
used to do that. But the idea of having an entire recital of folk songs

was something unprecedented. Now back on campus, 1947, the
American Youth for Democracy, which was the reconstituted
Young Communist League, disbanded and became Students for
Wallace. I'm not talking about George, I'm talking about Henry
Agard Wallace. I still think he would have been a better president
than Harry Truman. No, I'm no longer sure about that. Anyway,
one member of that organization was a nineteen-year-old sophomore girl whose acquaintance I was determined to cultivate.
Joining Students for Wallace improved my standing with her
impressively, and I got a load of the first *People's Songs* bulletin I'd
ever seen, and inside there was a song, the first topical song I ever
saw that I really loved. [Sings]

I get butterflies in my stomach
whenever I start to sing,
and when I'm at a microphone
I shake like anything,
but if you'll sing along with me
I'll holler right out loud,
'cause I'm awful nervous lonesome
but I'm swell when I'm a crowd.
Sing along. . .

That was the first song by Malvina Reynolds I learned.
        It was the first time that I had seen a song with a "tendency."
I'd been reading that stuff. I got myself a book by David Guest on
dialectical materialism, from which I learned that for art to mean
anything it has to have a tendency. You've got to show what side
you're on. And anything that helps the proletariat—What's the
classic formulation?—transfer the ownership of the means of
production from the hands of the bourgeoisie to the hands of the
proletariat, specifically its most class-conscious vanguard, the
Communist Party of the country in question—anything which helps
this transference is true, beautiful, good, valuable, immortal. And
anything which doesn't is undoubtedly paid for by the monarcho-
fascist running dogs of imperialism. I was gaining points with that
nineteen-year-old sophomore all the time. I'm working steady on
this. (You see I can still quote a little theory.) I married the girl and
we moved to Berkeley in 1948 so I could begin my graduate work
there. I used to go over to the California Labor School in San

Francisco. They had a real People's Songs group there. Pretty soon, we were singing those songs well. I'm talking about Barbara Dane, fabulous singer; her then "old man," a guy named Rolf Cahn; Jerry Walter, Jim Wood, a lot of guys who really sang well.

All of a sudden, out comes "Tzena Tzena." The first hit by the Weavers. We have "On Top of Old Smokey," "Goodnight Irene," "So Long (It's Been Good to Know Yuh)," "The Roving Kind," and somehow, behind it all I hear a tiny tinkle, the cash register. But an unfortunate thing happened at that time, known as the Korean War. About fifty thousand young American men made the ultimate sacrifice to contain communism. In connection with Joe McCarthy, we were living in the most repressive period I think that the United States has ever survived. It was the time of a real witch-hunt, there's no doubt about that. (Now that we see the real condition in which socialism has left some of the greatest countries in the world, we can understand that the threat was not as large as we imagined.) At any rate, there were a lot of people who suffered. They didn't suffer as much as Bucharin suffered, or as much as a few other people in the USSR suffered, but people like Albert Maltz and dear old Alvah Bessie, their careers were shot.

One thing I didn't know then was that Pete Seeger had brains enough to quit the Communist Party in 1950, before they gave him the dialectical materialist lobotomy, which would have guaranteed that he couldn't communicate with anybody. If I'd known that, I wouldn't have joined myself. By this time I was definitely a member of the Communist Party, and so was almost everybody else I was singing with. About two years thereafter they busted the Weavers. They couldn't sing anywhere. Anybody that hired them, the FBI would call them, say, "Your liquor license is gone." It was the end, right? So there were four of us who said, "Why not continue the great work?" And we formed a group first call the Reweavers, as a matter of fact. I took down "Kisses Sweeter Than Wine," "When the Saints Go Marching In." What other ones did I take? I took a whole bunch of them down. "Darling Corey," "Rock Island Line," took them down note for note and learned something about ensemble scoring. At one point the Communist Party came to us and said you got to get rid of your girl singer. That was Barbara Dane and we dumped her, just like that. It was thirty years 'til I talked to her again. Can you believe that idiocy? So we got a black woman named Elmerlee Thomas, who sang like Marian

Anderson, and the act really sounded better.

Now my whole life has been a group singer, and it took compromises, Tex, in spades. You really have to listen to what other people want to sing, or you won't have a group. I know that Pete could only take so much of that. Now let's go back and talk about Pete Seeger. Pete Seeger gave me my career, and I expect that's true of a lot of other people here. He was a completely unique entertainer. The only possible precursor was Bing Crosby. Bing Crosby never hid the fact that he was a graduate of Gonzaga University. And Pete never hid the fact that he had been an undergraduate at Harvard. He also was the antithesis of [sings] "I've got you under my skin, I've tried so hard," you know, the slick, the tuxedo-wearing Frank Sinatra, who was another great singer, but Pete was his absolute antithesis. He'd come out fully clothed and then take off his coat to start singing. He was the slickest professional amateur I have ever seen in my life. He avoided every conceivable cliche in the popular entertainment business, and I've loved every single minute I've been in his presence. Talk about goose bumps! Man, I saw him at a children's concert, the tears just wouldn't stop flowing. It was unbelievable. And curiously enough, like a great many performers, I think he's only really comfortable on stage. I mean on stage anything that *can* go wrong already *has*. And he knows what to do about it. But in an interpersonal relationship he's a little distant, I think we'll all agree. I mean he could really space out. He's got the same ol' lady. He's made plenty of loot, but never discusses it. I'm sure he's never been stoned on pot. Pretty damn sure. I mean, I'm sure one glass of draft beer and he's batso bug house. He is really straight, he is a real square, right? But squares like this should come along more often in my life, that's for sure.

I've never seen Pete Seeger when he didn't introduce something unprecedentedly new into the act. I'm sure those of you who have seen me more than once know that I am a robot. I do a verbatim act. Because that way you can, if you want, indulge in spirits or something and you won't goof too badly. Also I have found that when you work for money the product that you are selling is really consistency. I mean, if you are charging $15 in Bakersfield you have got to give something of the same value in Fresno for $15 the next night, so you tend to go with that which elicits a consistent reaction. You don't experiment much. Now there's a lot of people who find that revolting. But all the guys I came up with, I mean the comics, they did verbatim acts. Don Adams did a verbatim act. Irwin Corey did a verbatim act. All comics did verbatim acts until Lenny Bruce. I think if you can, in the course of your performance, crystallize your remarks out of successive improvisations and find a proper formulation, stick with it. The audience doesn't really want to pay to watch you "search," in my view. Other people have other opinions about that. Pete Seeger is anything but set. He may start out with "Darling Corey" or "John Henry" or something to get his chops up, but before long he'll do something that he's never done before in your presence. I loved everything he did.

Another name we were going to talk about is Paul Campbell. When the Gateway Singers made their first recording I had done a whole lot of work on that recording. And we know from the theory of surplus value that the only source of value is socially necessary labor time that is required to produce a product, right? Anyway, I put a whole lot of time in when we cut these records, but Decca Records kept all the tune money. Those tunes were getting paid two cents apiece. And they kept all the tune money on these public domain songs. Suddenly I began to wonder who is Paul Campbell? Guy writes a lot of songs, unbelievable, you know? Well, it turned out that Paul Campbell is the guy who copyrighted the arrangement. Paul Campbell, in fact, was the name used by the Weavers to indicate their joint authorship of their arrangements of public domain material. A fictional entity to whom the recording company could pay the royalties owed to the composer-lyricists of the songs they arranged. I suddenly learned that with public domain material, which has no known author and which has been circulating in the oral tradition for a while, you can make an arrangement of that and get the writer's money. That made a big impression. Suddenly Fred Regis showed up, and so did Cal Bagby. Those are two names I'm very proud of. They're rather euphonious in a way. But I still didn't get any money. You couldn't *give* the Gateway Singers' records away. It was the wrong time.

Soon, however, in the way that all children have of trying to irritate their parents and distance themselves and define their own personalities in contrast, a lot of kids were turning to liberal and left causes if for no other reason than to freak out their parents. And, mirabile dictu, the songs were being sung by people who weren't like that Elvis Presley, that Johnnie Ray. I mean, there were teenage girls who were having orgasms listening to these people. Elvis Presley was a young man who took his Negro pill early. He really could shake around. But Pete Seeger and those people around him, they didn't talk about sex and they certainly didn't shake around. They sang songs that were uplifting, moral. You could understand ever word. The groupies that I know now tell me that they were encouraged by their parents to listen to folk music to keep them away from the pernicious influence of those rock 'n' rollers.

Okay, so the Gateway Singers worked about seven nights a week, two and a half years, between three and five shows a night. Harry Bridges used to come in. He was a great labor leader, and he used to say, "I love what you're doing. The American working class no longer sings. I don't know if it ever did. But the Australian working class sings. The European working class sings." Everybody came to the hungry i. It was sort of *the* place to be. And yet it was not the only place where folk music was. Odetta was singing down the street at the Tin Angel. About 1957, my committee was beginning to wonder whether my dissertation was going to become a life's work. They encouraged me to quit singing and finish the dissertation. I got a grant, the Hertz Fellowship from the University, which came to about $300 a month, and finished the thing.

I had a wife and children, no money. And the entry-level jobs in the academic world were not really too attractive, so I started working as a stand-up comic and got a job at the Purple Onion. There were three guys there who used to hang around the hungry i all the time. In fact, they'd even be in the dressing room half the time. But they were cute. Dave Guard, Bob Shane, and Nick Reynolds. And they were the opening act at the Purple Onion. The guy that ran the Purple Onion hired me to do the comedy turn. Maya Angelou closed this show. It was a good bill. Well, sir, these kids really had something different. There was a magic about that act that was hard to explain. And I'll tell you how nice they were, when they made their first record, which was probably in February of '58, they needed a tune. I had a couple of old charts from the Gateway Singers that I quickly rescored for three voices. They did a song that I stole from Uncle Dave Macon called "Rock About My Sarah Jane" and put it on their first album. And they let me publish it. The royalties ultimately came out to thirty grand. And suddenly my eyes opened. You know, you have to teach a lot of musicology for thirty grand. For the next record they made, they needed some more tunes. They were down in L.A. working at the Coconut Grove. So I went down and went to work for Eddie Pearl, who is a groovy guy at the Ash Grove. He put me on, and the trio took two more arrangements for their second album. The loot kept coming in. But they couldn't read too well. So I figured if I could get two guys that could read and and sing these charts the trio could pick them up right away by ear.

So I was working for Eddie Pearl, and a guy I knew, Benny Shapiro, came over. He had this club called Cosmo Alley. He, Theodore Bikel, and Herbie Cohen, they had this place called Cosmo Alley. Benny came over and said, "There's some guys singing here I think you ought to hear." I went over after work one night and there was Alex Hassilev singing. Pretty soon a short, stocky cat came over and sang with him. They sounded real good. You know what they were doing? His material [pointing to Bob Gibson], I later found out. They had just come down from Aspen, where Bob had been working for Glenn [Yarbrough] at the Limelite. Glenn has always been able to detect a good song, that's for sure. When we got together they did these songs, and I had them sing some of my stuff with me. I said forget the Kingston Trio. We ought to try this ourselves. So we went up to Aspen and rehearsed the act. After about four weeks of that I called Enrico at the hungry i and he put us to work. This would be July, probably the 23rd, of 1959. That was a Wednesday. By Friday we had a few bona fide recording offers from major recording companies: Victor, MGM, Fantasy, and Decca. Anyway, that was because we had a hit singer. Yarbrough was a hit singer. The rest was very simple. I made a deal with these guys. I told them there'll never be a penny spent at any of our recording sessions for music preparation. I'll do all the arranging, copying, everything. Just give me the publishing. They went for it! That was Paul Campbell's influence.

Let me also stick in something on commercial music that I learned from Sheila Davis. Commercial music is music that is written by formula. Songs that are written to be sold must always put the singer in an attractive light, avoid making the singer sound selfish, egocentric, unethical, weak-willed, or judgmental or the like. It is vital to understand that a singer merges with the lyric, so write words to put into the mouth of a professional singer with all that implies. When you use the word "I" in a lyric, make sure you give the singer a statement that will make him or her appeal to millions. Reaffirm the fundamental tenets of our common experience. A deep-seated need to believe that love really can conquer all. [Sings] "Hang down your head, Tom Dooley." Now, every one of those tenets was violated by "Tom Dooley." You see, that was the rebellion of the time in the music business. [Sings] "I met her on the mountain."

[In answer to a question on the ethical dilemma of copyrighting songs in the public domain:] Well, you know what, I think Trotsky said, You could never tell about a fellow traveler which station they were going to get off at. And I got off with the Khrushchev revelations, which was about '55. So whatever caveats I had about making money from folk music were erased by the fact that I had two kids and a wife to support. I had been doing the same thing for five years. The last year I started making money. It's very difficult to understand why. But Frank Proffitt sang "Tom Dooley" for a long time, didn't make a dime. I sang "Tom Dooley" for a long time, didn't make a dime. But Bob Shane sang it, and suddenly the people could see there a dramatic character. Because Bob Shane could actually kill a girl who gave him syphilis. I mean, he ain't kidding. And it is something of that melding [of singer and song], you know what I'm saying. I don't know if Frank Proffitt wrote the song. He might have. It doesn't make any difference. But nothing—underscore, *nothing*—happened to it in terms of the music business until Bob Shane sang it. That's all there is to that. Now, who deserves which piece? Oh my God, there's lawyers just waiting to help you with that. They'll take that up any time you want.

[In answer to a question about his having a Ph.D. in ethnomusicology:] No, I'm not an ethnomusicologist. I mean, my dissertation was a transcription of twenty-three cyclic masses from the Trent Codex. This is a tremendous repository of the sacred music of the fifteenth century. I did the work under a man named Manfred Bukofzer, who was a real genius. He helped me all the way, but he made a bad mistake: He died before I got through. And then they brought a guy in named Edward Lowinsky, whom I almost killed. The hands were closing around his neck. You know, there are some victims of the Nazis who became Nazis, and Edward Lowinsky did just that. He let the dissertation sit on his desk for one full year without reading it. That'll test your mettle. And I didn't give you his A material. This is the way he lived, man. There were six gifted musicologists that split Berkeley after they saw what he did. He was a bad guy. Unfortunately, I must admit through clenched teeth that every suggestion he made improved the dissertation. That I can't deny. But he was a tough guy. Edward Lowinsky! He went to Chicago for eighteen grand a year. That was an unprecedentedly high salary if you were a musicologist in those days. He was a genius. But a bad guy. You know, have mercy, Lord have mercy.

[In response to John Cohen's statement concerning Lou's audition of the New Lost City Ramblers for the ABC *Hootenanny* TV show in 1963:] Now that was produced by two guys who are real hustlers, Fred Weintraub and Ted Ashley. I mean, they didn't particularly care about folk music. They cared about putting on a show that they could make some money with, see? Now at my suggestion, with pardonable lack of modesty, that show included Lester Flatt and Earl Scruggs. It included Mother Maybelle Carter, and it included the New Lost City Ramblers. That same week we [the Limeliters] had given a concert at Ann Arbor, and the guy who put it on said, "Well, I'm glad you made some money. Now we can get some folk music up here." That was what I call the "folk Nazis." They're all over. There's some kind of people who really feel that an entertainer is a vulgar person. An entertainer is a guy who involuntarily is popped into a peak experience by the sight of a paying audience. And his commodity is feel-good, feel-good, feel-good, feel-good. It doesn't matter whether he plays the guitar, dances on the trampoline, juggles, or dances the tango. A real entertainer says feel-good, feel-good, feel-good. Now, the New Lost City Ramblers were not entertainers. I never did get the feeling that they were really in a peak experience when they were playing. You hear John's testimony that I sat through two and a half New Lost City Ramblers' songs, all the way until I was interrupted by Bob Gibson. But I know that John has never listened to one Limeliters record all the way through. I'll promise you that. You [meaning John Cohen] can't take it. It's too crude. So I'm two and a half up on you, right? And what's more, I love the act. I love the act and I love Clarence Ashley. My Aunt Justine could remember slights for fifty years. That's right. And my Aunt Catherine was pretty near that good.

[Bob Gibson: Good resentment deserves time, by God.]

Oh, and let me tell you one other story. Talk about insult. When I was working at the Purple Onion with the Kingston Trio, Bob Gibson came in one night, one of my heroes, and I was doing some stuff, it wasn't that funny. He sat in the third row. About ten minutes into the act he got up and very slowly walked out in full view of everybody in the club. So I registered that, and I caught him one day up at the Hotel Jerome, and I sat down right in the front, you see what I mean. And I knew when I was gonna walk out. About midway through the second number. Well the first number was "Pastures of Plenty," and I stayed through the whole show.

[Bob Gibson: I have to make a public apology right now. There was a time in the '50s when I was touring with Dick Rosmini. And we were traveling up and down the West Coast in a station wagon and stuff and we called Enrico Banducci, who owned the hungry i, where the Gateway Singers were introducing a new single that they just cut for Decca. And Enrico Banducci said you could come down, you could open for them. I said great, because this was like a cocktail party at six in the evening. I went down, and the first number I did was "This Little Light of Mine." That was also the single that they were releasing. It was the most embarrassing moment of my life. I have to tell you right now that I'm still apologetic.]

The Ash Grove
8162 Melrose Ave.
OLive 3-2070

hoot!

Admission: $1.00, $2.00
No show limits, no minim

JACK ELLIOTT

A "folksinger's folksinger" and legend, in his own time, Jack is a globetrotter, raconteur first-class guitar picker who sings blues, yodels, mountain ballads, cowboy songs, Woodie Guthrie melodies, ragtime, and just about everything else. His humor's worthy of Mark Twain & Will Rogers combined!

BESS HAWES

Our most popular "hooter" and guitar song-teacher. The founder of Southern California's folk movement, Bess is joined by these three all-time local greats in a rare reunion....

FRANK HAMILTON

Los Angeles' brilliant and versatile folk instrumentalist, of "The Weavers" fame, returns to The Ash Grove with a song bag full of old favourites as well as new tunes to delight you for a long time!

&

SAM HINTON

Appearing August 9, 10, 11 Only......

three weeks only

Frank Hamilton

Jack Elliott

Bess Hawes

JULY 30 AUG 18

Sam Hinton will give a children's concert, Sat. Aug 10th at 1:00 p.m. & 3:00 p.m. Admission one dollar.

11 Frank Hamilton

I'm going to focus on the Old Town School. And this is what happened. In 1956 I played with Bob Gibson at the Gate of Horn in Chicago. I was the house musician and accompanied a lot of performers. And during that time I decided that I was going to get married and raise a family. In those days you couldn't do that on the salary of a professional folk musician, so I decided I needed something a little more stable. I started teaching guitar classes in the home of Dawn Greening in Oak Park, Illinois. Dawn was a magnet for the folk music community. She was the folklore center of Chicago. She was friends with many folk performers. She was an earth mother, socially gifted, and she attracted people from everywhere. Her legacy is still being felt in Chicago. It was in her living room that I taught guitar classes.

I'm not sure exactly if teaching was what I really wanted to do with my life, but I had an individual approach. In this particular class there was a very interesting elderly man, large, with a stentorian voice, and with a lot of show business experience as a folk singer in the Chicago community. His name was Win Stracke. He liked the way I was teaching. Win said, "I think we should start a school." And Win told me that this was one of his dreams, that he always wanted a folk school that offered a community feeling. He felt that Chicago was the right place for it, because it represented communities of different people. Old Town probably couldn't have worked in L.A. or New York. Chicago was right, because there was some interplay among the various ethnic communities. Of course, there was a lot of tension, too. There were ill feelings. Starting a school sounded good to me, because it was a way in which I could get across some of my ideas on what this folk stuff was all about.

We formed the school on November 29, 1957. We rented

rooms in an office building that held labor union meetings and Puerto Rican wedding dances in the Old Town area of Chicago on Sedgwick and North Avenue. Everybody in the Chicago folk music community was there on opening night such as Bob Gibson, George and Gerry Armstrong, and Studs Terkel. A potent force in the Old Town School was the late Big Bill Broonzy. He was there that night. Our articles of incorporation were signed by Win Stracke and Gert Soltker and myself. Gertrude Soltker was our accountant. She had worked for the Studebaker Theater, but she was now our original accountant. Dawn came in officially later.

Well, let me get to the goals. I'm speaking subjectively here, because I'm kind of a maverick in this whole thing called folk music. I never considered myself a folk singer. And I never really considered myself part of any folk music movement. I'm interested in jazz. I'm a musical eclectic and I love all different kinds of music. I go out of my way to study because I just love the music for itself.

For me, the school was an alternative to xenophobia. People who couldn't for some reason or other accept certain cultures that they couldn't understand—I wanted to change this attitude. The school gave me a chance to broaden some minds. It was an alternative to popular music, which I have no objection to. I think popular music's wonderful, but there are other kinds of music in the world. We could have taken the classical music route to educate people about music, but it's an elitist trip. It's too remote for most people. Jazz is a wonderful way to do it, but that requires a similar amount of discipline and study. Most people really don't have that kind of time and commitment. Folk music served a good function there. We could teach some really strong musical values and some social values without students having to work so hard.

It was an alternative to academia, where I've personally had negative experiences. In high school I used to get D's in music class, and I think there's a reason for that. There's an elitism in most academic music schools. They emphasize Bach, Beethoven, and Brahms. You're not allowed to take the music and use it creatively. It's paramilitary. The conductor becomes the general and the orchestra members become the rookies. You must interpret somebody else's music. It's considered better than music you create yourself. There's a non-participatory participation in conventional music schools. We saw the Old Town School as being different. People could have a hands-on approach to music and

could begin to understand what all music was all about. The vehicle
was folk music. Musical interaction was important in getting people
comfortable playing music with each other. It's pure "democracy."
There's sometimes tension when people play together and express
things, but the whole is usually greater than the sum of the parts.
I think that's true of the best musicianship. You find that to work
with others makes what happens musically better than what any
single person can do. This is what harmony really means. That's
what music theory really is predicated on, being able to harmonize,
bringing people together to make prettier music than they could do
by themselves.

I think that the folk-star syndrome was an oxymoron. It
didn't make any sense. What is a "folk star"? People should be able
to express themselves individually. That's not wholly where the
action is. We did encourage individuals to express themselves,
people who would not have had a chance otherwise. At one of our
first student concerts at the Old Town School, Roger McGuinn (later
of the Byrds) got up and sang "Lost Jimmy Whalen," a folk song
about a logging accident in the Northwest. This was one of the first
concerts he ever appeared in, publicly. Stu Ramsay, a young man
who was devoted to the blues, really got into it so that we were able
to feature him in a student concert. He began to record with some
of the Southside blues musicians, who affectionately called him
"Beef Stew." Hedy West traveled through the school. There are
countless names of people who eventually became so-called folk
stars, but that wasn't what we were about.

In spite of the fact that we call this folk music, musical
ignorance is no criterion for it. There is a musicianship level in all
music. It galls me to hear, "Hell, there ain't no notes to a banjo, you
just pick it." I think that's pretentious garbage. Study music all of
your life. A wonderful way to study is by singing folk music. The
more we appreciate traditional folk music the less chance we have
of throwing it away. There were Frankenstein monsters, instant
authorities on folk music. We diffused that. We had students
research their own lives and the folk music in their families. We said,
"Go back to your parents, your grandparents, and their ancestors.
Do your musical genealogy. Learn those songs." Today Izzy Young
sang a Jewish folk song that he learned from his parents. That's real
folk music, folks, not some recent imitation. That's what we
encouraged at the Old Town School of Folk Music in our classes.

We had a missionary doctor who had lived in Africa who played the
mbira, an African thumb piano. He retold a story he learned from
one of the tribe's people while he was there. A Japanese airline
hostess gave us a succinct lecture on Japanese music. A European
Jewish man played a mandolin and sang songs with the students.
We had other traditional folk artists involved in the school. Dick
Chase came by and told us folktales. We had international folk
dance taught by Nate Lofton, a great dance teacher. We had live
music accompany the dancing, by musicians from the Chicago
community.

I first had a narrow view of folk music, and then I began to
realize that it involves the whole world. America is composed of all
the word's cultures. Chicago, too. We began to reach out into the
ethnic communities. We'd go to Harrison and Halsted streets and
listen to the Greek musicians and watch the bouzouki players. We
ran across Milija Spassojevich, this wonderful Yugoslav accordion-
ist, a well-known virtuoso in his own country and unknown in
Chicago, except for the Yugoslavian community. He played at the
folk dances at the school. We supported the local blues musicians
at the time, Big Bill Broonzy, Mama Yancey, Big Joe Williams, Arvella
Grey. We just pulled them into the school and said, Hey, just interact
with these students. Play along with them, let's jam a bit. Local
Chicago Irish musicians came to the school. Dawn Greening
worked in the little office that was downstairs from the concert hall,
where we used to have the classes and concerts. And one time, Bill
Pittman came in from Tennessee, and he was gathering money for
the local mission where he was an evangelist, a fund-raiser. He had
his guitar with him, and Dawn started talking to him and literally
pulled him into the school. He sat down with the students and sang
some versions of "Barbara Allen" that not many had heard before,
a variant that he had learned from his family, his father. Today the
school has an involvement with the Spanish community of Chicago. Hispanic instructors teach classes in music from various parts
of the Hispanic world.

At first we taught a lot of the pop-folk stuff played on the
radio and featured at the Gate of Horn, the first folk nightclub in the
country. We used pop-folk as a vehicle for getting people interested
in the traditional music. Then we tried to wean them away from
pop by getting them interested in culture-based music. The Gate of
Horn was certainly a pipeline to the school. The way we structured

classes was like this. We had a "First Half" where we taught people at their particular level the accompaniments of songs on guitar, banjo and related string instruments. At the "Second Half" everybody joined from their respective levels to play and sing together. We had an Old Town School songbook which we went through. There were some real good guitar players on the advanced level who could take little solos in between the sung verses. We had children's classes, we had teachers' classes. We developed a tablature, a way of showing finger positions for stringed instruments using graphics, a way of annotating without referring to musical notation. That might have been a mistake, not to bring people into musical notation. Reading "Tablature" is like painting with numbers. It doesn't tell you anything about musical ideas. A lot of folk music is hard to annotate by conventional music notation, but on the other hand, a tab just approximates the sound of the music. You really have to hear it on record or played by representative traditional folk musicians. We organized song sheets with rhythm stresses, so that people could learn to coordinate the instrument playing and singing together.

We promoted great concerts. We went out of our way to get traditional performers like Horton Barker, one of the last of the great Appalachian unaccompanied ballad singers. We had Big Bill Broonzy. One memorable concert, I can't believe that this happened, was with the original Weavers, Big Bill Broonzy, and Mahalia Jackson and her accompanist, Mildred Falls. I don't think the school has ever really recovered from that.

I can't say enough about Win and his dream. He sold it through his personality and connections. He was a good organizer of materials. I'd say he was a great administrator of the school. Dawn Greening was the catalyst. She made people feel welcome, a part of the school, and she got to know a lot of people personally. Gertrude Soltker was a great financial advisor and a supporter of the school. She had this rich experience in the little theater movement. The lady who was responsible for what happened at the school in its entirety is Bess Lomax Hawes. She is the sister of Alan Lomax. As far as I know, she developed the first folk instrument accompaniment and singing class in the country in Los Angeles. She is an anthropologist and folklorist. She was one of the original members of the Almanac Singers. Before Bess, folk instruments and singing had been taught by private instruction, but large folk instrument classes should be attributed to Bess. She was my major influence. I think the Old Town School exists because of what Bess Hawes did in Los Angeles in the early 1950s. The school is ongoing now because Jim Hirsch, through his brilliant business acumen, has carried the original goals and ideals forward.

12 Dick Weissman*

My first introduction into American folk music was through Pete Seeger, the king of the pied pipers, I suppose. I saw him sing at the Progressive Party convention in 1948, when I was thirteen years old. I was fascinated by the sound of the five-string banjo, and after buying a mimeographed copy of Pete's banjo book I went down to a pawnshop in the Skid Row section of Philadelphia and bought myself a Weymann five-string banjo for $25. I broke some strings trying to tune the banjo to the piano, and put the banjo in a closet. Seeger's influence led me to the music of Brownie McGhee, Leadbelly, and Woody Guthrie, and I bought a number of 78 RPM records at drug stores and an Army surplus store that for some reason also carried records.

About six months after I graduated from high school, I bought Pete Seeger's first long-playing record, *Darling Corey.* Seeger sang a number of songs and played a medley of banjo tunes on this record. To this day it is the only record that I have ever literally worn out. I used to play it every day before I went to work, after I came home, and before I went to bed. I don't know where the record took me, but I remember being happy to go along for the ride.

I went to Goddard College in Vermont in 1952, and a student named Lil Blos taught me how to play the banjo, by showing me where to put my fingers and how to use the right hand. Like many of the people in the folk revival I had some formal musical training, in my case through seven years of piano lessons, but I learned how to play the banjo entirely by ear, and I picked up

*Parts of this essay previously published in "Confessions of an Unrepentant Banjo Player," Dick Weissman, *Music Making in America* (New York: F. Ungar, 1982), 21-47. Reprinted by permission.

some guitar by buying some chord books and watching other players at school.

Most of the people that I knew who played banjo or guitar learned quite a bit by imitating performers on records, but I never did very much of that because I wasn't that interested in literally duplicating what was already available and because I had neither the patience nor the talent to pick things off records. I don't think I was ever that concerned with duplicating existing music, and this later differentiated me from a number of people like the New Lost City Ramblers who wanted to reproduce fading or extinct traditions.

The Goddard program obligated students to work during January and February at whatever jobs were available. In my sophomore year, I got a job working at the New York Public Library. At the end of January I developed herpes virus in my left eye and had to go home to Philadelphia. I took atropine eye drops that were so powerful that I couldn't focus my left eye for six weeks. The only thing I could do was play the radio and the banjo. During this six-week period I became a reasonably decent banjo player because I spent so much time and energy practicing without distractions.

For my junior year I decided to study elsewhere, because Goddard was a very small school. I spent the fall at the New School for Social Research in New York and the spring semester at the University of New Mexico. As part of my academic program in New York, I studied banjo and guitar with Jerry Silverman, a well-known folk guitarist. He was also a fairly good banjo player, and he taught me to play chords up the neck. Jerry succeeded in turning some of my attention to the technical and theoretical aspects of the instrument.

In New Mexico I met an outstanding banjoist named Stu Jamieson. I spent two long evenings at Stu's house and watched him play mountain banjo styles. Stu had spent quite a bit of time in Kentucky with a famous player named Rufus Crisp, who played the banjo in a number of different tunings. Stu's playing was clean and precise, and he provided me with a lot of inspiration. He lived on a mountain overlooking Albuquerque, working as an engineer for the Sandia Corporation. Because he did not depend on music for a livelihood, Stuart played only the music that he enjoyed.

After returning to Goddard, during the winter work period I gave out toothpaste samples in New York and did some research for my thesis. A man named Bob Harris who ran a small record

store and folk record company called Stinson Records told me
about a guitarist and singer named Gary Davis. Gary played every
Tuesday night at Tiny Ledbetter's apartment on East Tenth Street.
Gary Davis was a blind street singer and preacher who made his
living in Harlem, playing music and collecting coins in a tin cup. I
went down to Tiny's apartment half a dozen times, listening to
Gary's singing sermons and sometimes trying to play banjo with
him. He used an unorthodox system of fingering with the left hand;
when I played with him, I had to listen rather than try to follow his
fingering patterns. This made me very nervous, because I literally
did not know what I was doing, but it also resulted in my playing
beyond my abilities.

I met quite a few fine musicians during these six weeks,
including Erik Darling, Woody Guthrie, and John Gibbon. Tiny
Ledbetter was Leadbelly's niece, and through her I met Martha
Ledbetter, his widow, and some other musicians. I cannot overes-
timate the influence that these sessions had on me. I got totally
caught up in the music. Gary played and sang blues songs with
religious lyrics. All the musicians listened to him carefully and
added little musical codas to his speeches. I didn't realize it at the
time, but this was the first inkling I had that I could devote my life
to a career in music.

When I returned to Goddard in March, I decided to write a
suite for the banjo. It was in five parts, including an opening theme,
a slow movement, a song, a blues, and a recapitulation of the whole
piece. I called it "A Day in the Kentucky Mountains" and practiced
it for hours, working out all the parts. It included specific themes
and extended improvisations, and most of it was written outdoors
in the Vermont woods. When we did our graduation concert people
seemed to like the suite, but they didn't know what to make of it.
I felt good about it because after three years of playing the banjo,
I had begun to develop my own voice on the instrument.

I spent the next five years in New York City. I started a
master's program in sociology at Columbia University. My parents
paid my tuition, but I paid for all my living expenses by teaching
banjo and guitar and doing occasional playing jobs. Through Bob
Harris, I made my first recording for Stinson Records, accompanying a West Indian folk singer named Dick Silvera. He had a
classically trained voice and a repertoire that included some interesting Ohio River songs. I think I earned $50 for playing banjo and

guitar on the album. I was not a member of the musicians' union
at that time, but shortly thereafter I got a chance to do an album
called *Banjos, Banjos, and More Banjos*, with Billy Faier and Eric
Weissberg. Eric became quite famous years later through his hit
recording of "Dueling Banjos," which he also played in the movie
Deliverance. In order to record for Riverside Records, the company
that did the banjo album, I had to join the musicians' union. The
New York local of that union had a residency requirement and an
audition procedure. The audition consisted of reading music; if you
didn't want to or couldn't read music, you simply told them that
you'd sing and accompany yourself. I didn't care to take the test,
and so I opted for the second alternative. The examiner asked me
to play for him, and so I sang and played an old mountain song
called "Pretty Polly." After he had heard about half a verse, he asked
me to stop, and he passed me. I was disappointed, because I had
psyched myself up to play for ten or fifteen minutes.

I was also commuting to Philadelphia, where I taught guitar
and banjo several days a week. In Philadelphia there was a
downtown coffeehouse called the Gilded Cage where people
would get together and sing on Sunday afternoons. I often attended
these sessions and met the local folk singers, including Lee and
Tossi Aarons, Joe and Penny Aaronson, George Britton, Ed and
Esther Halpern, and Harry Tuft. These were the semiprofessional
and professional folk singers in town, and many of them are there
to this day. People traded songs in a sort of round-robin way, and
many lifelong or short-term friendships and romances evolved at
the Cage. During the next five years or so a group of younger
musicians emerged, including Benji Aronoff, John Pilla, Jerry Ricks,
and Billy Vanaver. Pilla went on to produce a number of Arlo
Guthrie records, Jerry Ricks was profiled in *Living Blues* and has
become well known among musicians if not to the general public
as an outstanding guitarist, and Billy Vanaver was one of the first
folk musicians to explore world music. Benji was an outstanding
instrumentalist, whose whereabouts are unknown to me. During
this period Manny Rubin opened a club in Philadelphia called the
Second Fret, and Gene Shay began his radio show, which still
exists.

The scene in New York was much more professional and
business-oriented than what was happening in Philadelphia. It was
also extremely factional. There were the bluegrassers—Roger

Sprung, Lionel Kilberg, Artie Rose, Bob Yellin, Johnny Herald, and the Greenbriar Boys; there were the traditionalists, like John Cohen and Tom Paley; there were the political folk singers, the *Sing Out!* magazine people like Jerry Silverman, Irwin Silber, Betty Sanders, and Bill McAdoo; and a bunch of us who hung out in Washington Square, including Happy Traum, Barry Kornfeld, Dave Van Ronk, Roy Berkeley, Lee Haring, Dick Rosmini, and me. As the coffeehouse scene developed, singer-songwriters like Len Chandler and Tom Paxton appeared, as did Bob Dylan. Izzy Young started the Folklore Center on MacDougal Street around 1957, and almost all of us would drift in and out of there, talking with Izzy and each other and playing music informally. There was also a group called the Folksingers' Guild, which tried to establish an informal network of folk singers for mutual support and protection. On Sundays there were hootenannies at the American Youth Hostels office on Eighth Street and later at 190 Spring Street, where Roger Abrahams, a budding (and now famous) folklorist lived. Oscar Brand's radio show on WNYC gave folk singers an opportunity to promote themselves, and another group of revivalists were Columbia students, notably banjoist Art Rosenbaum. Izzy Young was promoting concerts in small midtown venues, and some of us got to play for him there or at his store, while others worked for him at Gerde's Folk City, originally called the Fifth Peg but later taken over by Mike Porco after he and Izzy and his partner Tom Prendergast had some sort of dispute.

Belafonte hit in the mid-'50s and shortly after that the Tarriers and Vince Martin had a couple of hits. Erik Darling was the leading folkie in the Tarriers, and their success created the first tensions about pushing the music into the pop arena among the New York crowd. Odetta's Vanguard record in the late '50s had somewhat similar although more complex effects, because Odetta was less directly involved in pop music, and also because she was both black and a woman people didn't tend to put her down. Besides, just about everybody liked Odetta, because she was a pleasant person with a great deal of dignity.

I think it was the tremendous success of the Kingston Trio from 1958 to 1960 that pushed many of us in the direction of pop music. It became clear that there was or at least could be a way to earn a living as a folk singer.

During the summer of 1958 I played on two network

television shows. One was an NBC special called "The Ragtime Years," and the other was an ABC Labor Day show. I got the first job through my friend Izzy Young, who had started the Folklore Center in New York. I played banjo for about five seconds, accompanying a folk singer named Robin Roberts, who sang a song illustrating the folk roots of ragtime. I suggested that my friend Eric Weissberg play fiddle with us, and he in turn recommended me for the Labor Day show. The ragtime show involved a week of rehearsals and tapings and featured many fine musicians, including the great pianist Eubie Blake and Hoagy Carmichael, the host of the show. This was my first contact with an expensive musical extravaganza.

Many of the rehearsals and tapings for "The Ragtime Years" were boring; even though I was playing for only half a minute, I was compelled to be there for the entire show. One day Hoagy Carmichael was having a very bad time reciting his lines without any flubs. As he missed another line, Eric leaned over to me and said, "Do you think in twenty years they'll do a show about us and call it 'The Folk Years'?" I broke out in laughter just as Hoagy blew his line. Carmichael turned to me and proceeded to tell me what a jerk I was, and did I think I could do any better than he could? I turned beet red and mumbled that I wasn't laughing at him. I'm sure he didn't believe me.

The music I enjoyed most at this point was music that reflected some sort of folk roots. I heartily disliked commercial music, although this did not prevent me from accepting studio work of all kinds. Studio musicians tend to develop a strong layer of cynicism and practicality, based on the knowledge that their work pays well and never lasts very long.

One person who influenced my musical attitudes was Hedy West. Hedy was a banjoist, singer, flautist, artist, and drama student. In 1959, she and I and two other musicians were picked to form what may have been the world's first and worst folk-rock group. It was called the Citizens, and it was put together by two Tin Pan Alley songwriters named Lou Stallman and Sid Jacobson to record an album of songs they had written about New York City. I played banjo and guitar and sang, Hedy sang and played the flute, and Lenny Levine sang and played guitar. The fourth singer, Al Wenger, was removed from the group during rehearsals, and Stallman himself sang on the record. We recorded for Laurie

Records, a small but successful rock 'n' roll label that had recorded Dion and the Belmonts and the Chiffons.

The Citizens represented my first real foray into commercial music. The music was not well written or interesting, and it turned out not to be commercially successful. The rehearsals were endless before we finally got into the recording studio. I also barely escaped signing a management and recording contract with Stallman and Jacobson that would have put me behind the eight ball later. Laurie eventually released the records in a very perfunctory way, and they faded into oblivion.

It was 1960, and I was twenty-five years old. I had been playing music full-time for about three years and supplementing my income by giving lessons. The music that I enjoyed most was southern mountain music and old blues. I wasn't interested in the successful folk singers of the time, such as Joan Baez. I felt that they were too involved in themselves and the commercial aspects of music. I use Baez as an example because she was one of the few successful folk singers who was interested in maintaining some authenticity of spirit in her performances. I was so alienated from the commercial world that she seemed commercial to me. I began to worry about what I would be doing to make a living ten years from 1960. I enjoyed playing music, I was living with two friends in a $105-a-month seven-room apartment, and my needs were relatively modest.

My own schizophrenia about entering the pop music arena was a result of my decision to become a professional musician rather than a sociologist, tempered with my minimally realistic analysis that revealed to me that I was never going to be able to make a living writing lengthy banjo suites, and that I wasn't a good enough singer or performer to pursue a solo career. The people that I looked up to were the individualistic instrumental stylists Frank Hamilton and Billy Faier, but I realized that they were having some difficulty in making a living themselves. I admired their ability to interpret tradition without distorting it, but I felt that this was not a viable long-term career path. And so I decided to "sell out."

There were several personal managers who were involved in the folk biz. Harold Leventhal managed the Weavers, and also handled Pete Seeger and later Judy Collins. Harold was widely respected by folk singers but was considered inaccessible by most of us downtown Villagers. More of a Village type, but lacking

Leventhal's impeccable folk credentials, was the mysterious Al Grossman, who owned the Gate of Horn club in Chicago and managed Odetta and Dylan, put together Peter, Paul and Mary, and also managed Ian and Sylvia and later Janis Joplin. Other managers on the scene were Art Gorson, who handled Phil Ochs, and Herb Gart, who I think managed Buffy Sainte-Marie and others. If Leventhal was renowned for his integrity and stability and Grossman for his shrewdness, it wasn't entirely clear to anyone what Gart or Gorson really did. The point that I am making here is that what had been a bunch of "beatniks" singing at hootenannies had indeed evolved into a business, and along with it grew Elektra and Vanguard Records, the former starting out of a small record store, and the latter an extension of a respected classical music company. Kenny Goldstein, who later became a well-known folklorist, began recording quite a number of artists, first for Riverside Records and then for Prestige. Both of these were jazz companies who sensed that they could enter the folk arena in a similar manner—in other words, without dealing in the pop music business. Kenny provided many of us, including me, with our first serious recording opportunities, and although he was tough and demanding he was also supportive and generally reasonable.

Through Izzy Young, I met a singer and songwriter named John Phillips. He was the leader of a male vocal quartet called the Smoothies. They sang in a jazzy Four Freshmen/Hi-Los style of harmony, but they hadn't succeeded in making any hit records. They wanted to try their hand at folk-pop music, and they were looking for guidance on folk styles. I went to a couple of their rehearsals, and we worked out a few musical arrangements. I suggested that we add Eric Weissberg to the band for the recording. They accepted that idea, and the recording date featured a blend of written arrangements played by some top studio players, such as guitarist Don Arnone, and Eric and me playing the folk-style solos. One thing led to another, and John and I started to hang out together, going to parties and playing music. John and Scott McKenzie, one of his singing partners from the Smoothies, decided to quit the Smoothies, and they asked me to join them in starting a new pop-folk group.

Given my orientation, this went against all my musical ideas. On the other hand, I had succeeded in ignoring such factors when I played with the Citizens. I was excited at the idea of traveling around the country, meeting new people, trying to make some hit records, and earning a lot of money. I felt that I had lived in New York long enough. It was time to try something new. We agreed to start the group, and John and Scott went to Windsor, Ontario, to play their last job with the Smoothies while I went to Los Angeles to play with an international folk singer named Martha Schlamme at a club called the Ash Grove.

I drove from Philadelphia to Denver with my old friend Harry Tuft and took the Santa Fe Railroad train the Super Chief to Los Angeles from there. At the Ash Grove, I opened the show, followed by a theatrical review called *Jewels by Feiffer*, which acted out some Jules Feiffer cartoons. Then Martha came on and closed the show, accompanied by me. I was very excited about playing at the Ash Grove and meeting the people in the Los Angeles folk scene. Playing for Martha was stimulating because she used written arrangements with quite a few of the guitar parts written out precisely. Although I could read music, I was a bit lazy about it and was used to interpreting music in any way I felt was appropriate. Martha was a very disciplined performer and didn't let me get away with that attitude. I did quite a bit of practicing and mastered most of the arrangements.

My own performances did not go as smoothly. I was not used to talking to the audience, and I felt embarrassed and ill at ease. Frank Mahoney, one of the actors in the company, took pity on me and showed me how to get the audience to relax. He taught me that it was possible for me to be funny if I used my own natural sense of humor. In the three weeks we played at the Ash Grove, I came a long way toward developing a style of performing, although I have never really gotten it all together in the way that Frank must have visualized it. At the end of the Ash Grove engagement, I turned down a tour of the West Coast with folk-blues singer Barbara Dane to go back to New York and sing with John and Scott. John in turn rejected a plea from a childhood friend to go to Spain and become a beach bum!

John Phillips moved into my apartment on West 106th Street, and he and I and Scott rehearsed eight hours or more every day for six weeks, trying to develop enough material for a record. We went through the Schwann record catalog and selected nine record companies to call for an audition. We also called Decca Records, because John and Scott were still under obligation to them through the Smoothies' contract. Of the nine companies we called, all requested sample tapes, except MGM Records, which agreed to see us live. They offered us a recording contract, but negotiations dragged on as they looked for a hit single for us to record. They felt that our style was good, but they didn't think we had any hit singles in our repertoire. Decca auditioned us, and true to John's guess, they turned us down. The staff producer who heard us was Milt Gabler, a noted jazz buff who, according to John, hated banjos.

In the midst of our dealings with MGM, we acquired a booking agency, International Talent Associates or ITA, and a manager, Rene Cardenas, then a partner of Frank Werber, manager of the Kingston Trio. Before we knew it, we were recording for Capitol, the same label that the Kingston Trio recorded on. We went into Capitol's New York studios, hired a bass player named Arnold Fishkin, and recorded our first LP. For the first time, I got to play banjo and guitar on some of the same songs, playing one part and then listening to it with headphones while recording the new part. There was a certain amount of freshness in the blend of Scott's high tenor, John's funkier baritone, and my instrumental abilities. We had to wait six months or so for the record to come out, and in the meantime we played our first live dates at folk clubs in New York and Philadelphia and on a Canadian TV show.

It is hard to explain how I felt about our group, which one of our agents had named the Journeymen. On one level it was sheer pop *fluff*, but I took pride in playing as well as I could and in learning a bit about group singing from John Phillips, who was an excellent though untrained vocal arranger. Both John and I were writing songs, but his were much more carefully put together, and I felt that I could learn quite a bit about songwriting from him. John benefited by picking up a number of guitar styles from me at our practice and jam sessions. After only four months, we picked up a booking at the hungry i in San Francisco. It paid $1,500 a week. By the time we got through paying commissions to our agent and manager, it came to about $1,000, but we were convinced that we were on our way.

The Journeymen lasted for three and a half years. In that time we bought out of our management contract while we were almost literally starving, moved out to San Francisco and back to New York, got another manager, and did three LPs for Capitol and a half-dozen singles. None of our records really caught on, although they did respectably. We were a musical improvement on the Kingston Trio, because we sang better and played better than they did, but for the most part our hearts weren't in it. We did good shows and people liked us, but we didn't have the special spark that a Peter, Paul and Mary seemed to communicate. The last year together was painful. We all had other plans, but we tried to hold the act together, doing concerts and radio commercials for Schlitz beer. Before the group broke up, Capitol decided to record me as a solo singer. Bob Dylan was just becoming popular, and apparently I was the only one on their label who seemed strange enough to record something similar. I put together an album of "protest songs," mostly topical songs I had written about various matters. The album was called *The Things That Trouble My Mind*, and it is not one of my favorite efforts. I still enjoy some of the songs I wrote for the album, but I never have developed much of an appetite for my singing.

In 1964 I rented an apartment in New York, and a few months later I got married. Toward the end of my Journeymen days, I had gotten very serious about writing songs, and I had more than fifty songs written. I was convinced that songwriting would lead me to fame and fortune, but I was wrong. Over the next few years I was under contract to two different (and respectable) music publishers; I received some reasonably good cash advances, and a number of my songs were recorded on successful albums. But I have never been able to make a living by writing songs as a full-time occupation, and I have never written a hit song. My most successful song, "Someone To Talk My Troubles To," was recorded by a dozen different artists, but there were many songs that never got recorded at all.

My financial status improved in 1964 and 1965. I did quite a bit of studio work as an instrumentalist. The folk boom was ending, but the record companies and advertising agencies weren't aware of it. As the popularity of the Beatles spread, I began to see a lot of my studio work dry up. I met a record producer named Dave Edelman while doing some studio work for a company called Cameo/Parkway. Dave was producing a "folk" album with Merv Griffin, and he asked me whether I'd like to co-produce it with him. I didn't know what that meant, but I agreed to do it. Through Dave, I met a brilliant engineer named Bill Schwartau, who took me under his wing and showed me how to use the recording studio as a

creative tool. Bill was absolutely fearless and adventurous, always
willing to try for a special effect or new sound. We became close
friends, and my wife and I used to go to his house in Greenwich
Village to talk about music and other things. Through my manager,
Stan Greeson, I got the chance to produce an album featuring the
Kentucky folk singer Jean Ritchie for Warner Brothers. I worked on
that project with Bill, and it was thoroughly enjoyable although not
commercially successful.

In looking back at the pop-folk revival I remember quite
clearly how and why I got into this area of "show biz." I had a
simple personal goal of trying to save $100,000, after which I
planned to move to Colorado and go to music school. People like
Eric Weissberg and I were in a peculiar place. The folk purists, or
folk Nazis as some called them, disapproved of us, and yet it was
those people that we tended to hang out with, rather than the
fraternity-party crew who made up the entourage of groups like the
Brothers Four. I remember seeing Frank Harris and Kay Oslin
performing Leadbelly tunes at a club in Houston called the Joker,
where I also met singer-songwriter Guy Clark, and I performed for
the fun of it at The Fox and The Hounds Coffeehouse in San
Francisco after my "straight" gig at the hungry i. During a brief
period when we lived in San Francisco I saw Al Young, now a well-
known novelist and poet, performing at the Blind Lemon. Marc
Silber always was on the Berkeley scene, whether it was through
owning a music store or playing his guitar. All around the country
were coffeehouses and guitar shops, like Lundberg's in Berkeley,
where the best old guitars could be found, and many of the best
players hung out there. These venues were tremendously significant for the aspiring performer because they enabled a young artist
to meet other enthusiasts, to develop an audience, and to make
professional contacts that led to musical collaborations and the
formation of potential performing groups.

My old friend Harry Tuft had moved to Denver and opened
the Denver Folklore Center in 1962. I used to visit him on the way
to or from the West Coast, and there were several clubs in Denver,
like the Exodus and the Satire, along with coffeehouses like the
Analyst and the Green Spider, and there was long-time folk singer-
actor Walt Conley, who was always playing somewhere or starting
a club.

There was something of a division among the '60s folk

singers that was based on their "purity" vs. commerciality. Groups like the Kingston Trio and the Journeymen were considered by many of the sincere folkies of the time to be sell-out artists trying to make a buck. In retrospect I feel that a good deal of that animosity was really about those of us who chose to make a living playing music as opposed to the "pure" but part-time musicians who had some other means of supporting themselves. I believe that people who were out there trying to play music professionally fifty-two weeks a year had a very different attitude than the part-timers with secure middle-class jobs. There were also people who fell in the middle of the two factions—like Judy Collins, who seemed to be accepted by both groups—but who were indeed professionals and, for want of a better term, pop artists.

I have to admit that some of the flak the pop-folkers got was a result of our style of dress, and the fact that we seemed to feel the need to run on stage, as though we represented eternal youth to our mostly collegiate audiences. And certainly there were those of us whose sole interest was making it in show biz, whether that entailed singing American folk songs or doing African chants or rock ballads. But some of us did have feelings about the music that we were "exploiting," and we did our best not to violate its spirit.

By 1964 the Beatles and Bob Dylan had hit the scene. They actually changed the direction of pop music, something that those of us who "went commercial," like Erik Darling, Eric Weissberg, and I, hadn't thought was possible. By 1965 the folk boom had pretty much evaporated and had planted the seeds of folk-rock and the San Francisco sound. Weissberg and I, among others, found refuge in the recording studios, and some of us also wrote songs and produced records. Dick Rosmini and Barry Kornfeld were involved in playing sessions and producing records, and Happy Traum started his Homespun Tapes in Woodstock, which developed its own colony of folk and folk-pop refugees, like Happy and his brother, Artie, John Sebastian, the Band, Bob Dylan, and Bill Keith. In 1973 I finally lived out my dream, moved to Colorado, and went to music school. I never did save as much money as I wanted to, but I managed to get there anyway. But that's another story.

Folklore Center presents
The

NEW
LOST
CITY
RAMBLERS

Mike Seeger, Tom Paley, John Cohen

FOLKWAYS
RECORDING
ARTISTS

&

ELIZABETH
COTTEN

Traditional Guitar Picker

FRI. DEC. 23 (8TH ST. & B'WAY) 13 ASTOR PLACE

TICKETS $2.00 & $2.25 AT FOLKLORE CENTER

110 MAC DOUGAL STREET TEL. GR 7-5987

New York Scene

Caravan

10¢

JUNE 1958

John Cohen

13 John Cohen II

One of the mainstays at Washington Square on Sunday afternoons was banjo player Roger Sprung. Around 1955, Roger persuaded Stinson Records to update an early 78 RPM album called *Folksay*. It was his desire to be on the same disc as Woody Guthrie, Leadbelly, et al., so he helped pay for issuing the album and it included several cuts by Roger and his band (Bob Carey and Erik Darling). They performed calypso-influenced versions of folk songs (à la Belafonte). One traditional Southern song they so arranged was "Tom Dooley," with Bob Carey crooning the melody while Roger played in a pseudo-Scruggs banjo style. Kenneth Goldstein wrote on the liner notes, "They join pretty illustrious company in this recording. Here's to their staying up there." Carey went on to join the Tarriers along with Erik Darling, who later joined the Weavers and then formed the Rooftop Singers; and Roger formed the Shanty Boys (with my brother Mike and Lionel Kilberg on washtub bass) while playing for years at Washington Square Park.

It was from that ten-inch LP that the Kingston Trio learned "Tom Dooley." Dave Guard told me this. It wasn't from Frank Proffitt or from Frank Warner, or from Alan Lomax's book, or from the old Bluebird 78 by Grayson and Whitter. It was Roger's introduction of the calypso rhythm jump in "Hang down your head, Tom Dooley" that moved the song out of Appalachian tradition and into the Revival—and into the mass media. One could say that Roger financed the commercialization of traditional music and the starting point of the "folk boom." I pointed out his contribution in 1988, and his response was, "Is there any way I can make some money from it?"

The folk song revival happened in Greenwich Village

alongside:

1) the growth and proliferation of coffeehouses, where people just "hung out";

2) the arrival of the Beat Generation and poetry readings;

3) the small art galleries on Tenth Street, where serious painting was shown (cooperative artist-run galleries to counter the uptown dominance);

4) the Cedar Tavern, where many Abstract Expressionist painters congregated;

5) the Limelight Cafe, which was the only gallery showing photographs in New York, at that time;

6) the White Horse Tavern, where Dylan Thomas had hung out and a tradition of chess, poets, and beer remained;

7) MacDougal Street at night, a magnet for people seeking an alternative to Uptown or the suburbs; and

8) Washington Square on Sunday afternoons, where guitar pickers and folk singers gathered around the fountain.

Although the Village had its earlier reputation as a place for artists, writers, and bohemians, there was truly a big change when the coffeehouses started around 1956. (Earlier there had been a few coffeehouses which served the old Italian community, and around 1956 the Figaro appeared, where people from outside the local community could sit and drink coffee and hang out.) But in 1957 things changed. People from the suburbs and Uptown came to Greenwich Village with certain expectations of observing bohemian behavior and people taking sexual liberties. These things were there, but they were not very visible. But the coffeehouses provided a scene which met the expectations of the visitors, although that was not necessarily the reason the coffeehouses opened originally.

The appearance of so many outsiders, of people dressing weirdly, and of interracial couples was disturbing to the old Italian community around MacDougal and Sullivan streets. There was tension between the new coffeehouses and certain Mafia elements, and the battle was played out in confrontations about permits—and between the political machines (of Carmine DeSapio and Ed Koch) representing the Democrats and trying to get the Italian vote. The Italian community was trying to have the coffeehouses shut down, and used liquor licenses, theater permits, and fire codes as the instruments for this. On the other side, the coffeehouse owners used the issue of free speech and treated folk singing as something

distinct from nightclubs and entertainment, or from theaters.
Poetry being recited in clubs became an issue of confrontation. The
question was whether it was cultural expression or a form of
commercial entertainment. The firemen, siding with the Italian
community, vowed to "throw the scum out." The coffeehouse
owners organized protests and marched on City Hall for the right to
have permits to present these things without liquor licenses or
theatrical permits. The press picked up on it, because the reputation
of Greenwich Village made for good "copy." According to Rick
Allmen, who founded the Café Bizarre (the first coffeehouse/
theater), the first march on City Hall was not successful, but the
press did publish a photo of someone with a beard and captioned
it a "Beat March on City Hall." Allmen figured that if that was the
image that would get press attention, he would play it up. Beards
were not in style at that time, however, so for the second march he
hired twenty rabbinical students. The press labeled them "beatniks," and so their image became synonymous with coffeehouses
and the Village—though there was no direct connection with the
Beat poets. Eventually, the city created a new form of permit for
coffeehouses.

In the coffeehouses, performers, especially folk singers,
entertained, although initially they were not paid. They passed the
basket instead and figured out how to attract a crowd and hold its
attention, using folk songs and performance. Many artists who later
developed successful careers in the entertainment industry used
the MacDougal Street coffeehouses as their training ground. Eventually there was a wide range of folk musicians available much of
the time, from newcomers passing the basket to featured performances at places like John Mitchell's Gaslight. There was Gerde's
Folk City, with its dedication to the folk scene; the Village Gate, with
a mixture of entertainment that was of interest to a more Uptown,
older, and more affluent audience; and eventually the Bitter End,
which connected more with the mass media aspects of folk and
popular music.

In the spring of 1957, Izzy Young opened up the Folklore
Center on MacDougal Street. Besides his experiences with Margot
Mayo and the American Square Dance Group, Izzy had worked in
the used bookstores on Fourth Avenue. The Folklore Center
opened originally as a bookstore specializing in folk music. It had
a row of record bins as well. I believe that Izzy and Kenneth

Goldstein were friends, and this provided a linkage between the academic side of folk music and the musical, entertainment/performance explosion that was about to happen. Izzy was very honest, idealistic, earnest, and nonaggressive. He was not driven by the profit motive, which characterized the rest of the scene along MacDougal Street. He was more of a chronicler and commentator than an activist.

Before the Folklore Center opened there were already one or two "coffeehouses" in the area. The Café Bizarre sometimes opened its doors to singers on Sunday afternoons. There were already folk singers around from Washington Square on Sundays, and there were a number of club and coffeehouse owners who saw the possibility of a new kind of market being attracted to the Village. Art D'Lugoff opened his cavernous club, the Village Gate, in the basement of an old hotel, and soon there were also the Kettle of Fish, the Café Wha?, and the Pussycat. Also located in the Village were the Folksingers' Guild, the Young People's Socialist League (YPSL), Elektra Records (Jac Holzman), Tradition Records (Diane Hamilton and the Clancy Brothers), Vanguard Records on Four-teenth Street, and Riverside Records.

From my small loft on Third Avenue and Ninth Street, I would take nighttime walks to visit Izzy, and I had the opportunity to observe the growth of the folk music scene from 1957 to 1963 (when my loft was torn down). Izzy's store became a true center, where you could find out about concerts, about who was in town or who was "making it" out of town. There were never-ending judgments made on the price of success, the compromises, the true line of folk music. Special venom was reserved for the Uptown managers, promoters, and artists who were making lots of money, softened by a belief that those rewards should come *our* way. Izzy could be very helpful, funny, and warm. Sometimes he would strap on bells and ribbons and do a joyful, jumping demonstration of Morris dancing in the store. Sometimes he would get annoyed and throw everybody out in order to have time inside with friends. Izzy used to refer to me as the conscience of the Folklore Center. Yet I viewed him as the conscience of a broader folk music scene that I wasn't part of.

The store was just one of the many distractions for night-time browsers along MacDougal Street. Possibly it was the only "bookstore" among jewelry stores and places which sold souve-

nirs, antiques, Italian sausages, and instant Jackson Pollock paint-
ings. It became a hangout for high school kids interested in folk
music. Izzy sold folk records, guitar strings, and accessories along
with the books and magazines. There were always posters for
upcoming events, and high on the wall were photos of many folk
singers. Rumors were passed quickly through the store. When the
Friends of Old Time Music presented the Stanley Brothers, this was
the first traditional bluegrass concert in New York. The rumor
among the kids was that this band also dressed up in white sheets
back in Virginia. Many of the rumors, along with news of promoters
and artists' record deals, became the basis for Izzy's column in *Sing
Out!* Various bands were formed among young people who met
at the store. I think the Even Dozen Jug Band, which recorded
eventually for Elektra, was one of these. Among the emerging
singers were the young Maria Muldaur, John Herald, and David
Grisman.

The interactions and nonsensical issues of that period are
best documented in the early copies of *Caravan* magazine, which
later became *Gardyloo*. These fanzines, edited by Lee Shaw, gave
an intimate, nonacademic interior view of what was on people's
minds, along with concert and record reviews, rumors, and opinions. It was interesting to see how *Caravan* became "serious" and
dealt with more significant issues of interest to folklorists, and how
the production of the magazine was shifted to other editors. Billy
Faier was involved in this shift. Roger Abrahams also wrote for the
later *Caravan*, and Lee Shaw continued the fun and gossip in
Gardyloo.

From the store Izzy produced a series of small concerts.
The first was with Peggy Seeger, who scootered into New York City
on her way from Swarthmore. There were also Robin Roberts,
Woody Wachtel, Billy Faier, Tom Paley, myself, Harry and Jeannie
West, and the New Lost City Ramblers' first concert, as well as Bob
Dylan's first concert. The Folksingers' Guild also sponsored con-
certs.

One evening when the Kentucky singer Roscoe Holcomb
was visiting me, we walked out to MacDougal Street and Roscoe
was amazed. He said there were more people on MacDougal Street
here on a Tuesday night than would be seen in all of Hazard,
Kentucky, on a Saturday afternoon. I remember taking Roscoe into
one of the coffeehouses, where Tom Paxton was singing his civil

rights song about the "High Sheriff of Hazard." Roscoe whispered
to me, "He shouldn't be saying those kinds of things about Charlie
Combs."

Roscoe was upset by seeing men with long hair. I
commented that in his home in Kentucky he had a picture of Jesus
with long hair. Roscoe said that it was okay for Jesus because he
was the savior for both men and women.

Memorable events:

Seeing Woody Guthrie with Jack Elliott in Washington
Square. Woody was in bad shape, his arm damaged in a Florida
kerosene stove fire, his head and beard scraggly, looking like a saint
or something that had stepped out of a Picasso blue period painting.
A legendary, tragic-heroic figure.

My first awareness of Dave Van Ronk, who appeared as a
prototype of new folk singers. I was from the suburbs, and recently
from Yale. My experience was shaped by concerts by the Weavers
and college singers at hootenannies, and I had never met someone
like Van Ronk, who was unlike any of the above. He played and
sang blues in a raspy voice that emulated black singers; his guitar
style was also blues. He was political, but not conforming to the
usual left-wing approach of *Sing Out!* His politics were between the
socialist YPSLs and the anarchist traditions of the Wobblies. Yet he
would sing old ballads with tenderness and make new chord
arrangements of old songs that had jazz progressions. He also
seemed tuned into the commercial pop music world, but with a
sardonic awareness.

Hearing a British skiffle band performing in the Folklore
Center.

The Washington Square protest and riot (in 1961) over the
cancellation of a permit which allowed the Sunday afternoon
singing.

The formation of Peter, Paul and Mary, handpicked by Al
Grossman from the right sort of coffeehouse folk singers. I knew
Mary Travers when she was a kid. I met Mary in mid-winter when
PP&M had returned from their first tryout in Florida, arranged by
Grossman in preparation for their New York debut. I told Mary that
she looked very pale for having just visited Florida. She told me that
Grossman instructed her to stay out of the sun. She was supposed
to have the image of a sophisticated, pale blonde.

The initial appearance of Mark Spoelstra and Bob Dylan at the Gaslight (or was it the Wha?). Maynard Solomon of Vanguard asked me my opinion of these new singers on the street. I said that Spoelstra was the better prospect because I recognized a Mississippi John Hurt song he played and thought that he might be a friend of old-time music.

In 1962, on my return from filming in Kentucky, Bob Dylan showed me the words for his new song "Hard Rain" at the Kettle of Fish upstairs. It didn't have a melody yet. I said, "If you're going to write like this, you ought to look at Rimbaud and Verlaine." He said, "Who's that?" and I invited him to my loft to see my few poetry books. I believe he was not entirely unaware, for he had already heard Allen Ginsberg at poetry readings.

The night of the Cuban missile crisis, joining Dylan onstage at the Kettle of Fish (downstairs) to sing "You're Gonna Miss Me When I'm Gone."

Izzy's (and my) book of punch lines to jokes. We'd read it every few years and try to remember the first parts.

The creation (by Izzy) of the word "folknik" to represent the pesky kids who hung around his store. It was following the appearance of the words "sputnik" and "beatnik."

Izzy and Tom Prendergast forming the first folk club at Folk City, initially named the Fifth Peg. This was different from the coffeehouses, which paid performers by passing the basket, and even more different from the Village Vanguard, which was a serious, "sophisticated" nightclub sort of place. Folk City was an already established restaurant-bar with a liquor license (which none of the coffeehouses had).

The poster for the New Lost City Ramblers and the Greenbriar Boys at Folk City. Dylan made the poster. It called the Greenbriars the best country group in the city, and the NLCR the best city group in the country.

Dylan's phenomenal following at Folk City, reviews in *The New York Times*, and all I could see was that he was imitating many of Woody Guthrie's jerky movements from the late stages of Huntington's chorea.

Judy Collins' first appearance at Gerde's. I heard her attachment to ballads and gave her a tape of traditional ballad performances from the Catskills.

The Folksingers' Guild, the YPSL, the early Jug Band, Maria

Muldaur and John Herald attempting rural jitterbug, or was it clogging?

The Saturday daytime sessions at Allan Block's sandal shop, where the store was packed with people playing old-time music.

The feeling at Izzy's store that Uptown managers and kids were all converging there for information and opinions. Odetta, Theo Bikel, Al Grossman, and Harold Leventhal were at the store being either consulted or insulted.

The thrilling letdown of meeting Harry Smith, the fabulous anthologizer of the Folkways set. We thought his name was fictional. He had introduced Allen Ginsberg to the type of poetic structures that came to exemplify Beat poetry, and which also influenced Bob Dylan's writing.

The appearance and audition at the Village Gate of the Stoney Mountain Boys, the first country bluegrass band to try to break the barrier into the folk song movement. I was trying to get people to show up and wandered into the Cedar Tavern, where there was no interest at all, except for Allen Ginsberg and several of his friends, who came over to hear.

Oscar Brand's Folksong Festival was held at Cooper Union during those times, and I remember bringing Woody Guthrie in from Greystone Mental Institution so he could be there and listen. We stopped at my loft and he ate up most of my peanut butter.

Roger Abrahams had an apartment on Spring Street before Soho came into existence.

The realization that during the '40s the Almanac Singers had a house in the Village, and during the '50s and '60s Alan Lomax had a fourth-floor apartment nearby, which Ralph Rinzler took over next. Various events and parties took place in that apartment: Mike Seeger's wedding party, and a music party after a New York City Folk Festival (1965) which had been in Carnegie Hall. Both Bill Monroe and the Blue Sky Boys were there. This was a historic meeting, and Bill Bolick (of the Blue Sky Boys) was so excited that he telephoned back to North Carolina to say that he was at a party with Bill Monroe.

The scene changed when the street took on an increasingly carnival-like atmosphere, as a place to stare at the freaks. Izzy claimed that Times Square was moving in. The national popularity of folk singing pulled many of the original performers away and opened the gate to any and all new singers looking to be discovered. The nature of the crowds likewise changed. Originally it was mostly Uptown and out-of-town couples on dates for a night out, but as MacDougal Street became sleazy, it also became an attraction for motorcycle gangs from New Jersey and for black groups from Harlem looking for excitement or trouble.

FOLKSINGERS GUILD *Presents*

Folkmusic at Midnite

Sullivan St. Playhouse

★ **TOM PALEY**

Esoteric · Folkways

★ **JOHN COHEN**

Traditional Folksinger

★ **ROY BERKELEY**

Nite Club Performer

Fri. June 27' Midnite

Sullivan St. Playhouse 181 Sullivan St.

Tickets $1.25 Available at...

Folklore Center 110 McDougal St. GR 3-7590 Sullivan St Box Office OR 4-3838

14 Roy Berkeley

I was active in the great folk scare of the '50s—more than of the '60s, I guess. I grew up with rather an eclectic assortment of music. My father was a lawyer; he wasn't a "folk." But he had played guitar and mandolin as a young man, and we had a lot of records in the house of people like Bradley Kincaid and Carson Robison and Frank Luther and a lot of Jimmie Rodgers, a lot of the Carter Family, later Burl Ives, people like that. I sang from the time I was very young. My father liked cowboy songs, so I learned a lot of cowboy songs.

By the time I was an adolescent I had turned my back on this music completely. I was writing poetry in Latin and found this music not only naïve but also embarrassing. At not quite seventeen, I made it to Greenwich Village and Morningside Heights and fell in with a bunch of people of the sort I'd been longing to mingle with from the time I was fairly young. They were intellectuals, thinkers, questioners. And what kind of music did they like? Folk music! I began to look at folk music with a different eye. It was so unelaborated, so unproduced, so uninvolved, it was just one person with an instrument and the song that he or she wanted to sing, without a lot of arrangement, without a lot of stuff that gets in the way. I began to like that.

I was at Columbia University. I went there not because of the core curriculum they had then, but because Columbia was in New York and that was where I wanted to be. It turned out to be a good thing, though, because of the core curriculum. We didn't read *about* Marx or Freud or any of the others who went into making up this civilization, we read *them*. We read the primary documents, pages and pages of them, until we owned that stuff. We owned those ideas. We lived with them. My pals and I used to make up songs about what we were reading, because we were always talking about it, always thinking about it.

When I was a senior I was in Charlie Mills' (C. Wright Mills') senior seminar. We put together *The Power Elite*. We did the research for it. That's why professors have seminars, right? And we got into Mills's peculiar sociology jargon and were writing songs like "Starving to Death on my Deference Claim," which vilified several of the more vilifiable professors and several of our classmates. At about that time I taught myself to play the guitar. I was irritated and offended by the deep piety that the Left attached to its connection with folk music. And I began to write parodies that poked fun at Pete Seeger and the unions and that sort of thing. I myself have always been very pro-union. I did a lot of labor education work. I taught at Rutgers University in the labor education school and worked for several unions as education director, teaching labor history. I'm certainly not anti-union. But when you're nineteen years old and there's all this piety, well, I began to think about a collection of my songs as the antithesis of *The People's Song Book*. It would be called *The Bosses' Songbook*, and just as the Wobbly songbook was called *Songs to Fan the Flames of Discontent*, mine would be called *Songs to Stifle the Flames of Discontent*. It was a gag, a joke.

At about that time, in my junior year at college, I used to go down to the Catholic Worker on Chrystie Street on Friday evenings. They would feed me a really good big meal and I would sing for them. I was putting myself through school, living on twenty dollars a week, and it made a difference having that one meal. And I fell in with a guy named Mike Harrington, who wrote *The Other America*. And shortly after that I joined something called the Young Socialist League, which was a funny combination of people who were too left-wing for the Norman Thomas Socialist Party and people who were too right-wing for the Trotskyist Socialist Workers Party. It was a very schizophrenic organization and a very uncomfortable marriage that did not last very long. But I was known for a time as the Traveling Trotskyite Troubadour—even though I was not actually a Trotskyite or even a Trotskyist. It's interesting to think about the connection between the Left and folk music at that time. Somebody once wrote that the Stalinists' songs were all parodies of, or written to the tunes of, folk-type songs while the Trotskyists were not much into the urban revival of folk music and all their songs were parodies of pop songs. So, in the '40s, before my time, they sang the following song:

O that Trotskyite mother of mine,
When we played in the school football line,
Every time that we'd win
She would shout through the din,
'O you fools, kill your captain and bore from within.'

      I began to sing my songs for the YSL. They were songs that poked fun at Pete Seeger among others, but I also wrote a marvelous song that vilified Eisenhower, called "The Right to Suffer Blues." It had this verse in it:

O the President's playing golf
Out at the Burning Tree
You know it warms the cockles of my heart
To know he thinks of me
And there he stands, putts.

      In the spring of 1956, Khrushchev made his famous speech to the Twentieth Congress of the Communist Party of the Soviet Union in which he admitted that everything people had been saying about the Soviet system, especially under Stalin, was true. Details soon came out about the millions of people who had been tortured and murdered and starved to death and all the rest of it. The YSL had an annual May Day show, and of course that year the May Day show was about the Twentieth Congress. I wrote some songs for that show. A couple of years later, some guys took the songs I'd written for that show and the songs I'd written in college and actually published *The Bosses' Songbook* (1959). Unfortunately, they added other songs that I did not write and did not agree with. One song they added was, I thought, pretty racist. And a few other songs they added were, in other ways, in poor taste. I'd like to disassociate myself from those.
      So there I was at Columbia, and Columbia at the time was kind of a boot camp for intellectuals, a really intensive educational experience. Especially for me, because, for a variety of reasons, I was able to take courses in almost every part of the university except the medical school. I had anthropology with Margaret Mead and history with Henry Steele Commager and Allan Nevins. I took

two years of Russian. I took courses in the Russian Institute when Brzezinski was there. And what happened was that because of the things in my life, the fact that I'm basically a storyteller and concerned with history, I approached the music somewhat differently from the way that my contemporaries did.

My attitude toward the music was, Sure I like the music, but I was interested in the music in many ways, in using the songs as primary documents to illustrate American, or world, or human, history. So when I did concerts—and I did a lot of coffeehouses back in the early days of coffeehouses—people used to joke that instead of the song that was current at the time, "I Come for to Sing," Berkeley's song was "I Come for to Talk" because I did more talking than singing. And I remember once, singing at some coffeehouse in a college town, in the middle of my set a guy raised his hand to ask a question. He thought he was in class! So I began thinking about using the songs in teaching. I taught at the New School for Social Research for four or five years—a course called "Folk Music: Mirror and Lamp to American History"— and at Wesleyan University in their graduate school summer program for teachers, and at a few other places.

I ought to talk briefly about the Folksingers' Guild. It grew out of my generation, my cohort, who were around the Village in the period 1955-57. We were a generation behind, say, Oscar Brand and Pete Seeger, and about a half-generation behind, say, Erik Darling and Roger Sprung. We wanted to sing. We wanted people to hear us. And we figured that the best way to do that was to put on our own concerts. So we got the Young Socialist League to let us use their hall, because we didn't have any money to hire a hall. And we did a concert, charging fifty cents admission. When we had enough money from the gate we could rent a hall for the next time. I was very scrupulous, I had asked the YSL to let us use their hall. But I didn't want to turn the Folksingers' Guild into a front for the YSL. I didn't want to do to the Folksingers' Guild and to our music what I felt the Communist Party had been doing to other organizations and to their music. So even though these people were my friends, I didn't want them to put out their literature and try to recruit.

After that, of course, we had enough money to rent a room at Adelphi Hall on Fifth Avenue south of Fourteenth Street, where a lot of radical organizations used to meet. The Folksingers' Guild put on concerts with me, Dave Van Ronk, Pat Foster, the New Lost City Ramblers, and a whole lot of other people. It was an interesting organization, completely voluntary. The idea behind it was, certainly, we wanted to sing and wanted people to pay to hear us sing. But as much as that we wanted to get the music out to younger people, to people of our generation. Then, of course, they'd meet us, and we'd sit around, and they'd also get involved in the Guild. It was kind of a nice organization.

I particularly remember the release of the Folkways *Anthology of American Folk Music*. When I was an undergraduate I was putting myself through school, working at various jobs and writing for the pulps, writing adventure fiction under fourteen different pseudonyms, but I never had any money. I borrowed some money from a friend to buy the *Anthology*. I didn't even own a record player. My girlfriend owned a record player. The *Anthology* made a great impression on all of us then. Just about everybody who was in that milieu at that time had physically assimilated the *Anthology*, had digested it, had made it a part of their corporeal being. Not just their intellect, but their actual physical essence. The *Anthology* was just so important to all of us.

In order to go to the hoots that Irwin Silber ran at the Masonic Temple on the Upper West Side, I either had to walk down from Columbia to the west 70s and take the subway back, or take the subway down and walk back. The fare was a dime then, I think, but I was cutting things so close that every dime made a difference. I made it my business to get to the hoot and buy *Sing Out!* magazine. I absolutely hated and still do hate most of what *Sing Out!* stood for politically, but it was undeniably an important magazine. Also it published a lot of good songs. And those hoots were really good. It was a chance to hear a lot of different musicians doing a lot of innovative and interesting music, including Pete Seeger.

Ten years ago I had thyroid cancer. I'm okay now. But surgery did some damage to my vocal chords and I was put on voice rest. A few years ago I was told I could sing again. But I'd gotten out of practice. I'd stopped playing. I'm thinking of getting back to it now. I'm primarily a writer, not a musician. I'm working on a big project now. When I get it finished I hope to get back to the series I started, on my own label, on folk and country songs of the Franklin D. Roosevelt years (*Folk and Country Songs of the FDR*

Years, with Tim Woodbridge [Longview Records L241, 1979]). But I'm thinking of that project with a different combination of words and music. Somebody once pointed out to me that I made records primarily as an excuse to write liner notes. So maybe instead of a record or CD with little liner notes, I'll do a book packaged with a cassette or two.

15 Ellen & Irene Kossoy

Irene: My mother remembers us singing when we were around three years old. We would just pick up everything we heard, much to her great embarrassment sometimes. And one time we were riding in a bus and we were singing, I don't know where we had gotten this record, who had given it to us, but it was the Strip Polka, and the verses went something like:

There's a burlesque theater
Where the gang loves to go
To see Queenie the Cutie
Of the Burlesque show.

And it goes on, "Take it off, take it off." We knew the whole song, and we were sitting on the bus singing this at the top of our lungs and my mother was embarrassed. But we sang everything we heard, and our mother sang a lot at home. Her sister, who lived with us also, would sing, and the two of them would sing in harmony. And my aunt played the piano. That was what we grew up hearing. My aunt also used to listen to opera, which we referred to as "that junk."

Ellen: She played tenor guitar also.

Irene: That's right. She played tenor guitar and piano, not at the same time. And so we grew up listening to that and it just became the natural thing for us to follow along, singing that. The songs that they sang were the old songs, just what my mother referred to as the old songs. The songs from the '20s and '30s, like "Rose of Washington Square." She sang "Rose of Washington Square," which is where we first heard of Washington Square. And songs like "Never Throw Stones at Your Mother," and other wonderful favorites like that. We started singing those kinds of songs and singing in harmony. And it was something that just happened; we never really learned to do it. I don't even remember when we first started doing it. We just did it. Seemed like we always sang in harmony. And when we were about fifteen we went to camp for the first time for the summer and heard what was then considered folk music. And actually our older sister—we do have another sister—used to take us to hootenannies on occasion, so we had seen Paul Robeson and the Weavers and Woody Guthrie. I think it was Woody Guthrie's last concert that we went to. And one or two other people like that, who left quite an impression on us. Although we never really got into the political part of it at all. But the music itself was very intriguing. Here was a whole new kind of music and everybody singing along. That really appealed to us.

When we went to this camp people were playing guitars and so forth and we, of course, felt that we had to learn how to do that. So we learned how to play three chords and convinced our mother to buy us guitars when we got home. And at this camp was a young man named Jimmy Gavin, who was about nineteen years old. We thought he was just the greatest thing on earth and when he mentioned that he used to sing on Sunday, that there was singing every Sunday afternoon at Washington Square Park, we had to go check this out, not so much because we were interested in the singing but more because we were interested in Jimmy Gavin. So we went, and as time went on we got less interested in Jimmy Gavin and more interested in the music. And as we did, it really became our life. Every Sunday we were there without fail. We would take the subway from Queens and go into Washington Square and check out the scene, see who was around. And I think Ellen will tell you a little more about some of the people we met and the influence that it had on us.

Ellen: I think one of the first people we met down there who took us under his wing was Roger Sprung, and I guess that he decided that our harmonies were very well suited to bluegrass-type singing. But we didn't know any bluegrass songs or anything about it, so he started giving us tapes and tapes and tapes to listen to. We got to know a lot of songs through him. He'd also come over to our apartment and sing with us and take us out various places and our mother thought he was such a nice young man, and she doesn't know to this day that when we were sixteen years old he used to take us to these bars in Newark that were just scuzzy places. I mean, the type of bands that they had playing there—well, they had a bass player who played the bass with his toes. I mean, that's how weird it was. We used to sing songs like "Dim Lights, Thick Smoke, and Loud, Loud Music," and all these wonderful western twangy kinds of songs, bar songs. My mother had no idea, still to this day has no idea that we were going to places like that. But she thought that Roger was really nice. We also met Ralph Rinzler, who also started giving us lots of tapes of more traditional kinds of music. And between the two of them we just learned an awful lot of songs and were really exposed to a lot of different traditional music styles. Ralph used to come over to our house, or we would go over to his house. He would have just learned some wonderful new song that we all had to sing together, and somehow it was never okay to just sing it once—we would sing it for the whole day. I still have a recollection of one day over at our house. The three of us in a closet, literally in a closet with a tape recorder. And I think the reason we were in this closet was because the acoustics were good in there. We sang this song called "Watermelon Hanging on the Vine" for about six hours. Just over and over and over and over again until we really learned it. And we've never sung it since.

I think it was interesting in Washington Square in those days. We were in high school. We weren't really politically conscious; it was the music that was so appealing to us. The people we met down there became our social life. This music became like part of us, really. It was almost by osmosis that we were learning it. We were just drinking it in. The people we met became so important to us, like Lee Haring, Frank Hamilton, Roy Berkeley, and Tom Paley. We went to the Folklore Center when it wasn't a Sunday afternoon. When we had to get some kind of music fix we'd go the Folklore Center and always find somebody there to sing with. Or we'd go to Allan Block's Sandal Shop, and he always had people sitting around playing music. It was just an absolutely wonderful atmosphere. It was a very nurturing atmosphere for us, because people really took to us and were wonderful about teaching us songs that they knew. Dave Van Ronk was another one. We used to call him our mother hen, because we'd walk down the street with him and we felt like he was—he'd tower over us, and we felt like he was almost literally taking us under his wings.

Irene: This was the '50s, and I think there was really no

feminist consciousness, at least none that we were aware of at the time. Mary Travers was around Washington Square. She had this wonderful big dog and she just really looked the part, besides having a really great voice, which she still does. But she was the only woman that I remember being down there. We never really thought much about the fact that there were few women around. I guess we were never close friends with Mary because I was so in awe of her. She was so sophisticated compared to us. She was also a year or two older. But I just felt like such a timid little soul next to her.

When we were down in the Village, singing in Washington Square, a woman named Lucia Walker came up to us and asked us whether we would like to do a concert. And it had never occurred to us to do anything like that. But we said sure. And I believe it was at Circle in the Square that she put on a concert of us, and pretty soon we were doing a number of concerts around, a lot of them with Ed McCurdy, some with Erik Darling, and some with Erik Darling and Ed McCurdy. These were mostly midnight concerts. They were at small theaters in the Village. After the regular show was over and the audience cleared out they'd have a midnight folk concert. So it's amazing. I guess in New York you could do that. In most other places who would come to a midnight concert? But in New York you could do that. The places were always filled. It was amazing.

After doing some of these concerts somebody approached us and said there was somebody who was interested in doing a record of us. And we were very excited about that. And that again was something that had never occurred to us, that that was something we could do. And it turned out that it was Pat Clancy, who was just starting up Tradition Records. And so we met with him and we arranged this recording session and Erik Darling was on it. We recorded the whole thing in two days, if that even. No, it was one afternoon. One afternoon, maybe. And this is a record called *Bowling Green and Other Folksongs from the Southern Mountains,* which up until five years ago was still in print. The company has since been bought by Everest, and all kinds of weird things have been happening with it. They keep coming out with anonymous recordings and copies that we are on without our names. But that's a whole other story. Anyway, we did do this one record, which people still come up to us and say, "Hey, I just found a record of yours in a record shop for two dollars." So it's still around in some places. And we also, in 1959, were approached by Al Grossman, I guess, about singing at Newport. They were going to be starting this big new festival, and did we want to sing there. So of course we said yes. And we sang in the first Newport Folk Festival, which was another very exciting moment in our lives.

Ellen: One of the concerts we did, one of the midnight concerts we did, we just happened to do a Woody Guthrie song. Our mother was in the audience, and this was very exciting—I mean, this was one of the first concerts we'd done and we were really excited and we even had our hair done. And got new dresses. The weather was such that the minute you had a new curl in your hair it was immediately wilted out by the humidity. By the time we got on the stage we were just feeling very bedraggled. But we did this concert, and at one point we sang a Woody Guthrie song and there was all this loud hooting and hollering in the audience, and we realized while we were singing it that it was Woody Guthrie sitting there listening to us. We forgot about our wilting hair and our dresses that didn't look quite right, and we were just thrilled to death. After the concert was over our mother came over to tell us that well, it was too bad that our hair didn't hold up. She said that there were some people in the audience who were so rude—I mean, they just kept shouting, and we were beaming. We couldn't do anything except grin from ear from ear, we were so excited that Woody was there and enjoying our singing.

We would go to the Village almost every single week all the time we were in high school. And then, when we went away to college, we would always spend all of our vacations in the Village. Around the beginning of the '60s we both independently got married and had families and moved to different parts of the country and stopped going down to the Village on a regular basis and we really haven't done all that much singing since then, but every few years, we do get together either to give a concert somewhere or just to sing.

Israel G. Young ✣ Autobiography ✣ The Bronx ✣ 1928-1938

Photographs by David Gahr

16 Izzy Young

As a kid I learned one Jewish song. My parents came from Europe, from Poland, and we had a bakery, we worked in bakeries, and there was a baker's union in the thirties and they had a strike and they won. They had a song that was sung on WEVD in New York. And I heard it as a kid at union meetings, which they don't have anymore. I think I sang it the last time at a Pennywhistlers concert or something. Now everyone's Jewish in New York City, and they have special courses on how to sing Jewish. Twelve different styles of classical guitar. It wasn't always that way. In my day, when I put on concerts and we decided to have ethnic music we got an old Irish lady from the Bronx and my mother. Anyway, I'll translate the song first and then I'll sing it. The translation is:

Sitting down at the breakfast table
Eating bread with a union label
International union bread
Makes the cheeks blushing red.

And they were very proud when I sang it. I think it's a Mozart tune or something.

When I was young I was secretary of the Junior Astronomy Club. One night it was raining in Central Park so we couldn't see the stars. That's about as close as you could get to the stars in New York at that time. Someone said let's go square dancing. I said, I'm not that kind of a person. You know, I grew up in the Bronx and everything. But we went and I really liked it. And then the next week I visited the American Square Dance Group. And I, who just thought it was weird, square dancing—who grew up, like Joe Hickerson, listening to the top ten hit parade every Saturday night—after three weeks I thought I was the best square dancer in the United States. I was terribly disappointed when Margot Mayo's American Square Dance Group did a program for the United States Armed Forces and filmed square dancing and I wasn't in it. Well, anyway, I became a member of the American Square Dance Group, and then there were these other groups which I knew very little about, the Folksay group and the hootenannies. And I still remember going to my first hootenanny, and Pete Seeger even remembers it. Me, coming from the working class, I go to this hootenanny and they're singing, "O you can't scare me, I'm sticking to the union." And I got so angry, growing up in the Bronx, that I yelled out, with my stentorian voice, "O you can't force me to join the union, the union, to join the union, the NAM is enough for me." I still don't understand why I got so angry, working-class kid that I was, to bring up the NAM (National Association of Manufacturers).

Anyway, I became a nut, or folknik—a word I created in the year 1959, after the sputniks and beatniks stuff. I had been reading all the books and reading all the magazines and I was very serious about it. I went to every single square dance, whether it was good or bad, except the left-wing square dances. I never went to Folksay, and when Dick Reuss came to me in the '60s and taped forty hours of conversation with me, he'd ask about Margot Mayo and ASDG, and he'd throw in a question about some square dance group with a name that sounded like a "front" and I'd be shocked that I didn't know of it or couldn't recall it. Anything that had to do with the Left I'd never heard of. And here I was brilliant. I kept up with everything.

At ASDG the important thing was dancing. We danced for about two to three hours and then we took a break, and then we danced some more and then we sang at the end of the evening. The hootenannies were just the opposite. They sang a lot and then they had some square dancing at the end, with Irwin Silber as caller. I preferred ASDG, because to me that was traditional. We did play parties, the running sets and square dances, but at the hootenannies the caller would sing, "Swing your union maid around." I didn't understand what he was talking about.

My life was getting ruined very quickly and I wasn't getting anywhere, and I worked fourteen summers as a waiter in the "mountains" wondering what I was going to do in the future. I met Kenny Goldstein, and I followed him around the way Leadbelly followed Lomax around. I had a car then, and Kenny and I would sometimes go on "trips." I'd visit him in the Bronx, where his collection formed the basis and idea for my first catalog of folklore books sold by mail order. I'd sit in his kitchen while he recorded Reverend Gary Davis, and that recording is as good as any recording made of Reverend Davis. The Clancy Brothers were also first recorded in his kitchen. And so it was exciting for me to meet all these people through Kenny, and I also met a lot of these people, including Josh White and Leadbelly, through Margot Mayo's ASDG.

I published a book by Patrick Galvin, *Irish Songs of Resistance*, and I issued two book catalogs. And I actually started to make money selling scholarly books on folk music, jazz, dancing, proverbs, anything. All the books that you couldn't find anywhere else. Somebody told me of a small bookstore on MacDougal Street that was available. I went to the worst street in America, MacDougal Street, really crowded, really touristy. I was always attracted to Greenwich Village. I opened the Folklore Center, and it was filled with books that you could sell only to scholars. It was the dumbest thing I ever did. I tried to sell records, too. A few weeks before I opened my store, in April 1957, I filled a notebook with "A New Secret History of Folklore USA"—a revelation for me, at the age of 29, that there was a cold, hard outside world and my life wasn't just to be dancing and having fun.

I opened my store, and within weeks I'm a world-famous personality. I get a call from Al Grossman, in Chicago, that Peggy Seeger is passing through and can I do a concert for her? So that's how I started my concert series. Jack Elliott was coming back from Europe, so I had a concert with him. And Alan Lomax was coming back after cooling off for six or eight years from the communism stuff in America. I made a party for him in my store as well as for a woman I was in love with who had just returned from Israel, and they left the party together. And I was alone. Then I had concerts with Tom Paley and John Cohen. Even then there was a dichotomy. Everyone knew that when I did concerts that John forced on me with his philosophy, his cosmos, I lost money. But all the concerts I did with Tom Paley and his friends made money. I put on hundreds of concerts. There's no way to count them. I'll put that series against anybody's. I had only one rule: The artists and I shared the gate equally. I never had to sign a contract. It turned out that I was paying people more than folk singers were getting paid at the famous baskethouses, and everyone understood that people at my concerts "listened" to the music, so my store became the place to play. And I put on everybody. The only English skiffle group that ever played in America played in my narrow store. They sang mostly Leadbelly and Woody Guthrie songs. But when they spoke you didn't understand a word they said.

I put on Bob Dylan's first concert, but he was just part of the whole series of concerts. Nineteen sixty-one was a big year. We started the Friends of Old Time Music. John Cohen, Ralph Rinzler, and me. John Cohen and Ralph Rinzler were the brains. I was the one who followed orders. We did something that was unheard-of in New York—brought Doc Watson, brought Joseph Spence. We made available music for the first time in New York City, for urban people, that would not be possible otherwise. We can still be proud of that. John would have his things that he liked and Ralph would have his things.

My store was the only place in America where you could get every folk magazine. You could get *Sing Out!*, *The Little Sandy Review*, *Broadside*, magazines from England, magazines from the West Coast, folk magazines from anywhere. Dick Reuss used to come into my store a couple of times a year. Ed Kahn used to come in to buy everything new. Harry Tuft started his Folklore Center in Denver with scholarly books I couldn't sell in New York City. So that was really a fabulous thing that went on for a long time. Then in 1961 was the riot in Washington Square when Newbold Morris, who was my hero as a child—he was the second man to Mayor La Guardia—decided we couldn't sing songs in Washington Square. And we decided we could sing songs. So we had a big fight, and a film, *Sunday* by Danny Drasin, was made about it. Everybody was there. There was a headline in the *Daily Mirror*, "10,000 Beatniks Riot in Greenwich Village."

The best account of that to this day is in Oscar Brand's *The Ballad Mongers*. New York was the center of the folk music universe. And the only book that came out of it from New York that's any good is Oscar's. The only good book that's come out of the whole folk music thing is the book from Boston, *Baby, Let Me Follow You Down*, by Eric von Schmidt and Jim Rooney. So it's interesting for me that we in New York screamed more. We thought we did more. But we didn't come up with many good books. In 1963 there was a blacklist against Pete Seeger appearing on the

Hootenanny TV show. And there was a folk singer's committee. Everybody was there. And I was the secretary. The only complete notes of those meetings are to be found in my notebooks. There was a question brought up at the meeting. I don't remember who brought it up. What's Izzy Young doing here? He's not a folk singer. So the folk singer's group voted on the question. The vote was 31 to 1. So I'm a folk singer. An honorary folk singer.

In 1969 I heard Swedish folk music for the first time, and because of a whole series of questions and problems which I have not answered I have yet to figure out why I left America, why I moved to Sweden, why I'm coming back more and more often now. I left America to "work" with Swedish folk music. And I have exactly the same problems in Sweden that I had in America. Except that in America everybody was smarter than me and in Sweden everybody's more qualified than me. I put out a little newsletter of folk music in Sweden, with a circulation of 3,000, which is one-third that of *Sing Out!* In Sweden, instead of having the progressives, the intellectuals, the folklorists, it is mostly just people who "like folk music" that subscribe. I'm proud of my 3,000 circulation and I try to work with folk music from the whole world, with Swedish "folk music" as a shaky starting point.

REALLY SING THE BLUES

BROWNIE McGHEE
& SONNY TERRY
REV. GARY DAVIS,
BARBARA DANE,
JOHNNY HAMMOND,
ERIC VON SCHMIDT

JOHN HANCOCK HALL

FRIDAY, JAN. 8

8:30 P.M.

Send mail orders with stamped self-addressed envelope to:
Folklore productions, P. O. Box 227, Boston 1.

Tickets:
$3.50, 2.80, 2.20

ibliography: Folk Music Revival

Baez, Joan. *And a Voice to Sing With: A Memoir.* New York: Summit Books, 1987.

Baggelaar, Kristin and Donald Milton. *Folk Music: More Than a Song.* New York: Thomas Y. Crowell Company, 1976.

Barlow, William. *Looking Up at Down: The Emergence of Blues Culture.* Philadelphia: Temple University Press, 1989.

Bartis, Peter T. "A History of the Archive of Folk Song at the Library of Congress: The First Fifty Years." Unpublished Ph.D. Dissertation, University of Pennsylvania, 1982.

Bastin, Bruce. *Red River Blues: The Blues Tradition in the Southeast.* Urbana: University of Illinois Press, 1986.

Becker, Jane S. and Barbara Franco, eds. *Folk Roots, New Roots: Folklore in American Life.* Lexington, Mass.: Museum of Our National Heritage, 1988.

Blake, Benjamin, Jack Rubeck and Allan Shaw. *The Kingston Trio on Record.* Naperville, Ill.: Kingston Korner, Inc., 1986.

Boyes, Georgina. *The Imagined Village: Culture, Ideology and the English Folk Revival.* Manchester: Manchester University Press, 1993.

Brand, Oscar. *The Ballad Mongers: Rise of the Modern Folk Song.* New York: Funk & Wagnalls Co., Inc., 1962.

Cantwell, Robert. *Ethnomimesis: Folklife and the Representation of Culture.* Chapel Hill, N. C.: University of North Carolina Press, 1993.

Cantwell, Robert. "When We Were Good: Class and Culture in the Folk Revival," in Rosenberg, ed., *Transforming Tradition*, 35-60.

Carawan, Guy and Candy Carawan, eds. *Sing for Freedom: The Story of the Civil Rights Movement Through Its Songs.* Bethlehem, Penn.: Sing Out! Corporation, 1990.

Clarke, Donald. *The Penguin Encyclopedia of Popular Music.* London: Viking, 1989.

Clark, Jim, ed. *The Folk Music Yearbook of Artists.* Fairfax, Va: Jandel Productions, 1964.

Cohen, Norm. *Folk Song America: A 20th Century Revival.* Washington, D.C.:Smithsonian Collection of Recordings, 1990. (Accompanying four-CD boxed set of recordings.)

Cohen, Norm. *Long Steel Rail: The Railroad in Americana Folksong.* Urbana:University of Illinois Press, 1981.

Cohn, Larry, ed. *Nothing but the Blues: The Music and the Musicians.* New York: Abbeville Press, 1993.

Collins, Judy. *Trust Your Heart: An Autobiography.* Boston: Houghton Mifflin Co., 1987.

Country: Pickers, Slickers, Cheatin' Hearts and Superstars; The Music and the Musicians. New York: Abbeville Press, 1993.

Cray, Ed. *The Erotic Muse: American Bawdy Songs.* Second Edition. Urbana:University of Illinois Press, 1992.

Crosby, David and Carl Gottlieb. *Long Time Gone: The Autobiography of David Crosby.* New York: Dell Publishing Co., 1988.

Dane, Barbara and Irwin Silber, comp. and ed. *The Vietnam Songbook.* New York: The Guardian, 1969.

Denisoff, R. Serge. *Great Day Coming: Folk Music and the American Left*. Urbana: University of Illinois Press, 1971.

Denisoff, R. Serge. *Sing a Song of Social Significance*. Second Edition. Bowling Green, Ohio: Bowling Green State University Popular Press, 1983.

DeTurk, David A. and A. Poulin. *The American Folk Scene: Dimensions of the Folksong Revival*. New York: Dell Publishing Co., 1967.

Dunaway, David King. *How Can I Keep From Singing: Pete Seeger*. New York: McGraw-Hill Book Co., 1981.

Dunson, Josh. *Freedom in the Air: Song Movements of the Sixties*. New York: International Publishers, 1965.

Eliot, Marc. *Death of a Rebel*. Garden City, New York: Anchor Books, 1979.

Ennis, Philip H. *The Seventh Stream: The Emergence of Rocknroll in American Popular Music*. Hanover, N.H.: Wesleyan University Press, 1992.

Ferris, William and Mary L. Hart, eds. *Folk Music and Modern Sound*. Jackson:University Press of Mississippi, 1982.

Gahr, David and Robert Shelton. *The Face of Folk Music*. New York: The Citadel Press, 1968.

Gillett, Charlie. *The Sound of the City: The Rise of Rock and Roll*. New York: Pantheon Books, 1984.

Grafman, Howard and B. T. Manning. *Folk Music USA*. New York: The Citadel Press, 1962.

Grayson, Lisa, comp. *Biography of a Hunch: The History of Chicago's Legendary Old Town School of Folk Music*. Chicago: Old Town School of Folk Music, 1992.

Green, Archie. *Only a Miner: Studies in Recorded Coal-Mining Songs.* Urbana: University of Illinois Press, 1972.

Green, Archie, ed. *Songs About Work: Essays in Occupational Culture for Richard A. Reuss.* Bloomington: Indiana University Press, 1993.

Green, Archie. *Wobblies, Pile Butts and Other Heroes: Laborlore Explorations.* Urbana: University of Illinois Press, 1993.

Green, Victor. *A Passion for Polka: Old-Time Ethnic Music in America.* Berkeley: University of California Press, 1992.

Greenway, John. *American Folksongs of Protest.* New York: A.S. Barnes and Company, Inc., 1960.

Grossman, Victor. *If I Had A Song: Lieder und Sänger der USA.* Berlin: Lied der Zeit, 1990.

Guthrie, Woody. *Pastures of Plenty: A Self-Portrait.* Ed. Dave Marsh and Harold Leventhal. New York: HarperCollins Publishers, 1990.

Halberstam, David. *The Fifties.* New York: Summit Books, 1993.

Hood, Phil. *Artists of American Folk Music.* New York: William Morrow, 1986.

Johnson, Joyce. *Minor Characters: Coming of Age in the Beat Generation.* New York: Washington Square Press, 1983.

Kahn, Edward A. "The Carter Family: A Reflection of Changes in Society." Unpublished Ph.D. Dissertation, University of California-Los Angeles, 1970.

Klein, Joe. *Woody Guthrie: A Life.* New York: Alfred A. Knopf, 1980.

Lawless, Ray M. *Folksingers and Folksongs in America.* Revised Edition. Westport, Conn.: Greenwood Press, Publishers, 1981.

Lieberman, Robbie. *"My Song Is My Weapon": People's Songs,*

American Communism, and the Politics of Culture, 1930-1950. Urbana:University of Illinois Press, 1989.

Lomax, Alan. *The Land Where the Blues Began.* New York: Pantheon Books, 1993.

MacKinnon, Niall. *The British Folk Scene: Musical Performance and Social Identity.* Bristol, Penn.: Open University Press, 1994.

Malone, Bill C. *Country Music U.S.A.* Revised Edition. Austin: University of Texas Press, 1985.

Malone, Bill C. *Singing Cowboys and Musical Mountaineers: Southern Culture and the Roots of Country Music.* Athens: University of Georgia Press, 1993.

Miller, Jim, ed. *The Rolling Stone Illustrated History of Rock & Roll.* Revised and Updated Edition. New York: Random House, 1980.

Patterson, Daniel W., ed. *Sounds of the South.* Chapel Hill: Southern Folklife Collection, University of North Carolina, 1991.

Pescatello, Ann M. *Charles Seeger: A Life in American Music.* Pittsburgh: University of Pittsburgh Press, 1992.

Phillips, John. *Papa John: An Autobiography.* New York: Dell Publishing Co., 1986.

Rahn, Mildred L. "Club 47: An Historical Ethnography of a Folk-Revival Venue in North America, 1958-1968." Unpublished M.A. Thesis, Memorial University of Newfoundland, 1993.

Reagon, Bernice Johnson. "Songs of the Civil Rights Movement, 1955-1965: A Study in Culture History." Unpublished Ph.D. Dissertation, Howard University, 1975.

Reuss, Richard A. "American Folklore and Left-Wing Politics, 1927-1957." Unpublished Ph.D. Dissertation, Indiana University, 1971.

Reuss, Richard A., ed. *Songs of American Labor, Industrialization* and the Urban Work Experience: A Discography. Ann Arbor: Labor Studies Center, Institute of Labor and Industrial Relations, University of Michigan, 1983.

Reuss, Richard A., comp. Woody Guthrie: Bibliography. New York: The Guthrie Children's Trust Fund, 1968.

Rodnitzky, Jerome L. Minstrels of the Dawn: The Folk-Protest Singer as a Cultural Hero. Chicago: Nelson-Hall, 1976.

Rogan, Johnny. Timeless Flight: The Definitive Biography of the Byrds. Brentwood, Essex: Square One Books Ltd., 1990.

Rosenberg, Neil V. Bluegrass: A History. Urbana: University of Illinois Press, 1985.

Rosenberg, Neil V., ed. Transforming Tradition: Folk Music Revivals Examined. Urbana: University of Illinois Press, 1993.

Sallis, James. The Guitar Players: One Instrument and Its Masters in American Music. Lincoln: University of Nebraska Press, 1994.

Sandberg, Larry and Dick Weissman. The Folk Music Sourcebook. Updated Edition. New York: Da Capo Press, Inc., 1989.

Seeger, Pete. The Incomplete Folksinger. New York: Simon and Schuster, 1972.

Seeger, Pete. Where Have All The Flowers Gone: A Singer's Stories, Songs, Seeds, Robberies. Bethlehem, Penn.: Sing Out! Corporation, 1993.

Seeger, Pete and Bob Rieser. Everybody Says Freedom: A History of the Civil Rights Movement in Songs and Pictures. New York: W.W. Norton & Co., 1989.

Shelton, Robert. No Direction Home: The Life and Music of Bob Dylan. New York: William Morrow and Co., 1986.

Spitz, Bob. Dylan: A Biography. New York: McGraw-Hill Publishing

Co., 1989.

Stambler, Irwin and Grelun Landon. *The Encyclopedia of Folk, Country & Western Music*. Second Edition. New York: St. Martin's Press, 1984.

Sukenick, Ronald. *Down and In: Life in the Underground*. New York: William Morrow, 1987.

Tilling, Robert, comp. *Oh! What a Beautiful City: A Tribute to Rev. Gary Davis, 1896-1972*. St. Saviour, Jersey: Paul Mill Press, 1992.

Tribe, Ivan M. *The Stonemans: An Appalachian Family and the Music That Shaped Their Lives*. Urbana: University of Illinois Press, 1993.

von Schmidt, Eric and Jim Rooney. *Baby, Let Me Follow You Down: The Illustrated Story of the Cambridge Folk Years*. New York: Anchor Books, 1979 (reprinted Amherst: University of Massachusetts Press, 1994).

Wakefield, Dan. *New York in the Fifties*. Boston: Houghton Mifflin, 1992.

Willens, Doris. *Lonesome Traveler: The Life of Lee Hays*. New York: W.W. Norton & Co., 1988.

Wolfe, Charles K. and Kip Lornell. *The Life and Legend of Leadbelly*. New York: HarperCollins Publishers, 1992.

Woliver, Robbie. *Bringing It All Back Home: 25 Years of American Music at Folk City*. New York: Pantheon Books, 1986.

CCNY CORE + FINLEY BD. of MANAGERS
PRESENTS A BENEFIT

¡¡CONCERT!!

STUDENT NON-VIOLENT COORDINATING COMM.
~ GREAT FUN ~
TARRIERS
DAVE · VAN · RONK
THE HARVESTERS
RAMBLING JACK ELLIOT
JOHN HERALD ○ BOB DYLAN
NEW WORLD SINGERS
JERRY SILVERMAN
FEBRUARY 23, 1962 ~ 8:15 PM
GRAND BALLROOM   DONATION $1.50
$1.25
TICKETS FOR SALE (!) FEB. 13-23 (108 FINLEY)
DO NOT LITTER THE CAMPUS   15-16 (TROPHY LOUNGE)

CCNY
UPTOWN

Contributors

ROY BERKELEY went to New York to attend Columbia College, became involved in the folk scene during the 1950s, was the first folksinger to sing in a MacDougal Street coffeehouse, and was a founder of the Folksingers' Guild. He has performed extensively and lectured widely, was a member of the Old Reliable String Band with Tom Paley and Artie Rose (Folkways Records, 1962), and appears on numerous recordings, most recently *Songs of the FDR Years* (Longview Records).

One of the more active topical songwriters of the 1960s, **LEN CHANDLER** recorded extensively for Columbia, Folkways, Broadside, Blue Thumb, King and and FM Records, and performed widely. He was particularly involved in the civil rights movement. He was the co-founder of the Los Angeles Songwriters Showcase in 1971 and has continued as its co-director. He maintains a busy performance and lecture schedule.

JOHN COHEN has been a member of the New Lost City Ramblers since its inception and continues to perform with the group. As a filmmaker and folklorist he has documented, on record and on film, traditional cultures in the United States and South America, and recently has issued two CDs of "Huayno Music of Peru" as well as the film "Dancing with the Incas." He is currently writing a book on Huaynos.

RONALD D. COHEN has taught in the history department at Indiana University Northwest since 1970 and is the author of three books on the history of Gary and public schooling in the United States. He is writing a book on the folk music revival in the United

States, currently titled "Rainbow Quest: Folk Music and American Society, 1940-1970," and is working (with Dave Samuelson) on *Music for Political Action: Folk Music, Topical Songs, and the American Left, 1926-1954*, a ten-CD reissue (Bear Family, BCD 15720, forthcoming).

Gadfly of the folk revival, **LOU GOTTLIEB** first formed the Gateway Singers, then the Limeliters, with whom he still performs. A Ph.D. from Berkeley, when not working with the Limeliters he creates the illusion of solvency as a forensic musicologist in copyright litigations and in desktop music publishing. He recently moved back to Northern California, sings bass with the Bach Choir of Sonoma State University, and teaches piano at his Morningstar Ranch, site of the infamous hippie commune during the late sixties.

FRANK HAMILTON was a seminal figure in the folk revival, a talented multi-instrumentalist who performed and recorded extensively, was the founding teacher of the Old Town School of Folk Music in Chicago, and replaced Erik Darling in the Weavers. He currently performs folk music for the schoolchildren of Atlanta in the trio Meridian, is a member of The Uptown Strollers, which plays popular music from the 1920s, 1930s, and 1940s, and he also performs Irish music. He is composing the musical score for a local theater musical and has his own music production company.

Known to millions as the radio personality "Dr. Demento," **BARRET E. HANSEN** early became involved in traditional music in his native Minneapolis. He was a record reviewer for *The Little Sandy Review* and its later editor, worked at the Ash Grove in Los Angeles and with the John Edwards Memorial Foundation at UCLA, then joined Specialty Records and compiled 35 reissue LPs of blues, gospel, and rock 'n' roll. He worked for Warner Brothers Records during the 1970s while initiating *The Dr. Demento Show*, which has continued to the present.

Currently Head of the Archive of Folk Culture, American Folklife Center, Library of Congress, **JOE HICKERSON** assumed that post in 1974, after an 11-year tenure as its Reference Librarian. He has been Chairman of the Committee on Archiving of the American Folklore Society, an advisory board member for *Foxfire* and *Sing*

Out!, and author of "Folk Music of the United States," which has appeared in the *Encyclopedia International* since 1972. He has performed on numerous albums for Folk-Legacy and other labels, and continues an active concert and lecture schedule.

ED KAHN was the Executive Secretary of the John Edwards Memorial Foundation from 1964 to 1969, while writing his dissertation at UCLA on the Carter Family and continuing his fieldwork in the South. He has written extensively on Southern white music, produced six albums, and is currently working on two CD reissues of the Carter Family. He is also a computer expert with a monthly column in *MicroTimes* and a computer book published by Ten Speed Press.

Twin sisters **ELLEN KOSSOY CHRISTENSON** and **IRENE KOSSOY SALETAN** as teenagers began singing in Washington Square in Greenwich Village. **ELLEN** settled in St. Louis in 1961 and performed with her husband Robin. While working as a secretary, she also continued her singing as a member of the Mississippi Mudcats string band, then with the Harmony Grits. **IRENE** moved to Boston in 1960 and performed with her husband Tony Saletan and in a trio. Since 1985 she has worked in tourism, first as a travel agent, then as an adventure tour specialist. Most recently she has served in the Peace Corps in Costa Rica.

Currently an administrator at the University of Minnesota, with a Ph.D. in American Studies from the university, since leaving *The Little Sandy Review* **JON PANKAKE** has continued to be musically active. He has written for *The Old-Time Herald*, published with Marcia Pankake *The Prairie Home Companion Folk Song Book* (1988), and has had a hand in reissuing recordings by the New Lost City Ramblers on Flying Fish and Smithsonian Folkways, as well as the album *Folk Song Types* for New World.

Most recently editor of *Transforming Tradition: Folk Music Revivals Examined* (1993), **NEIL V. ROSENBERG** has published widely concerning Canadian and American folk music. He received his Ph.D. in Folklore from Indiana University in 1970, and is currently professor of folklore at Memorial University of Newfoundland. Perhaps best known for *Bluegrass: A History* (1985), he has published scores of essays in books and scholarly journals, and provided program notes for over thirty sound recording albums. He is also a musician and singer.

DAVE SAMUELSON was early exposed to folk and country music in Chicago, and while attending the University of Illinois fell under the influence of Archie Green. He initiated Puritan Records in 1972, and has produced and annotated more than thirty folk, country, and bluegrass albums for Bear Family, Copper Creek, County, and Rebel. Currently a free-lance writer in Battle Ground, Indiana, he is producing *Music for Political Action: Folk Music, Topical Songs, and the American Left, 1926-1954*, a ten-CD reissue (Bear Family, BCD 15720, forthcoming).

Since co-directing American Folksay Group from 1943 to 1947, **IRWIN SILBER** has continued to be active in the field of politically oriented music and, in recent years, more overtly political writing. He was Executive Director of People's Songs (1947-1949), editor of *Sing Out!* (1951-1967), publisher-editor of Oak Publications (1960-1967), and the editor of a number of song collections, including *Lift Every Voice* (1952), *Songs of the Civil War* (1960), *Songs of the Great American West* (1967), *The Vietnam Songbook* (with Barbara Dane, 1969), and *The Folksinger's Wordbook* (with Fred Silber, 1973). He was co-owner, with Barbara Dane, of Paredon Records. Cultural Editor (1968-1971) and Executive Editor (1972-1978) of *The Guardian*, and currently Associate Editor of *Crossroads* magazine, he has written *The Cultural Revolution* (1970), *Kampuchea: The Revolution Rescued* (1985), and most recently *Socialism: What Went Wrong?* (1994).

DICK WEISSMAN currently teaches at the University of Colorado in Denver, and remains very active as a performer, composer, and writer. He is co-author with Larry Sandberg of *The Folk Music Sourcebook* (updated edition 1989) and has issued the CD *New Traditions* (Folk Era), as well as appearing with the Journeymen on a recent Capitol Records CD reissue. He has written numerous books on instrumental techniques and the music business, including *Making a Living in Your Local Music Market* (1990) and *Creating Melodies* (1994).

ISRAEL G. YOUNG opened the Folklore Center in Greenwich Village in 1957, and remained its proprietor until 1973, when he moved to Stockholm, Sweden. His long-running *Sing Out!* column "Frets and Frails" was avidly read for its information and gossip. He currently operates the Folklore Centrum in Stockholm, publishes a newsletter, in Swedish, on folk music and folk dancing throughout the Scandinavian countries, continues to teach square dancing, and hosts a radio program. He is currently editing for publication his numerous columns for *Sing Out!* and other writings.

Sing Out!

A PEOPLE'S ARTISTS PUBLICATION

VOL. 1 NO. 10   MARCH, 1951   25¢

Index

A

Aarons, Lee, 164
Aarons, Tossi, 164
Aaronson, Joe, 164
Aaronson, Penny, 164
ABC (television), 152, 166
Abrahams, Roger, 63, 165, 181, 184
Acuff, Roy, 49
Adams, Don, 148
Adelphi Hall, 190
Akron University, 127, 128
Alden, Ray, 43, 45, 46
Allmen, Rick, 179
Almanac Singers, 16, 84, 90, 93, 94, 159, 184
Alper, Jackie, 133
Alper, Joe, 133
Amberg, George, 110
American Banjo Scruggs Style, 38
American Banjo Tunes and Songs with the Stoneman Family, 38
American Folklore Society, 28, 97; Historiography Committee, 13
American Folksay Group, 90
American Square Dance Group (ASDG), 20, 31, 50, 51, 179, 199, 200, 201
American Youth for Democracy, 145
American Youth Hostels, 165
Anderson, Marian, 146-147
Angelou, Maya, 149

Ann Arbor, Michigan, 14, 36
Anthology of American Folk Music, 34, 40, 52, 80, 118, 191
Archives. *See* Indiana University; Library of Congress
Arhoolie Records, 41, 45
Ark, The, 14
Armstrong, George, 156
Armstrong, Gerry, 156
Arnone, Don, 168
Aronoff, Benji, 164
Asbell, Bernie, 9
Asch, Moe, 8, 13, 19, 35, 38, 50, 52, 55, 89, 101, 102, 104, 123
Ash Grove, 37, 53, 62, 109, 115, 121, 150, 169
Asheville, North Carolina, 57
Ashley, Clarence "Tom," 30, 34, 40, 49, 59, 152
Ashley, Ted, 152
Asimov, Isaac, 107
Atlanta, Georgia, 136
Avon Books, 101, 104

B

"Back Where I Come From," 19, 50
Badeaux, Ed, 101
Baez, Joan, 3, 42, 55, 74, 138, 167
Balfa, Dewey, 45, 56
Band, The, 173
Banducci, Enrico, 150, 153

Index